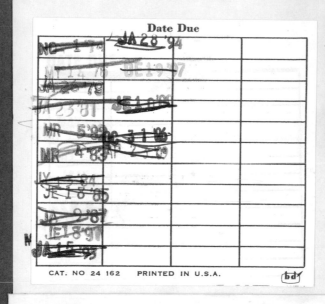

# Sartre and Camus

# Sartre and Camus

## Literature of Existence

**LEO POLLMANN**

*Translated by Helen and Gregor Sebba*

Frederick Ungar Publishing Co.   *New York*

Translated from the original German *Sartre und Camus: Literatur der Existenz,* © 1967, by arrangement with Verlag W. Kohlhammer GmbH, Stuttgart

# Foreword

Without doubt Sartre and Camus are the most discussed contemporary writers in French—or any other—literature. Proust is read, and his literary qualities are appreciated, but he provokes little discussion. Every reader with sound instincts recognizes Valéry and Mallarmé as excellent poets; yet, different as their poetry is, the difference poses few problems. Writers such as Michel Butor, Alain Robbe-Grillet, Samuel Beckett, and Nathalie Sarraute certainly inspire heated discussion for and against the new novel or, more generally, the dynasty of form, to which they are committed. They certainly produce enthusiastic if sometimes less than adept supporters, as well as critics who predict the imminent death of the movement. This, however, applies to the problem as a whole, whereas in the case of Camus and Sartre the writers themselves constantly arouse controversy (some of it violent) through their work, their philosophy, and their lives. It might almost be said that they are an intellectual watershed, and this is partly because each of them stands for an ideological complex of meaning which his name has the power to call to mind in its totality.

Not long ago I mentioned to a colleague that I was preparing a lecture on Sartre. He literally groaned—in fun of course—and charged me with adding my stone to the building of the *Grande Sartreuse*. I soon discovered the reason for his strong (though perfectly friendly) reaction. In the course of our conversation it emerged that my colleague was preparing a seminar on Camus. Obviously he could not be indifferent. One can hardly say "Sartre" without the name "Camus" insinuating itself, and vice versa. And since I have always had a special love for Camus, whereas Sartre is a more recent love, born—perhaps not entirely by chance—in Berlin, which, as Sartre says himself, has some of the qualities he attributes to Bouville, it occurred to me to combine these *deux amours* in a single study and to set the discussion of Sartre and Camus, so often conducted by way of anemic "positive" and "negative" arguments, on a more solid basis of literary criticism.

The subtitle "Literature of Existence" says a great deal about the level of comparison at which I propose to begin. The literary works of Sartre and Camus will be treated not as depicting detached reality but as the esthetic formulation of what existence means to these writers. We shall see that they have very definite, diametrically opposed views on this, that the literature they create, as a union of form, content, and meaning, stands in a very close, inescapable interrelationship with their ontological and metaphysical positions. Hence, Sartre and Camus, precisely because their aim is to create literature of existence, face very similar esthetic problems, which, however, they solve in quite different ways.

These esthetic problems can only be made concrete with the aid of categories which permit a verifiable analysis of the various dimensions of literary reality in terms that are equally applicable to the formal aspect of the work, to its content, and potentially to a "third dimension" of philosophical meaning beyond these, to a statement which has ontological implications. The terms "horizontal" and "vertical" will prove helpful here, signifying a notion as applicable to the formal and material components of the work as to its philosophical meaning.[1] Since in Sartre and Camus this philosophical meaning can, moreover, often be derived from the content, this method will also provide an interesting opportunity to see, inversely, how they master the technical problems of the genre from their respective metaphysical positions. It will turn out that there is often an inescapable link—to the embarrassment of both writers—between form and metaphysics. To see how Sartre himself feels about this in retrospect one merely needs to turn to *Les Mots*.

These considerations, however, are not at all the purpose of this book; they simply happen to emerge as a by-product. Even a cursory glance at the chapter titles will show that this study is principally devoted to the individual works as such, so that Sartre is not from the outset being compared with Camus; the comparison arises by necessity from the course of the study. The section dealing exclusively with Sartre (Chapters I through VII) is therefore more or less self-contained and can perfectly well be read independently. The same applies to each individual chapter in this section, with the single reservation that anyone not familiar with Sartre should read the basic opening chapter first.

This independence of the component parts, however, is less valid for the Camus section (Chapters VIII through XII), since this section depends to some extent on the findings of the Sartre chapters. Yet even here every chapter has deliberately been made relatively independent. Hence all chapters can be read alone as brief guides to the structural reality of any particular work of Sartre or Camus, independently of the overall thesis of the book.

This book is essentially an introduction to the work of Sartre and Camus. It is intended to stimulate rather than replace the reading of the works themselves.[2] It also tries to call attention to the problems inherent in a literature which seeks to be, not a world *à part*, but a living dialogue with human existence, and it thus tries to lay the groundwork for a comparison of Sartre and Camus on the plane of literary criticism, but no more. Finally it is hoped that it will stimulate a re-examination of other phenomena in modern literature, such as the new novel.

*Berlin*                                    LEO POLLMANN

                                            January, 1967

# Contents

ix

## chapter 1

# Introduction
# to the Philosophical Problems
# of Sartre's Work

Without doubt we can read Sartre's fiction, as he himself insists, in the way it presents itself: as literature; and this applies to the plays, to *Les Mouches* and *Les Mains sales*, for instance, no less than to *La Nausée* and *Les Chemins de la liberté*. Conversely, it is certainly also legitimate and in no way erroneous to regard his work as a documentation of philosophical theses.[3] It is, however, questionable whether either a purely philosophical or a purely literary approach can do full justice to the work, can apprehend and evaluate what it truly is. For this is precisely its special quality: that it is both things at once, that it presents itself as a literary reality which as such carries a philosophical meaning, but is also, in its form and content, intimately related to its philosophical meaning—and to a certain extent *is* in fact that meaning. It would therefore seem quite legitimate to say that a purely literary analysis of this work is not capable of exploring even the full literary reality because the philosophical reality is inextricably implicit in it.

**Word and Meaning**

In fact, we are in danger of misunderstanding the meaning of this work if we look at it purely in the light of its literary reality. Where the meaning is implicit in the work it is just as much an integral part of it as form and content are. And a philosopher who is also a writer will quite naturally extend meaning beyond form and content. He cannot stop at a self-sufficient work of art; for him writing demands what the Neo-platonists called "the lie," justification through meaning.[4]

Everyone who reads Sartre senses that such a meaning is there—must be there—but we must be very careful in seeking out where it lies, for the danger of misunderstanding is great. The meaning is, in fact, never to be found on the literal level; it is never a practical—that is to say, practicable, moral meaning —but always an epistemological, philosophical one.

The fact that humanists, Christians, and Marxists agree in rejecting Sartre is partly due to such misunderstanding. Certainly we are justified in being shocked by his depicting so much killing, so much hopeless and total failure, so much decadence and perversity, but it is wrong to regard this material and factual actuality as anything more than a medium which is not identical with the meaning of the work. Of course it would also be false to say that the choice of this medium has nothing to do with the meaning of the work, that no inferences can be drawn from it, or that medium and meaning are unrelated. On the contrary, the choice of medium is symptomatic and ex-emplary of a meaning which, however, is still brought out.

To take an example, Sartre did not write the three vol-umes of *Les Chemins de la liberté* so far published in order to posit as ultimate meaning the freedom to kill wantonly, which Mathieu finally achieves. But we misunderstand him if we try, as it were, to save something indubitably meant to be a blind act of murder inspired by revenge by attributing to it the "supreme ethical significance" of political engagement in the Resistance.[5] Indeed the text will hardly support such an interpretation.[6] Here, as always, what Sartre is after is not a practical solution but an epiphany of exemplary meaning, an epistemological, not practical, understanding of what freedom means or, still better, of what it is.

### Literature and Philosophy: The Problem

Whether we accept the idea that literature may, as exemplary reality, point to a specific, philosophical mode of cognition as its meaning is something else again. Although Sartre insists that his work can be read and understood as literature (and if this were not so, his work would not be a legitimate subject for literary criticism), the work by its very nature invites interpretation, a search for what lies behind it. But if the nature of the work at the same time forces the reader to make a false interpretation of what lies behind it, unless he has access to certain fundamental concepts and structures in Sartre's philosophical thinking, then we may well ask whether a purely literary reading can ever be satisfactory.

The problem is as old as literature itself. Literature that eludes the uninitiated has always existed and has not necessarily been qualitatively any the worse for it. But in this case the problem is particularly acute since what an uninitiated mind might get from Sartre's work could be not merely a harmless misunderstanding but a completely false direction.[7] I remember reading recently in the newspaper of a case in which a young murderer asked the judge to take into consideration the fact that he had read *L'Etranger* and was trying to imitate its hero, Meursault. Here it was Camus who gave rise to the terrible misunderstanding, so fraught with responsibility; but it is by no means impossible that *Les Mouches* or *Les Mains sales* might produce in an uninitiated reader the idea, and all the tragic complications it might entail, that murder is an ideal manifestation of freedom and that the essential thing is to prove oneself sovereign, like Orestes after his deed, and not yield to the temptation of remorse. Obviously, misunderstanding will rarely go as far as this, but we cannot ignore the fact that Sartre's work is disquieting and dangerous. How easily such misunderstandings occur can be seen from the fashionable antics of so-called existentialists who have probably never asked themselves—and some of whom are perhaps not even capable of asking—what exactly it is that they profess.

### Literary Work and Life

Taking a look at Sartre's life, we see quickly enough that extreme actions like those he depicts in his work have no parallel there. Sartre is without doubt an existentialist—an existentialist who, born into a good middle-class Parisian family in 1905, does brilliantly at school, graduates from the Ecole Normale Supérieure in 1924, places first in the class of candidates for the *agrégation* in philosophy in 1929, teaches philosophy in *lycées* in Le Havre, Laon, and Paris, spends the years 1933 to 1934 at the Institut Francais in Berlin, is drafted, like everyone else, in 1939, is taken prisoner, but manages to get released on medical grounds, and resumes his position as professor of philosophy at the Lycée Pasteur while playing an active part in the French Resistance. Obviously Sartre was far from being a young gentleman of independent means who decided at the age of thirty that since there was plenty of existence in the world already, it would be irresponsible to work at creating more of it. Sartre did work; he sought professional security; he set about writing his works over and above his full-time professional activities. He continued this until 1945, and even after that he did not devote himself entirely to writing but became chief editor of *Les Temps Modernes*.

So we should not be misled if Sartre's heroes, Roquentin, say, in *La Nausée* or Mathieu in *Les Chemins de la liberté*, show biographically recognizable features, if Mathieu is a professor of philosophy at the "Lycée Buffon" or Roquentin lives in a city which is obviously Le Havre, and if they are both the same age as Sartre was at the time of writing. A great and fundamental gulf separates these heroes from the author's life: the gulf between practical, everyday reality and literary reality posited and created in order to find life within itself but intended at the same time to be the exemplary expression of a philosophical insight.

This literary reality thus pertains to morality, especially to the practical morality of life, only insofar as the philosophical insight, the view it takes, say, of freedom, itself points toward a posture of responsibility. This, however, is a conclusion divorced from the meaning of the work, which emerges only on a second level. The happenings we encounter in Sartre's writings never mirror model conduct, cannot mirror it because according to Sartre there is no such thing.

### Freedom and Action

Every man stands perennially and inescapably on the brink of new, still-to-be-posited action. He is condemned to a monstrous freedom which he cannot escape by shifting responsibility to values or standards by which he was guided. In the strict philosophical sense nothing worth emulating exists—and this philosophical sense is intended in Sartre's literary work, once we penetrate the literal surface and try to get at the meaning. He would thus be contradicting himself, refuting his own position, if his work were meant to provide norms for conduct—or were even capable of providing them. This is precisely what he wants to evoke as the first principle of knowledge for potential action: that there can be no given criteria for me, for action in the specific case, for determining my choice. I am absolutely free; my action alone posits values.

One might think that this would lead to arbitrariness, that I can do as I like, since it is I who am the sovereign arbiter of value, whose choice makes good or evil that which I have chosen. This, however, is not so. Sartre himself expressly refuted this potential charge (which has in fact frequently been made) in his lecture *L'Existentialisme est un humanisme*. On the contrary, the absolute, inescapable freedom of positing values creates a disquieting responsibility: through my actions I decide not only what represents value for me but what represents value for man, for all men. By making plain through my actions what man is, I define man. Nothing can save me from this inescapable, momentous choice—no commands, no value criteria, not even other people's actions, no model I may follow. Here nothing can help me, for even if there is in practice such a thing as the exemplary model, even though it may be practically important, in essence it does not exist.

*L'existence précède l'essence* is the maxim which formulates this first principle of existentialism, and we recognize now, or we can sense, the ethics behind this maxim. It is an ethics that would not permit one to say that a man of one race is worth more than a man of another, that a senator is worth more than a whore *(La Putain respectueuse)*, an ethics in which the excuse that one was forced to become a party member is meaningless *(Les Séquestrés d'Altona)*. *L'homme est ce qu'il se fait* (man is what he makes of himself). This is purely a consequence of the maxim that existence precedes essence.

Thus the ethics of existentialism is as demanding as it is absolute. It is not derived from concepts given in advance. Whether there is a God or a supreme good is immaterial and irrelevant to it. But this does not mean that it must necessarily be atheistic. For Sartre, well known to be an atheist, the problem of a God simply does not arise. Toward the end of the above-mentioned lecture he says: "Even if a God existed, this would not alter the facts." On the other hand, it is interesting to note that without calling upon God's existence Sartre breaks through to a magnificent concept of human dignity—a dignity which is, of course, not an inherent possession but something man creates. Here the Christian might almost speak of a hitherto unsuspected side of man's being made in the image of God, of a quite genuine creative function which allows man to create himself, as might be expected of a "divine" being. (There would then remain only the question whether this "divine" dignity of man's is itself taken to be a gift of God. But this, as has already been suggested, is a question not of knowledge but of faith.)

### Being and Nothingness

One further potential misunderstanding must be cleared away before we turn to the analysis of Sartre's work, a misunderstanding connected with the magic word "nothingness." This word, in fact, exerts a peculiar spell over us. It is like a deep pond which attracts and fascinates us irresistibly but which under the cold breath of "objectifying" abstraction all too easily freezes to ice on which we can safely tread or even trample. And yet this word has nothing to do with what is commonly meant by nihilism; it should now be quite clear that Sartre's ethics is not nihilistic.

We must go back a little to clarify this. First, it is important to establish that Sartre distinguishes between several modes of being, between the *en soi*, the being of things, and the *pour soi*, the being of men, existence. Whereas things are definable in space as what they are, existence and man are undefinable because man exists only as an individual, and this individual is not something fixed but a reality which stands in the dialectic between being and nothingness. The moment I try to comprehend this man conceptually, he becomes something else, and that too is merely a manner of speaking, because he *is* not any more this new something than he *was* what he was before. The reality of existence partakes of something which from the viewpoint of the being of things is nothingness. The word "nihilism" should not mislead us into seeing this nothingness as something ethically negative, for all this has nothing to do with ethics. In fact, we should not be far from the truth in conceiving of this nothingness in man, this dynamics which constantly drives him out of himself, as soul. "*Quelle belle absence que mon âme*" (What a glorious absence my soul is), says Orestes in *Les Mouches*, and we deceive ourselves if we take this for parody or an assertion of what is commonly called nihilism. To put it somewhat paradoxically, nothingness has a quite positive meaning in Sartre.

On the other hand, though, nothingness is not only a given fact of existence: it is also something that man creates and must create in order to realize his existence. For man is essentially choice, a constantly redrawn preliminary sketch for something else, both in knowing and in acting, and this posits the annihilation or, to put it more understandably, the bracketing out and subjective nullification of everything that is not known and not chosen. If I am studying chemistry, for example, this presupposes that I more or less isolate this project and bracket out many other things—ignore them as not existing for me. I must isolate my project with nothingness, surround it with nothingness, just as I must let the mass of the people in a crowd be submerged if I consider it important to recognize one man.

Not only does man carry nothingness within himself; he also carries it forth into the world, and this carrying forth and embodying in himself of nothingness is just as much man as is his factual reality. Thus, man is neither the one nor the other, neither thing nor nothingness. Neither can he be defined, say, as flux, for flux is predictable, whereas man is at every moment new, free choice. Still less, of course, is man an ideal reality, according to Sartre. Indeed, for him it is impossible to speak of "man" because there is no such thing. I decide, my actions decide, what man is. To repeat: *L'homme est ce qu'il se fait.*

### "Mauvaise Foi"

One point remains to be clarified before we can turn to the literary reality of Sartre's work. (Other points are, of course, bound to come up later.) That is the concept of *mauvaise foi*, (literally: bad faith and here meaning intellectual dishonesty), which is so important for the understanding of Sartre's ideas, and its "positive" counterpart, authenticity. From what we have said, it is almost self-evident what this *mauvaise foi* is: the refusal to admit man's limitation and his existential reality, an evasion of what *is*. One typical example of this which Sartre cites is the title of an essay by Jacques Chardonne: *L'Amour c'est beaucoup plus que l'amour.*[8] This is an attempt to ascribe to love more than it is; love is represented as something *a priori* lofty and to be sought after, an "ideal" never concretely attained. In reality, however, love is what we make of it.

*Mauvaise foi* is the turning into a thing of a phenomenon inseparably linked with, or to, the mode of existence, inasmuch as this act takes place for the sake of evasion, out of dishonesty. Thus a woman is in bad faith when she divides the unity of loving into a physical and a psychological-sentimental or psychological-idealistic experience, when her hand, resting in the hand of her beloved, becomes a thing which is no longer directly within the circuit of her existential unity but is apprehended as something separate and thus materially alien, something foreign which is surrendered to the partner while the intellect rises to the heights of speculation.[9]

We now understand that for Sartre *mauvaise foi* and sincerity ultimately amount to one and the same false posture, to the same misapprehension of the truth, that in their ultimate effect they cannot be separated from one another. (We must, however, add that by "sincerity" Sartre always means a sincerity which desires to be sincere, that is, an explicit effort toward sincerity.) Anyone who wants to be sincere breaks, by definition, the unity of an existential reality. He makes an object, a thing, of something that is not a thing at all but an integrated component of an effective dialectial reality, of an existence. In wanting to be sincere, to "look into my conscience" and apprehend myself, I turn myself into a thing, disregard my existential being, and act as though I could define myself. In reality, however, this is only possible with reference to the man I no longer am, the man I was. If I do this in full knowledge that I am not defining myself as existence but as something past, something that has enjoyed some pleasure or other or had some intention or other, that is legitimate with regard to truth. But if I claim to be making a valid statement about myself, even if I do this in good faith, I am, in the event, to be equated with the man who is in bad faith.

This completes the circle of our very brief preliminary analysis. Everything points back to the fundamental maxim *l'existence précède l'essence*, to the being condemned to freedom that is a necessary part of it, and finally to the distinction between existence and thingness as a synthesis of the dialectic between being and nothingness.[10]

# chapter 2

# Nausea

*La Nausée* (Nausea) —
*Le Mur* (The Wall)

### The Function of Nausea

One of the charges most frequently made against Sartre's literary work is that it stresses the negative, indeed the revolting and the repulsive, that it leaves out the sunny sides of life—the positive and the beautiful—which, after all, are there too. The argument is quite understandable, and there is plenty of evidence to support it. We need only think of the short stories in *Le Mur*, of the panorama of life histories unrolled in *Les Chemins de la liberté*, or of the work whose very title programmatically suggests disgust: *La Nausée*. Never a child's smile, as has justly been objected, never the sun of a meaning! None of Sartre's works, neither the epic ones just mentioned nor any of the plays, offers a meaning in the literal sense, a livable reality. They all demonstrate total failure; they all arouse disgust with existence, or at any rate they are capable of arousing it.

On the other hand, the systematic way in which Sartre arouses such disgust gives us pause, especially when we remember that in *L'Existentialisme est un humanisme* he says that existentialism is a form of optimism. And in fact, he originally intended to call his first and best epic work *"Mélancolie,"* not *"La Nausée."* Nevertheless the latter title, suggested by Gallimard, his publishers, was by no means fortuitous. It stems from the reality of the book, picking up a word which recurs almost like a leitmotiv, though without the theoretical function that might be attributed to its Italian counterpart, Moravia's *La Nausea*.[1] This nausea is, rather, a reality which pervades the whole novel and in which the "hero," Antoine Roquentin, matures to an understanding of himself and of what existence is. Roquentin is in a way a medium for the understanding of existence.[2] Nausea creates the condition man needs in order to become aware of the absolute meaninglessness of existence. As the concrete sense of orientation which man has given himself is muted in this nausea, existence shines forth in its true character, and it becomes obvious that it cannot offer any meaning, that meaning still remains something yet to be made real.[3] Roquentin reaches this conclusion (or at least it is suggested that he reaches it) at the end of the book.

To put it somewhat pointedly, to reproach Sartre with arousing nausea is like reproaching a mystic with using the dark of night or the desert or being faced with a blank wall as a device for depicting his encounter with the absolute. Let us make no mistake: the dark of night, the desert, the blank wall are unquestionably symbols not only for the silence of the senses but for the silence of all sense as well. Thus, in the context of existential thought, nausea takes on a very positive significance.[4] This is what permits being and existence to shine forth in their essence.

### The "Hero"

Of course, Roquentin, the "hero" of *La Nausée*, never fully understands these relationships. He is not in fact a hero in the exemplary sense, but rather as an autonomous existential reality which freely determines its own course.[5] Roquentin has come to Bouville in pursuit of an entirely concrete goal: he wants to write a book on Rollebon, a shadowy eighteenth-century figure supposed to have played a role in the assassination of Peter I, and he hopes to find valuable material on him in the Bouville municipal library. Roquentin will fail in his task, not because the material is not there, but because, beyond it, he is trying to find and grasp Rollebon himself. But existence cannot be fixed; it eludes the grasp which seeks to define it. The material at his disposal does not enable Roquentin to construct a clear portrait. It seems to him to apply not to the Rollebon whom he is trying to portray, but to several personalities[6]. The material thus still reflects the freedom that is inherent in existence.

Thus Roquentin fails because he is too essential, because he is tied to the existence of existence, because he cannot be content with depicting the figure as a historical one, for example, as something from the past, something objectified, simply to be recorded in its facticity. Not only will he not achieve his goal; his inability to do so will also make him questionable to himself, for, as a historian, he has by and large understood himself in the light of this goal. Thus when he says, "Rollebon bores me to death," this is quite literally true. The elusive existential reality of Rollebon destroys his own definition of himself, disillusions his historian's being, throws him back upon his sheer existence.

Roquentin saves himself from this brutally overwhelming realization by turning, in his search for something to hold on to, to something that lurks everywhere in Sartre as a seductive temptation, a trap in which one becomes a thing, as Roquentin would have liked to make Rollebon a thing through words: "On the wall is a blank hole, the mirror. It is a trap. I know I am going to get caught in it. There! The gray thing has just appeared in the mirror. I approach and look at it. I can't get away." [7] Indeed, in this mirror Roquentin so completely becomes a pure thing that he feels the terms "beautiful" and "ugly" (which express ideas) to be no longer appropriate. After all, it would be just as senseless "to call a clod of earth or a chunk of rock beautiful or ugly." [8]

Thus Roquentin is by no means "authentic" in what he is doing; he sees himself as something which he *is* not in essence.

He is not an ideal incarnation of Sartre's ideas on human freedom and the awareness of responsibility which they engender.
He is not predetermined by the ideas of his creator, and he
cannot be, unless Sartre wants to belie his own ideas on human
freedom through his fictional character.[9] Roquentin is an
autonomous novelistic figure which, being existence called
forth in a work of art, has the freedom to go plainly wrong.

Nevertheless Roquentin bears the mark. Even if he makes
the great mistake of seeing himself as something which he is
not, as a thing, he does not go so far as to define himself by
way of this thingness, as can so easily happen before the
mirror; he does not placate his thinking, as it were, by classify-
ing his objective reality as ugly or beautiful, thus re-relating it
to the ideal. In the existentialist sense Roquentin is oriented to
being; if he feels this dull flesh and its pores to be senseless and
inhuman, this demonstrates what his failure to attain his high
goal has already demonstrated: that in principle he is oriented
toward authenticity, toward an understanding of what existence and thingness are.

### La Nausée as a Novel [10]

Thus Roquentin is concerned with authenticity from the first.
He is on the way; he is seeking, and this makes him a genuine
fictional character. His story is a story of failure to achieve
high aims, but of a failure which will lead him step by step, by
way of disillusionment with the possibility of finding meaning,
to the knowledge of what existence, according to Sartre, is. His
way is, as it were, a search for the ideal on a negative plane, a
search which amounts to the liquidation of the ideal and its
rechanneling into the plane of essence. For Roquentin's demands for the book he was about to write showed that he had
set his sights very "high." The decisive importance that Sartre
attaches to these demands shows in the structural technique he
uses here. He makes a point of repeatedly confronting the high
goal with an almost ridiculous reality, as Roquentin's eyes are
forced, as he goes to and from the library, to face the reality of
a monument representing an insignificant historical figure, one

Impétraz, dressed in a frock coat and top hat—a representation which excludes his existential reality so that he stands there as a man who thinks "just like everybody else." [11]

But in addition to Roquentin's illusory aim, this Bouville which he has chosen is also a token of his being one of the "chosen," for this town, which, as its name alone suggests (*la boue*—mud), hardly offers meaning, elicits nausea. It is a town with streets "such as are normally found only in capital cities, in Berlin around Neukölln or toward Friedrichshain, in London behind Greenwich." [12] It is a city which we have good reason to believe stands for Le Havre, where Sartre worked from 1931 to 1933, but which can also be taken quite generally as evoking a certain type of town in which any newly arrived human being who has a relation to what is meaningful will be thrown back upon himself, where he becomes eminently aware of the existential nature of his existence.[13] Thus this town contributes to the destruction of Roquentin's redeeming, structure-creating orientation toward concrete meaningfulness; it helps to make him wholly absolute, turning his years in Bouville into one great search for ultimate, authentic meaning.

Everywhere, not merely in the library, Roquentin is seeking a value that can meet the breaking test of his thinking. He is constantly on the lookout. However much time he spends sitting in cafés, his eyes are always searching, not least among the people he watches there. He tests them all for authenticity: the couples, the waiters, the proprietresses, and the solitary customers too. Most of them have totally surrendered to objectification or to *mauvaise foi*; they betray the predictability of an ambulatory waiter's existence or the bad faith of a divided way of loving, so that Roquentin asks himself: "After all, is it absolutely necessary to lie to oneself?" [14] But there are a few who are actually on the way, who, while they fall short of ultimate good faith and authenticity, are oriented toward it and toward truth, though with varying degrees of consistency and pertinacity. These are the great unforgettable characters of *La Nausée*: Anny, the autodidact, and Antoine Roquentin himself. (Perhaps Monsieur Achille should be included too, although he appears only briefly.[15]) These are the three central characters, although Anny, Roquentin's former mistress, does not become important until the concluding phase. They have all passed the "positive" high point of their search when the story begins. Crisis has engulfed all of them, Antoine Roquentin most deeply and relentlessly, because of the three he is the one who recognizes most plainly the spuriousness of the temptations which arise. But all three of them are far from giving up the search. At first the continuity of their search is suggested only occasionally, and then only in Roquentin and the autodidact. (Anny, as we have said, does not appear until the end.) But halfway through the novel their search becomes noticeably more concentrated.

Until then Roquentin has had his experiences more or less alone. The others, including the autodidact, have been merely a backdrop in front of which his failure was enacted, his justifying goal disappeared, and his own existence became *de trop*.[16] Now that he has written off his failure and realized perfectly clearly that his book was merely a pretext [17] to get away from the unbridgeable loneliness of being nobody but himself,[18] now that he has been inescapably thrown back upon his existence and, proceeding from himself alone, must make a fresh start by way of the Cartesian *cogito ergo sum*,[19] he realizes among other things that his existence is something imperfect ("*l'existence est une imperfection*" [20]). This realization will drive him into three final temptations which amount to structuring himself upon living people and brotherhood and thus overcoming the isolation of being himself.

As we might expect, these temptations now bring into play the other two heroes of *La Nausée*, Anny and the autodidact, no longer as backdrop or memory, but actively. Here Sartre will alternate temptation and mystical, almost ecstatic absorption in the nature of existence in a broad design which points toward the end as the climax and is worked out in the structure of the novel as well. The first temptation,[21] the weakest of the three, is the temptation of "humanism," as represented by the autodidact, and this is really more like a caricature of humanism. For the autodidact is basically just as absolute as Roquentin. He belongs to the world of authentic seekers and goes astray only through ignorance, as Roquentin himself explicitly states. His warped, tortured humanism is an escape from being, which refutes itself. For the autodidact has discovered a system which provides him with an illusion of order and meaning: he is reading all the books in the municipal library in alphabetical order and noting down on a pad remarks that seem to him worth remembering. In this way he creates around himself a world of "humanistic" ideology. But it is easy enough to see how spurious it all is, how artificial. Fundamentally and from the first he belongs among the naked, undefined existences. The collapse of his constructionism is only a matter of time.

In the café where the two meet, however, things have not yet reached that point. Here the autodidact can still play the tempter, challenge Roquentin to attach a label to himself, call himself a misanthrope or an antihumanist, allow himself to be seized and made into a thing. But Roquentin resists, and when the autodidact throws out the most insidious bait—"One must love men. Men are admirable"[22]—he is racked with nausea, with *"cette aveuglante évidence"* (this blinding certainty),[23] this heightened and enlightened moment in which things pitilessly show their true face, their underside.

Thus in a first temptation Roquentin liquidates the autodidact's humanism, and almost as a fruit of this annihilation of possible meaning he now has the marvelous experience of existence induced by watching the root of a chestnut tree.[24] Roquentin experiences the ecstasy of being absolute, and like every ecstasy this one, too, primarily denotes understanding.[25]

Somewhat as the mystic transcribes his vision, this vision of essential being is proclaimed as the attainment of wordless knowledge: "Words had vanished and with them the meaning of things, their uses, the faint bench marks which men have traced on their surface." [26] What Roquentin is now experiencing is no longer the journey; it is ecstatic anticipation of arrival: "I have reached my goal: I know what I wanted to know. Everything that has happened to me since January I now understand." [27] Up to now he has always used things as tools, taking their surface for the things themselves. Now, however, he is overcome by the realization of the too-muchness (*être de trop*) of things and of himself, their un-related isolation,[28] what might be called their horizontality, their absoluteness, or—and in this case it amounts to the same thing—their absurdity.[29] It is now clear to him that any form of constructivity—interpretations, explanations, or the positing of any kind of relationships—leads away from the world of existence, runs counter to the nature of existence: "The world of explanations and reasons is not the world of existence." [30] Roquentin calls this moment, in which he is overwhelmed by evidence of what existence is, an "extraordinary moment," a "terrible ecstasy." He sums up the fruits of the insights so gained as follows: "The essential thing is contingency. I mean that, by definition, existence is not necessity. To exist means simply to *be there;* those who exist appear and can be *encountered,* but one can never *deduce* them." [31] Thus the absolute horizontality of all being is once again stressed, its unrelatedness, its nonde-ducibility: "Everything that exists is born without reason, continues to live out of weakness, and dies by chance." [32]

Then comes the second temptation,[33] the temptation of the quest for magic meaning and the resignation which results from it.

Roquentin meets Anny, his former mistress, and together they revive for one last time their past of illusions and dis-appointments. What was for Roquentin the adventure, orienta-tion toward meaning falling to his share, was for Anny what she called the game of "perfect moments." Michelet's *Histoire de France* had led her to seek to fix the moment into absolute validity. In Michelet a few pictures, illustrations, had been given a whole page to themselves and even a blank page on the back too. For the whole sixteenth century, for instance, there were only three: one showing the death of Henry II, another the murder of the Duc de Guise, and a third the entry of Henry IV into Paris. What fascinated Anny in these pictures was their rigorous unity. She took this to mean that there are "privileged situations" in which one can push forward to the unity of valid meaning, to the structure of a solid connection: being a king and dying. These are moments in which one is raised above oneself and can escape from mere existence. Later Anny added other privileged situations: among others the act of love. Such a "privileged moment" could then be heightened to a "perfect moment" if one succeeded in willing an order commensurate with the exceptional, a kind of magic harmony of circumstances.[34] Again and again she had tried to bring this about in her friendship with Roquentin, to create with him a real-life work of art, but something had always prevented it. Above all, Roquentin himself, whether he acted one way or another, had never understood what the issue was and what was at stake in it. As a person he was simply too horizontal, too odd and unique, to enter into such a context.

Nevertheless in their first kiss she achieved a "perfect moment" with Roquentin. All the time he was trying to get her to kiss him she was sitting on a stinging nettle, and she had succeeded in sovereignly fitting the constant stings into the given order of a "perfect moment," not only suppressing any utterance of pain but not even feeling any pain.

All these illusions, however, lie deep in the past. In the meantime Anny has resigned herself to the impossibility of acting: "One cannot be a man of action."[35] But she has not reached the authenticity of conscious aloneness which is beginning to be—and will become more and more—characteristic of Roquentin. She has sought methods for producing a structure of pseudo-meaning, at least in her dreams. Here, Loyola's *Spiritual Exercises*, the handbook of contemplative verticality, has been very useful to her; here she found the methodological instructions for elevating her past through contemplation into a series of "perfect moments." Roquentin is perplexed by her desperate constructivity. They have lost the same illusions, followed the same way, but the radical difference between them is that Roquentin is neither despondent nor resigned: he is simply astonished: "Astonished at this life which is given to me—given to me for *nothing*." [36] The reason for this is evidently that he never expected much. Once again he reacts "horizontally." He feels a desire simply to take Anny in his arms and through a straightforward, nonproblematical action to let love be its own answer. But Anny draws back; she cannot help demanding more of love: that it create a transcendent, valid meaning. And since she genuinely loves Roquentin, it is impossible for her to silence this demand while she is with him. She therefore gives him up for the illusionless eroticism of a liaison with a handsome young foreigner.

Thus love and the search for magic meaning are liquidated, and now for the first time Roquentin is afraid of solitude.[37] This second temptation has taken him deeper into the understanding of what existence is. Now for the first time he becomes completely aware of his existential situation of exile, of his bridgeless isolation.[38] In the three years he has spent in Bouville he has not come to feel at home there. Bouville has not become *his* town; he is still a stranger.

The third and last temptation still awaits him.[39] It leads back to the setting where so many scenes of *La Nausée* take place: the Bouville library, with its few readers and its assistant librarian. This is Roquentin's last visit to the reading room; he has come to take his leave of it. His disillusionment is apparently complete; yet he still cherishes a great hope. He still has to learn that the solitude of existence to which he is condemned is unbridgeable, that there is no such thing as a "community" of loneliness, no such thing as brotherhood.

Roquentin has in fact often noted in his diary that somebody, the autodidact for example, is really on his side, and this feeling used to give him a sort of sense of belonging, the possibility of establishing a relationship to someone else and thus fixing and structuring mere existence by means of inter-relationships with others, moving it out of itself, pushing it beyond itself toward some available meaning. Now, when Roquentin wants to say good-bye, the autodidact's suffering seems to offer him an opportunity for this. For a long time the librarian and a studious old lady have been awaiting their chance to expose the autodidact as a homosexual, for it is all too obvious that he is vulnerable on this score. This time they are successful. Roquentin tries to prevent the misfortune by coughing loudly, forcing the autodidact to pay attention. But this does no good. Sitting between two young boys, the autodidact commits a slight impropriety in the reading room. Amid the general indignation, Roquentin seizes the opportunity of taking his side. But the autodidact wants no part of it and rejects Roquentin's support. He is absolute freedom. He rushes out into the loneliness which alone is in keeping with man's essence, and here through a symbolic touch Sartre seems to suggest the existentialist standing it confers on him: "The setting sun illuminated his bent back for a moment, then he disappeared. On the doorstep was a bloodstain in the shape of a star." [40] Roquentin's search has reached its lowest point, its negative climax. Every possible meaning seems to have been cleared away. All that remains for him to do is to sum up his three years in Bouville, and this he does in the "Rendez-vous des Cheminots," a bar and restaurant where he often goes. This is the moment when he has become geographically placeless too; to all intents he has already left Bouville, but he was not yet set foot in Paris, and the *dénouement* of this moment, described in the final pages of *La Nausée*, is to bring him a remarkable experience of meaning.

Madeleine, the waitress, trying to cheer him up a little, offers to play his favorite record, a jazz recording of *Some of These Days*. Roquentin has listened to it many times before, but at this moment, as the notes of the saxophone again reach his ear, he understands for the first time the true and for him the embarrassing meaning of this tune. These notes are validly apprehended, restrained suffering. In them existence has been successfully transcended. This melody does not exist; it is not contingent; it is not imperfect. It simply *is*. And confronted with this success he confesses that his whole life is a quest.

> And I too wanted to *be*. Indeed that is all I have wanted. That has been the whole point of my life. Beneath all those apparently unrelated attempts I discover the same desire: to drive existence out of myself, to rid the instants of their fat, wring them out, dry them up, to purify and harden myself, and in the end to give out the clear, precise sound of a saxophone note.[41]

We may ask why it should be a jazz tune that triggers this experience in Roquentin, why Sartre wanted it this way. It could be an antibourgeois stance, certainly also his predilection for the discordant. Ultimately, however, there is something else, something more essential. Sartre is determined to make it impossible to take this tune as a concrete combination of statement and meaning, as an existing thing which itself decomposes into meaning and existence. In this jazz melody the individual notes are in unbroken identity with themselves, as they are not in a classical melody. They are absolute; they are not a means of creating something else, something comprehensive, a structure of meaning. They form a horizontal series. This jazz melody is horizontal transcendence.[42]

An American Jew, sweating from the heat on the twentieth floor of some New York skyscraper, has thus succeeded in overcoming existence, in saving himself as well as the Negress who sings his song.

> Those two at least are saved: the Jew and the Negress. Saved. Maybe they thought they were completely done for, drowned in existence. Yet nobody could think of me as I think of them—with this tenderness. Nobody, not even Anny. . . . They are cleansed of the sin of existing. Not entirely, of course—but as much as a man can manage.[43]

This is what Roquentin has been seeking too. He wanted to cast off the existential element in his existence ("to drive existence out of myself"). He wanted to escape contingency, to become pure and absolute ("to purify myself") like the hard note of the saxophone. He wanted to be redeemed, and the terms Sartre chooses to express this need for redemption are astonishing. He speaks of the "sin of existing," of "being ashamed of existence" [44] and of catharsis ("they are cleansed"). This awareness of the sinfulness of existence had also prevented this thirty-year-old man of property from working creatively: "To do something is to create existence—and there's already plenty of that as it is." [45] Now, in the concluding lines of La Nausée, the potential task reveals itself: instead of trying to resuscitate Rollebon, he must write a book that will be like the notes of the saxophone, hard as steel, so that, confronted with it, people will be ashamed of their existence.[46]

### The Inner Structure of *La Nausée* [47]

It is not difficult to guess what book Roquentin has in mind as his redeeming goal when Sartre's novel ends. It is *La Nausée*, the diary of failure which he has in fact just written. Thus *La Nausée* is to be taken as more than just a novel: as a novel it is to fulfill the same function as the jazz melody: to reveal the existential nature of existence so absolutely that existence is overcome and pure being is attained.

It was therefore vital that, despite its necessarily vertical novelistic structure telling of development and search, *La Nausée* should be horizontally designed and that the epic principle of horizontality should so far as possible outweigh the vertical structure. Here the choice of diary form is significant.[48] In this essentially serial arrangement the individual entries are to a great extent autonomous, something like the *laisses* of the Old French epic—at any rate much more autonomous than a sequence of numbered chapters. It was no accident that Lamartine chose this form for his sentimental epic *Jocelyn*.

Moreover, a syntactical analysis shows a predominant use of parataxis, of apparently irrelevant juxtaposition, although not as consistently as in, say, Camus's *L'Etranger*. Let us take the following paragraph as an example. (The scene is the Bouville Library at closing time.)

> The old man had finished his novel. But he did not leave. He was tapping the table with his finger in a staccato, regular beat.
>
> "Gentlemen," said the Corsican, "we're about to close."
>
> "The young man started and darted a quick glance at me. The young woman had turned toward the Corsican, then she picked up her book again and seemed absorbed in it.
>
> "Closing time," said the Corsican five minutes later. The old man shook his head uncertainly. The young woman put her book aside without getting up.
>
> The Corsican was at a loss. He took a few hesitant steps, then turned a switch. The lights went off at the reading tables. Only the central bulb was still on.
>
> "Must we go?" asked the old man softly.[49]

The brief sentences follow one another loosely, formally expressing the disconnectedness and isolation, the horizontality, of their content. From time to time hypotaxis intervenes, and the verticality of deductive thought seems to predominate. But this is never anything but a temporary shift which soon leads back to the horizontality of pure statement of absolute facticity. To quote again:

> I am surely going to see Anny again but I can't say that the idea makes me exactly happy. Since I got her letter I feel at loose ends. Luckily it's midday. I'm not hungry but I go to lunch to pass the time. I go to Camille's in the Rue des Horlogers.
>
> It's a cosy little place; they serve sauerkraut and *cassoulet* all night. People come for supper after the theater. The police recommend it to travelers who arrive late at night and are hungry. Eight marble tables. A leather seat runs along the walls. Two mirrors covered with reddish stains.[50]

In the first paragraph hypotaxis—syntactical connection—predominates. The infinitive phrase "to pass the time" also falls into this pattern. But the words "I go to Camille's" prepare the substantive as well as the stylistic transition to the next paragraph. The thought, up to now effortlessly reflective, has through an action attached itself to an object which it pauses to consider, and this is expressed quite logically by parataxis.[51] This reflective dwelling on the object, this horizontal form of thinking, is definitely the one that characterizes Roquentin.

This becomes particularly clear in the decisive experience in which Roquentin becomes aware of his absolute dropping out of "positive" relatedness. First there is that trifling occurrence which Sartre even refuses to call an "event," reported in an undated and fragmentary entry which, like a torn-out, absolute page from a diary, serves in form and content as an introduction. Roquentin was about to pick up a pebble, as he must often have done before, and skim it over the surface of the water to watch it jump. Then something remarkable happened. He was about to throw it, but dropped the stone and went away. And now, thinking over what actually went on, he can arrive at no deduction, no link between cause and effect, for what had happened to him with the pebble was precisely the suspension of this ability to see himself related. In his search for an explanation he can therefore only describe the sheer objectness of a thing in horizontality, both linguistic and conceptual: "The pebble was flat, dry on one side, damp and muddy on the other. I held it by the edges with my fingers far apart so as not to get them dirty." [52] Just as unrelatedly absolute was whatever it was that prevented him from picking up a piece of paper on the ground, taking it in his hand, and enjoying the rustling freshness of its paper being.[53]

The two cases point to the same thing: the constructivity of his subject-object relationship is broken; what Heidegger calls "*das Zuhandensein der Dinge*," the being-there of things, eludes him. (At the time of writing *La Nausée*, Sartre was still very much under the influence of the German phenomenologists, of both Heidegger and Husserl.[54]) He experiences the objectness of things as a reality separated from himself, one which by its very nature cannot be brought into relationship with himself. Hitherto objects have been useful to him; he has made use of them. Now they are moving up toward autonomy, *touching* him (the word *toucher* is of central importance in Sartre): "Objects ought not to *touch*, since they're not alive. You use them, put them back in their places. You live among them. They are useful, nothing more. But in my case they touch me, and that's intolerable. I'm afraid of making contact with them, just as is if they were live animals."[55]

And this breaking up of cohesiveness, of this "so regular world" (p. 13), this sudden intuitive awareness of the horizontality, the *pour-soi* of man and object, is what arouses his nausea: "And it came from the pebble, I'm sure. It was transmitted from the pebble into my hands. Yes, that's it, that's certainly it: a kind of nausea in my hands."[56] The formal horizontality largely maintained in the syntax parallels the subject matter: to a certain extent they are identical.

This process whereby things become autonomous in relationless confrontation is not confined to objects in the narrow sense. It includes man too in his material, physical reality. This applies above all to the members through which man actualizes the being-there of things and draws them into relatedness: the hands. One day, for example, it takes Roquentin a long time to realize that what he is holding in his hand is not a white worm but the extremity of an arm belonging to the autodidact (p. 16). The absolute isolation of objects, their removal into essential untouchability, their elevation into *"personnalités"* which themselves have the property of touching, makes hands seem useless, annuls in a way their integration into the human consciousness, turns them, like the objects themselves, into independent phenomena which exist by themselves, independently, simply hanging fortuitously and irrelevantly at the end of an arm: "At that moment a hand began to move downward across the skirt at the end of a stiff arm." [57] And this by no means applies only to other people's arms.

> I see my hand opening out on the table. It's alive—it's me. It opens. The fingers unfold and point upward. It is on its back. It shows me its fat belly. It's like a turned-over animal. The fingers are the legs. I amuse myself by moving them very quickly, like the legs of a crab which has fallen over on its back. . . . Now I feel its weight at the end of my arm. It drags a bit, hardly at all, gently, limply. It exists.[58]

Obviously passages like this, evoking the sheer existence of existent things, have an extraordinary charm, the poetry of the being-for-themselves, beyond all meaning, of things, and there is no need to emphasize how much in keeping this horizontal charm (which Sartre uses frequently in *La Nausée*) is with the spirit of epic writing.[59]

A final example may also show that existentialism and humor can be quite compatible, that here the laughter of things, so to speak, if not the laughter of a child, can be captured. The case in question is one of evoking the reality of pure planeness, on its way to becoming an indeterminate color sensation, of a pair of suspenders which simply insist on remaining themselves and nothing but themselves.

The suspenders can hardly be distinguished against the blue shirt; they are completely effaced, absorbed by the blue. But this is sham humility: in fact they don't let themselves be forgotten. They irritate me with their sheeplike obstinacy, as if, having set out to be purple, they had stopped on the way without abandoning their pretensions. You feel like saying to them: "Go ahead, *become* purple, and let's not talk about it any more." But no, they remain neither one thing nor the other, stubbornly persisting in their unfinished effort.[60]

### Novel and Existence

Unquestionably in *La Nausée* Sartre has respected the horizontality of his concept of existence both formally and in content—has in fact given it visible form. *La Nausée* is literature of existence. Yet as such it is not completely satisfying. Remembering what we said of it as a novel, we are left with a certain uneasiness about the formula, or at least it is understandable that a philosopher or structuralist should feel this way. Sartre himself has spoken of this uneasiness in *Les Mots*, although, of course, without restricting it to *La Nausée*.[61] After all, we have just seen that besides inner horizontality, *La Nausée* also has a relatively continuous plot, even if it "builds up" in reverse order. Indeed—and here we become extremely dubious—its last few pages present an unmistakable deliverance which allows us quite naturally to see everything that has happened as leading up to that deliverance—and which perhaps even must be seen this way, esthetically speaking. It makes no difference that this accepted possibility of deliverance that suddenly emerges toward the end is exemplified by an essentially horizontal jazz melody. The solution itself remains vertical in any case, because it leads out of the oppressive contingency experienced as sin.

These reflections, which imply no disparagement—for nothing is farther from my mind—may perhaps throw new light on the fact that Sartre has made only one really successful attempt at the novel as a genre. He sensed that a novel, in order to become completely convincing *as a novel*, in order to become a *grand roman*, must lead to a vertical transcendence.

*Don Quixote, La Princesse de Clève,* the novels of Chrétien de Troyes, as well as works such as Malraux's *La Condition humaine* and François Mauriac's *La Fin de la nuit,* all have this "vertical transcendence." [62]

Philosophically it is thus entirely rational that Sartre should have sought to reorient the genre immediately after *La Nausée.* (In fact, in the novella *Le Mur* he had already attempted it.) He branches out in two directions, away from the novel as novel, though without departing from the epic genre. On the one hand he experiments with the novella, and he also tries, in *Les Chemins de la liberté,* to overcome the technical requirements of the genre from within. The novella gave Sartre an opportunity to take as point of departure an event needing little or no development in order to illustrate a phenomenon in its isolation—as he does in *Le Mur* [63]—and thus to obviate the necessities of structural totality inherent in the novel.

But it cannot be said that the results are very convincing. *Le Mur* (The Wall), *La Chambre* (The Room), *Erostrate* (Erostratus), and *Intimité* (Intimacy) are disappointing; they provide no satisfactory esthetic solution.[64] *L'Enfance d'un chef* (The Childhood of a Leader) is the exception, and this is really more than a novella. The longest of the stories, this miniature novel deals with Lucien's development from infancy to early manhood or, as the title says, with the childhood of a man born to be a chief. This "novel" too ends with a kind of conversion of the hero which, like the one in *La Nausée,* leads away from the existentiality of existence, this time through the reassuring structuring of bourgeois values: "For a long time he had believed that he existed by chance, drifting at random, but that was because he had not thought about it enough. Long before he had been born, his place had been marked out in the sun, at Férolles." [65] If the meaning which Roquentin discovered at the "Rendez-vous des Cheminots" was already suspect, if it looked like a structural relic of a scheme from which Sartre cannot free himself completely without violating the character of the genre, "vertical transcendence" is here presented with obvious irony: "In the same way whole generations of workmen could scrupulously obey Lucien's orders; they would never exhaust his right to command. Rights were beyond existence, like mathematical objects and religious dogmas." Here Sartre's existentialism is completely turned around and offered in unmistakable irony, not to say parody, as the redeeming realization that *l'essence précède l'existence*. For Lucien's saving insight does indeed imply that his right to give orders is something that precedes existence, that is inalienably his own, something whose essence generations of workmen can never exhaust with their existence. Thus the "childhood" of the future "chief" is over. He is now "the chief," and all he needs is a mustache: " 'I'll grow a mustache,' he decided."

But the other stories, revealing as they are of Sartre's philosophical position, are hardly convincing. In *La Nausée* nausea was given shape as a phenomenon; there it could almost rise to song, holding the whole together and giving it unity. Here nausea remains confined to superficialities, to disgusting things, to those sides of human nature which, brutally pulled out into the light, may shock and nauseate, but after all only as something accidental, concretely founded, and not as an absolute. The humiliating failure of bodily functions suffered by the condemned men in *Le Mur* and observed in their fellow prisoners, the oppressive, self-enclosed world of madness in *La Chambre*, the sexual perversion of the hero of *Erostrate*, the stress on the vulgar aspects of the erotic relationships in *Intimité* are well designed to arouse disgust, but it is a dischargeable, justifiable disgust, a disgust that lacks the smile which in *La Nausée* and perhaps in *L'Enfance d'un chef* too actually proves Sartre's mastery.

In these stories Sartre also made the mistake of allowing certain basic tenets of his philosophy to stand out too obviously. Lulu in *Intimité* is first and foremost an unequivocal incarnation of a Sartrean concept, so that the dialectic of the plot, which takes four chapters to develop, is only an apparent one. Lulu is a clear-cut exemplification of the thesis that in love one partner tries to objectify the other, to make him into a thing: "Lulu liked to feel this big captive body against hers. 'If he could stay like this, paralyzed, I'd take care of him, I'd clean him up like a baby, and sometimes I'd turn him over and give him a spanking. . . .' "[66] This is how Lulu thinks about her relationship to her husband. What she loves in him is the soft, yielding, unmasculine element that permits her to regard and treat him as a thing. But this does not throw either Lulu or her husband into relief as people, as existential reality.

No doubt this shadowless horizontality of "being-only-this" goes better with Sartre's horizontal philosophy than novelistic connectedness. On the other hand, as we have already said, the existential nature of existence is abandoned in these characters. They are no longer incarnations of the freedom of "choice"; instead they are a reality predetermined by philosophical thinking. Theoretically, to be sure, Lulu could leave her husband and agree in turn to become an object in Pierre's eyes, a chattel of her essentially "more masculine" lover. But she is far too strongly drawn as an "ideal" reality for this danger to be taken seriously. Her *"je ne suis pas un chien"* (I am not a dog) is the long-awaited return to her "ideal" essence.

Neither is *L'Enfance d'un chef* entirely free from this "ideality"—as the title already implies. But Lucien, far more than any of the other characters in this volume of novellas, represents a true dialectic of existential reality. This spoiled baby, who, while still sitting on the pot and despite all the structural life-aids offered to him, penetrates to the solitude of authentic humanity, feels the summons to something else in a completely genuine way: "He thought he had had enough of playing at being Lucien."[67] He perceives the existentiality of existence, its character of being there, and yet he is deeply rooted in a milieu and a way of thinking which foist unauthenticity upon him. There is no way of telling what decision he will come to. Nothing ties him to the existentialist short circuit in which—though through a genuine act of choice—he finally decides in favor of what Sartre calls nonauthenticity.

**chapter 3**

# Freedom and Engagement

*Les Chemins de la liberté*
(The Roads to Freedom) —
*Les Mouches* (The Flies)

Until the war the problem of freedom apparently did not pose itself pressingly enough for Sartre to become a major theme in his novels. His war experiences—military service and captivity and finally his role in the Resistance—probably played a part in making it a central literary problem for him. It is not by chance that *Les Chemins de la liberté* leads into precisely the straits of free existence that Sartre himself had passed through during his military service and captivity and in the Resistance. Neither was it chance that led him in 1943 to write a play, *Les Mouches,* in which the hero's thinking revolves around the concept of freedom and which depicts a nation that has relinquished this freedom to wallow in collective guilt under a usurper. Nevertheless the topical nature of *Les Chemins de la liberté* and *Les Mouches* should not be overstressed, for both works are after all logical continuations of a dialogue begun in *La Nausée* and *Le Mur* but interrupted by the war. This also applies to the choice of genre. So far as *Les Mouches* is concerned, the stories in *Le Mur* are already clearly oriented

30

toward a dramatic constellation. (The themes of *Le Mur*, for instance, anticipate *Morts sans sépultures*. The point of departure of *La Chambre* is a situation developed dramatically in *Les Séquestrés d'Altona*, and *Erostrate* is not unrelated to the theme of *Les Mains sales*.) Thus Sartre's turn to the drama form was a logical one which had been in the making for some time. As for *Les Chemins de la liberté*, this leads into the alternative still open to him within the epic genre if he wanted to avoid the compromise of *La Nausée* and the weaknesses of his novella collection. Here Sartre decides to widen the narrative basis so that the structure of the work will correspond to the horizontality of what he has to say.

This work was to comprise four volumes: the three extant ones, *L'Age de raison* (1945; The Age of Reason), *Le Sursis* (1945; The Reprieve) and *La Mort dans l'âme* (1949; Troubled Sleep), and another *La dernière chance*, still to come, a fragment of which has been published. The narrative technique of this work, as well as its scope, leads into the "dispersion" of horizontality. The classical unity of action and place that marks *La Nausée* is lacking in *Les Chemins de la liberté* as a whole and in its individual volumes. In form (diary) and content (nausea) *La Nausée* emanated from the reality of a single consciousness; in *Les Chemins de la liberté* we have plurality in both title and form. In this way Sartre tries to make form too express the objective character of the freedom of existences, and it is revealing that here, quite in contrast to *La Nausée*, the threads do not gradually—especially toward the end—link up into a firm pattern of meaning. They continue at first on a relatively straight and continuous path, but by and by they lead ever more deeply into "dispersion," into the pathlessness of absolute freedom.

Whereas *L'Age de raison*, for instance, presents various groups made up of clearly profiled individuals, Mathieu, the central hero, is still a pivotal character unifying the action. Daniel too has a considerable degree of independence, as do Boris and his aging mistress Lola at times, but their connection with Mathieu is never completely broken. In *Le Sursis*, on the other hand, unity of action has been completely disregarded. Modes of behavior are registered by various individuals and groups kaleidoscopically.¹ The mosaic of an epoch is jumbled, and the pieces are rearranged in a multicolored, meaningless chain. Thus the separate elements become completely autonomous and attain a much enfeebled continuity only by way of far-flung bridges across nothingness. What matters is the obligation to choose, the freedom to which each man is condemned.

This structure is certainly co-determined by the subject of the book. As the title, *Le Sursis*, indicates, Sartre takes as his point of departure the week of September 23 to 30, 1938, a momentous week of danger and excitement in world politics when war seemed to be imminent and all customary understanding seemed to be at a halt for a week. Yet, on the other hand, this conferring of autonomy on individual happenings is also a formal consequence of a way of thinking. In *La Mort dans l'ame* Sartre will go a step farther in completely divorcing two parts at the intersection of which the hero, who has so far dominated and unified the action to a certain extent, dies. We should also remember that although the title of this whole work is in the plural, it contains the crucial word "roads." Thus the book is also trying to present a journey, something that by its very nature entails continuity, systematic orientation toward a goal, perhaps even a search. Whether *"de la liberté"* is to be interpreted objectively in the sense of roads *to* freedom or subjectively as roads *of* freedom, the word "road" is unquestionably there. Probably it does not explicitly mean either the one or the other: Mathieu is on the way to a freedom which he already is.

### L'Age de raison

*The Age of Reason* is the title of the first stage of this journey. Mathieu, having reached so-called maturity, really ought to settle down, marry, and acquire proper status, as his brother Jacques, a lawyer, plainly tells him: "You've reached the age of reason, Mathieu—or you ought to have. . . ."² Jacques has picked the moment to tell Mathieu this diplomatically yet very badly, casting himself so obviously in the role of the tempter, not to say the blackmailer, that there is little risk of his seriously threatening Mathieu the idealist. Mathieu needs money, four thousand francs. He needs it for an abortion for Marcelle, his mistress for many years, and Jacques seizes the opportunity of reiterating his old advice: Mathieu should settle down and marry Marcelle; then he'll get the money and more besides. Jacques offers him ten thousand francs. He plays his cards cleverly, but Mathieu does not respond. The thirty-four-year-old philosophy professor is too attached to his freedom to enter into this social commitment. To show himself with Marcelle would then seem to him unauthentic because it could no longer express what he is: choice.

He rejects another, doubtless more dangerous attempt to lure him into engagement. The Communist Brunet tries to persuade him to enlist in the Spanish civil war, in which he himself has given meaning to his life through political commitment: "Now nothing can deprive my life of its meaning; nothing can prevent it from being a destiny." [3] He challenges Mathieu to do the same: to yield to a need he is sure Mathieu feels too: "You need to commit yourself." [4] Mathieu must commit himself if his freedom is to serve any purpose. He has freed himself from bourgeois society, but the freedom he has acquired is the freedom of "an abstraction, of someone who isn't there." According to Brunet he should commit his freedom to "engagement"; only in this way will he truly achieve it: "You have renounced everything in order to be free. Go one step farther: renounce your freedom itself, and all will be given to you." [5] But Mathieu thinks abstractly, not practically. He feels a need to tell himself that what Brunet is proposing leads to objectification, to a renunciation of the dialectical nature of being which prohibits man from tying himself down; he believes that he would be denying an essential part of himself if he were to become like Brunet: "A man with powerful, slightly knotted muscles, who thought in brief, rigorous truths, an erect man, closed, sure of himself, a man of the earth, resistant to the angelic temptations of art, psychology, politics, a whole man, nothing but a man" (*ibid.*).

Brunet has become an entity, something tangible and definable, something which fills space, which is space. In confronting him Mathieu is handicapped by weakness, by his undefinable, unstable position: "And Mathieu was there facing him, irresolute, not properly grown up, not properly baked, a prey to all the vertigoes of the inhuman" (*ibid.*). He is open and therefore vulnerable, an image of what man by essence is, condemned to be more and at the same time infinitely less than just a man. In declining Brunet's proposal he opts for this nongravitational freedom of human existence. This decision (which, for all its significance in the context of Sartre's ideas, in no way reflects Sartre's own practical position) is not easy for him, first because the temptation to give his life a concrete meaning is a strong one, and second because it is by no means evident that it is really only a temptation. Though at the moment of declining he feels a kind of elation, this soon recedes, yielding to a disturbing realization: " 'I am one of the irresponsible ones,' he thought." [6] And he imagines an incident of war from which he has just excluded himself: bombs falling on the innocent while he avoids engagement.

Mathieu misunderstands freedom. He wants to remain free, but a freedom which becomes its own object is no longer freedom. Moreover, he reveals all too plainly what he cherishes in this "freedom," what it means to him: "I like my green curtains; I like taking the air on my balcony in the evening, and I don't want that to change." [7] Mathieu has yielded to habit, erected a framework to support his life, and for him freedom means being able to retain these habits; freedom is the vicious circle of self-chosen limitation. Going back to his room, he finds *his* chair, *his* furniture, the possessions with which he has "set himself up," as the phrase appropriately puts it, and he remarks with some justification: "I am a lousy wash-out" (*ibid.*).

### The Structure

Perhaps it now begins to be clear that the roads in *Les Chemins de la liberté* are also roads *to* freedom, or at least they represent themselves in this way, as a quest which knows defeat and false directions. Since this is a novel, it had to be so. Although the scope is broadened, the orientation toward an ideal to be realized persists. The ideal will be submerged from time to time, but sometimes it will rise to a high point. Mathieu has a long way to go before he realizes—and then not definitively—that he already *is* freedom.

What difference does it make that Mathieu and the young woman philosophy student Ivich are taken for representatives of freedom and admired as such? In a night club, acting in full freedom, they stick a knife into their hands, first Ivich, then Mathieu. When the blood spurts in such a silly way from the flesh surrounding the blade, *their* blood, which they wanted to shed, Mathieu is forced to recognize that his action is ultimately no more than defiance of his brother Jacques, the bourgeois lawyer, of Brunet who sought political engagement, and of Daniel who is flirting with religious meaning. His action is a demonstration of his sovereignty of action—but it is no more than a demonstration. It is not reality but just a demonstration which does not even convince him: " 'I'm a bloody fool,' he thought. 'Brunet's right to call me an old child.' " [8] Mathieu makes the mistake of seeing freedom as an ideal he must attain, as something toward which he must move. Freedom seems to be a grace constantly eluding him and ultimately unattainable: "And suddenly he seemed to *see* his freedom. It was out of reach, cruel, young, and as capricious as grace." [9]

In another passage, however, the meaning of freedom dawns upon him, and he realizes that he is inalienably free:

> Even if he let himself be carried off, helpless and in despair, even if he let himself be carried off like an old sack of coal, he would have chosen his own perdition. He was free, free for everything, free to act like a fool or a machine, free to accept, free to refuse. . . . For him there would be neither Good nor Evil unless he invented them.[10]

But this realization does not show him the way to freedom of action—not by any means. It is a useless, absolute realization which does not answer his quest; it will raise new hopes without halting his effort to make himself a thing and to rob himself of that infinitude in whose name he rejected engagement.

The consequences are inevitable. When the action of *L'Age de raison* closes, Mathieu certainly feels himself alone, but he has to admit that he is no freer than he was *("Seul, mais pas plus libre qu'auparavant")*.[11] He has not advanced a single step. His life is meaningless ("this life was given to him for nothing"), and his purpose has still not been achieved: "He was nothing, and yet he would not change any more: he was finished" *(ibid.)*. It only remains for him to recognize that his resistance to yielding to reason has been in vain: "He took off his coat and began to undo his tie. Then he repeated to himself with a yawn: 'It's true. It's true after all: I've reached the age of reason.' "[12]

### Le Sursis

Thus *Le Sursis* opens on a very resigned Mathieu who has almost reconciled himself to being "just anybody." Yet he still harbors a trace of his tendency to seek elevation and meaning, for when his sister-in-law Odette tells him that one gets used to it *("on s'y fait")*, he exempts himself from this rule: "I suppose so. I haven't yet." [13] Just at this moment—symbolically, it seems—he gets his little sand castle to hold firm, despite the dryness of the sand, which up to now has frustrated all his attempts.

Yet this faint tendency toward a possible construct of meaning, toward success, should not be overrated. In an early chapter of *Le Sursis* (September 24) Mathieu, as he is getting up, asks himself, "What's the use?"—and this basic attitude will not change essentially throughout the novel. Later that day, as he reads a poster announcing the mobilization of his age group for military service, he is again overcome by a kind of tendency to see possible meaning: "There it is. I'm about to become interesting." [14] But it does not last, and fundamentally it refers only to the possibility of becoming an object. Thus he explains to Jacques a short time later: "I'm going because I can't do anything else." [15] It is as if the mobilization had revealed even more clearly the meaninglessness of his existence, which is now objectifying itself in its encounter with the possible offer of meaning. Now the vacuum of meaning in which he lives reaches its greatest intensity, expressing itself in complete indifference: "War or peace, what's the difference?" [16] Whether there is war or peace, whether thousands of people die or not, mankind will always remain the same, following the same pathless course, because it cannot go anywhere, because it has no direction: "It will keep on going nowhere" *(ibid.)*. On the level of language, this is what would follow from absolute horizontality, from absolute unconnectedness, if such a thing existed. Mathieu does not realize that he is faced with an inescapably responsible choice. He will accept war as an illness, as something which simply befalls you, toward which you cannot take a position. In this way he thinks he can escape his responsibility.

So Mathieu evades engagement in *Le Sursis*, just as he did in *L'Age de raison*. Sartre probably makes him evade it because he did not wish to obscure the philosophical nature of freedom by letting Mathieu discover a meaning. This can be better expressed formally by having Mathieu in a state of nonengagement. And in fact the formulations arrived at by Mathieu come closer and closer to the essence of what freedom is for Sartre: "Halfway across the Pont Neuf he stopped and burst out laughing: 'This freedom—I looked for it so far away. It was so close that I couldn't see it, that I can't touch it. It was nothing but myself. I am my freedom.' "[17] Freedom is not the ecstatic oneness with the self that he had sought; it is the freedom in which he *is*, nonsituational freedom, the freedom of the drifting cobweb, the freedom of the exile, of hopeless unrelatedness: "Freedom is exile, and I am condemned to be free." [18] This freedom is not one which brings deliverance, but one to which one is condemned. It is freedom *for nothing:* "*Je suis libre* pour rien" *(ibid.)*. Thus *Le Sursis* leads to the same conclusion, somewhat heightened, as *L'Age de raison*. Expectations have dropped a little; the peaks have flattened out; but insight into the essence of freedom is the sharper for it.

### La Mort dans l'ame

As mentioned, the third volume of *Les Chemins de la liberté* introduces, even in its design, a new factor. This novel falls into two parts, the first (pp. 9–197) being essentially broader in scope and having a strongly pluralistic narrative structure, and the second (pp. 201–298) having a more closed one. In the first part we meet Mathieu, the familiar central hero, as well as other no less familiar characters such as Daniel and Jacques. In the second part, however, the action centers on a single theme: the Communist Brunet, whom we have already met in *L'Age de raison* as Mathieu's friend and opponent in argument.

The first part takes place during the "phony war" and Germany's blitzkrieg against France. It is characteristic that Sartre chooses not the beginning of the war but the moment when everyone has *la mort dans l'âme* (death in the soul), when hopes have become "memories of hopes." Ever since his childhood Mathieu has been waiting for a chance, but it has never offered itself. He makes one last—and vain—attempt to summon up some sense of brotherhood: "Mathieu yawned. He looked sadly at the others submerged in the darkness. 'Us,' he murmured. But it didn't work any more: he was alone." [19]

They await the arrival of the Germans in the city hall, wait to be taken off as prisoners of war. But events take a new turn. Pinette, who, like Mathieu, is attached to a staff unit, decides to put an end to the senseless waiting. He decides—the date is June 17, and Pétain has already offered an armistice—to fight. He takes a rifle from the armory, and without comment Mathieu does the same. They leave the *mairie* and go to the church tower, where some soldiers have set up a last pocket of resistance—actually little more than a gesture of protest. Even the physical setting indicates an approaching climax. At first the regular soldiers still under orders stare in bewilderment at the two amateur staff officers so that they begin to have doubts about their action. But after sharing a last meal, and after Pinette explains that they simply could not stand this passive waiting for the end, they attain a kind of togetherness.

Then comes the battle—or more accurately the action—

the hopeless battle which is yet so extraordinarily meaningful to Mathieu. The reserved, skeptical, intellectual Mathieu comes out of himself and experiences the rapturous, ecstatic meaning of killing. Sensing that this experience will be short-lived, he tries to give it finality in the imagination, to frame it in a form-giving context which will raise it above existence and trans-form it, as it were, into a "perfect moment." He sets himself the goal of holding out for fifteen minutes. If he succeeds, he will take this as a magical corroboration of this high point, the achievement of his goal.

Thus the search for magical meaning breaks through. Mathieu has opted not for resistance, not for engagement, but for an action designed to help him overcome the existen-tiality of existence. Moreover, this action is a revenge for his various failures: "It was a tremendous revenge. Each shot wiped out a former scruple." [20] The text says this in so many words, and there is no need to cite further passages, some of which exceed esthetic limits, showing the low animality with which Mathieu celebrates his great "discovery" that "freedom is Terror . . ." (ibid.).

It is nevertheless remarkable that Sartre should allow Mathieu's quest to end like this, for he is presumably killed after these fifteen minutes. This may prompt us to stop and examine the meaning of this scene. Obviously climatic in char-acter, this episode is intended to illuminate in a single flash the motivation of Mathieu's whole existence. If he kills in order to avenge himself, he acknowledges that the target and the motive of his revenge are what determines his thinking and acting. His revenge on human beauty (his last act is to shoot down with particular gusto a handsome officer) shows that this ideal of beauty lived and still lives within him too, that he merely cannot cope with it. Thus the apparent absoluteness of his killing cancels itself out in the perverse meaning of his revenge. Mathieu has been pursuing a phantom. Again and again he has drawn back from acting, from commitment, be-cause he thought he must protect freedom, his freedom. This was a false start, for freedom is not a possession which man can or should guard; it lies beyond everything that is guardable.

Freedom that has been made an object is therefore a contradiction. Now, at the end of the road, this kind of freedom emerges not only as an illusion but as something that can enslave man and lead him into bondage and nonfreedom.

In practice, therefore, Brunet, to whom Sartre returns in the second half of *La Mort dans l'âme*, comes much closer to the essence of freedom through his engagement, and Sartre is obviously trying to stress this through the contrast with Mathieu.[21] Brunet is in the same position as Mathieu, with the significant exception that he experiences the military collapse as a member of a combat unit; he is not a staff officer. But Brunet acts quite differently from Mathieu. At the point when Mathieu decides to fight, he lays down his arms: "The fighting's over now. The war's lost, and there's work to be done." [22] Brunet fought while Mathieu yawned and felt conscious of his emptiness. Now it is Brunet's turn to yawn, and this too has a reason and a meaning: " 'A lot of work.' He lay down in the hay, yawned and fell asleep" *(ibid.)*. To fight now would be senseless; it would be to fight irresponsibly. Therefore Brunet must take care of himself now; he must sleep and gather strength for the tasks awaiting him. Even in the prisoner-of-war camp which looms inescapably before him, Brunet will not be robbed of his freedom; the worst adversity will not determine his destiny. For man is not predestined; he is always free to make something of his situation. As Sartre explains in *L'Etre et le neant*, he can regard the boulder blocking his way as an obstacle—the pessimistic attitude of the determinist—or use it, climb up on it in order to obtain a vaster view.[23] Even in the prisoner-of-war camp Brunet has an opportunity to work for the Party, to recruit people to prepare for the coming tasks, chiefly those of the Resistance. And this freedom is so great that Brunet is able to look forward—though naturally not without suffering—to his imminent and then actual deportation to Germany, knowing that there his fellow prisoners will be much more receptive to his plans, that there they will not be in danger of capitulating to the fraudulent "normalization of life" already in the making in Pétain's France.

All this is summed up in a brief encounter with the eyes of a little girl whom the prisoners glimpse from the railroad car:

> In the park a little girl holding a hoop watched gravely. Through her young eyes all France, innocent and antiquated, watched them pass. Brunet looked at the little girl and thought of Pétain. The train cut across her field of vision, across this future, full of mannerly games, good thoughts, and trivial cares, speeding on toward the potato fields, the factories and armament works, toward the dark, real future of men.[24]

Brunet makes his freedom, the freedom of party engagement, very strong. He practices that responsibility for the whole of which Sartre speaks in *L'Existentialisme est un humanisme*: "Make my escape? Write off twenty thousand men? Leave them to rot in their own shit? Has one ever the right to say: there's mothing more to be done? . . . There's always something to be done. You will have to work wherever you are with the means at your disposal." [25] He will not try to escape because he sees his task here in the prisoner-of-war camp. But Brunet is not alone with his thoughts; he exchanges ideas with other Communists, and they reflect his own unacknowledged uncertainty. Schneider is skeptical, unable to follow Brunet in his party idealism. Russia's nonaggression pact with Germany sticks in his craw, and it is useless for Brunet to talk of temporary expedients and propose that Russia and the party are two separate things.

Then there is the young typesetter, with his fear and despair. *La Mort dans l'âme* ends tragically, in keeping with its title. Brunet's constructivity, solid as it looks, is already cracking. The prisoners roll along the tracks in their freight cars, trying to kid themselves that they are being shipped to Châlon, not Germany. But then they reach the crucial switches, and the truth is inescapably obvious. The others are overcome with despair. The young typesetter has just one thing in mind—to jump from the car—and Brunet is not going to be able to hold him back much longer. Brunet realizes how limited his possibilities are; his freedom exists, as it were, only within the Party.

He would have liked to talk to him, urge him, help
him. He could not. His words belonged to the Party. It was
the Party that had given them their meaning. Within the
Party Brunet could love, persuade, and console. The typesetter had fallen outside this immense beam of light. Brunet
had nothing more to say to him.[26]

He grips Schneider's hand—the last hold for his sense of
solidarity. But Schneider breaks away and disappears in the
darkness of the freight car. Now Brunet is alone, quite alone
for the first time, with nothing to hold on to: "He stood on
one foot. The other was caught just above floor level in a
tangle of legs and boots. He made no effort to free it. He
needed to maintain this provisional state. He was passing
through. His thoughts were passing through his head. The
train was passing through France." [27] The future lies omi-
nously before him: "Tomorrow the black birds will come."

### La Dernière Chance

So ends *La Mort dans l'âme*, and Sartre has now intimated that
the last volume of *Les Chemins de la liberté*, *La Dernière
Chance*, will never appear. Did he come to realize the difficulty
of presenting a hero who is simultaneously free—infinitely
free—and engaged? Was this paradox of human existence incapable of being given esthetic shape? Did Sartre find that
man's philosophically, logically inferred absolute uncommitted-
ness, that is to say, his freedom, is an abstract reality which
cannot be given esthetic treatment when linked with the practical demands of engagement and responsible behavior? Did he
find here an antinomy to be resolved only in the dialectic of
thesis and antithesis which could never lead to a convincing
synthesis?

Sartre has said in an interview that the solution he had in
mind for *La Dernière Chance* was too simple for esthetic treatment. This last volume was originally intended to deal with
engagement in the Resistance, an engagement whose end is
freedom. But this engagement, he suggested, seemed too obvious and did not represent a real choice (*Observer*, June 18,

1961, p. 21). This is certainly true. On the other hand, judging by what is available to us, *La Dernière Chance* looks complicated rather than simple. In *Drôle d'amitié*, a fragment published in *Les Temps Modernes* (November and December 1949), we meet a Schneider who has meanwhile turned out to be the Marxist writer Vicarios, a man who has left the Party in protest against the nonaggression pact. Brunet's friendship with Schneider-Vicarios is by now so deep that he is prepared to escape from the camp with him, for his attempts to work for the Party inside the camp have failed. But they are betrayed. Vicarios is shot during their attempted escape and dies in Brunet's arms. "The Party has killed me," he says, and under the impact of his death Brunet realizes that men are alone and will remain so, even if the Soviet Union wins. The conclusion he comes to is: "To hell with the Party!" He walks back to the German guards in despair. Here the fragment ends. Thus the solution Brunet seemed to offer in *La Mort dans l'âme*—freedom stemming from commitment—is negated by events in *La Dernière Chance*. Here the Communist Brunet joins Roquentin, the autodidact, and Mathieu as one of the "elite" composed of those who are hopelessly alone.

Perhaps the "last chance" was meant to be the chance of choosing, as a man condemned to freedom, total commitment in the Resistance. Sartre was certainly right to reject this solution as simplistic. And would it have been convincing? Would it have been capable of "saving," by way of synthesis, Mathieu's grasp of essential understanding and Brunet's essential experience and realization—which is what brought both of them to perdition? A synthesis of this kind would demand a scope which the novel cannot offer; it would demand a genre which would permit the merging of the horizontal and the vertical, of statement and exposition and thematically speaking, of aloneness and relatedness, in one self-contained formal concept. The drama offered this scope, and Sartre was already making use of it long before his epic phase drew to a close in *Les Chemins de la liberté* and literally exhausted itself in *La Dernière Chance*.

### Les Mouches

Sartre wrote this play after his release from the prisoner-of-war camp (a release he managed to obtain on medical grounds), and we are certainly not wrong in seeing in *Les Mouches* (1943) a statement of what he intended to say in the last volume of *Les Chemins de la liberté*. While the city of Argos, acknowledging its collective guilt under the rule of the usurper Aegisthus, has something of German-occupied France, the France of Pétain, it must also be said that the parallel is by no means imperative.[28] As a work of art, *Les Mouches* is absolutely timeless. It is a formula for human existence itself, a formula also for freedom and engagement, aloneness and togetherness.

This becomes clear right at the outset in the impressive introductory scenes. Orestes, heir to the House of Atreus, arrives, with his tutor, in Argos as a stranger, but a stranger seeking what is his, bent on discovering what home and community can mean, seeing in city and palace a welcome chance to call something *his* city gate, *his* palace, one who wants to find his place but feels that his freedom is boundless, his soul a nothingness: "I am free, thank God. Oh, how free I am! What a glorious absence my soul is!" [29] If he had grown up here as a child he could call this gate *his* gate; it would have become in effect *his* gate, a gate that places him, gives him his bearings in space: "I would have gone in and out through this gate ten thousand times. As a child I would have played with its panels and braced myself against them. They would have creaked without yielding, and my arms would have learned their resistance" (*ibid.*). As it is, however, he is an exile, in both the literal and the figurative sense. He has been an exile since he was seven: "The scents and the sounds, the patter of rain on the roofs, the flickering of light—I let them slip down over my body and fall all around me" (*ibid.*). The things that surrounded him did not belong to him; they glanced off him, kept to themselves, leaving him to his absolute separateness.

Now he has come to his city, the city that should be *his*. He is on the way from the absolute freedom of abstraction to the tension of finding his place, which is the tension of engagement. For this Argos is not just any city, different only in that it is the lost home of Orestes: it is a city in need of a savior, a city which will lure Orestes to the highest form of engagement: redemption. Thus when he "comes into his own" as a stranger and "his own people do not recognize him" it seems that a still blind fate hangs over him: "I was born here and yet I have to ask my way like a stranger." [30] Yet his work of redemption is quite different from that of Christ—the exact opposite, in fact. Orestes' task is to "de-redeem," to liberate the city from the mechanism of redemption imposed on it by King Aegisthus. What has happened is this: Aegisthus, the lover of Clytemnestra, murdered her husband, Agamemnon, Orestes' father, upon his return from the Trojan War. He then married Clytemnestra and made himself king. In order to establish a hold over the people and give himself the status of a divinely appointed ruler (and here the specifically Sartrean slant begins to emerge[31]), Aegisthus, with the help of Jupiter, has transferred his personal guilt to the people as a whole and hammered into their consciousness their guilt for past events. Since a nation is in any case prone to feel that it shares the responsibility for the murder of its king, Aegisthus has succeeded in this and also in arousing in the people of Argos a need to wipe out their guilt, a need for atonement, thus putting them in the hands of the high priests, of Jupiter and of his ally Aegisthus. This guilt-atonement mentality keeps Aegisthus in power. Jupiter for his part has given this power an ominous aura by loosing a plague of flies over Argos as an outward sign of guilt. These flies are something like goddesses of vengeance —Furies who keep the people's sense of guilt alive or, if necessary, arouse it, forcing them all to seek deliverance again through penitence.

Orestes is about to encounter this rigorous structure of spellbound thinking—Orestes who is as free as the thread of a spider web in the wind (p. 26), as free as Mathieu, who Brunet says "lives in parentheses, as it were." Like Mathieu he has achieved the freedom which books can bring, the freedom of abstraction. Like Mathieu he has the feeling of seductive strength of those born for engagement: "There are men who are born committed. They have no choice. They have been thrown onto a road and at the end of it an action awaits them—*their* action. They trudge along, and their bare feet press hard against the ground and are lacerated by the rocks." But Orestes, very much in contrast to Mathieu, is a man compulsively given to action, even though this action at first seems merely a dream hanging over the course of his life: "But you know, if there were some action that would grant me the freedom of the city, if I could gain possession, even by a crime, of their memories, their terror and their hopes, to fill the emptiness of my heart—even if I had to kill my own mother. . . ." [32]

Something else too, something structurally significant, separates Orestes from Mathieu. He does not face an enduring commitment such as war service or support of party policy, but rather the "one-shot" engagement of a single act which, while not formally excluding the horizontality of being free, will yet be totally binding, as Sartre requires action to be: "And you'll know at last that you have staked your life on a single throw of the dice, once and for all." [33] In the first act of the play, of course, this commitment to an act is still a long way off. This intellectual weakling from Corinth seems quite unfitted to make Electra's dream of an avenging brother come true. Even when Clytemnestra, who fails to recognize him, just as Electra did, begs him "for his mother's sake" to leave Argos and he decides to stay, he is not thinking of the deed to be committed. On the contrary, Clytemnestra's "for your mother's sake" tempts him with the idea of being able to call something his own. Thoughtfully he repeats the words "for my mother's sake" and makes up his mind to stay, to participate as a spectator in the public festival of penance to be held next day.

Aegisthus, in collaboration with Jupiter and the high priest, has introduced this religious festival, at which the spirits of the dead are conjured up. It is held every year and serves as a kind of psychological safety valve for the guilt-atonement mentality, both relieving and reinforcing it. For at this festival the inhabitants of Argos are confronted with the dead, with the spirits of their guilt. In the confrontation all their accumulated guilt feelings can be discharged in an orgy of self-accusation, while acquiring enough new impetus to keep them going for another year. Hence the people fear this day as much as they look forward to it.

Orestes is not following any plan in attending this public festival of penance. When Electra flouts the strict regulations (and Aegisthus' own command) and appears dressed in white, thus confusing the people in their penitent mood, when at the last moment Jupiter contrives through a spectacular miracle to regain control of them so that Aegisthus can take the offensive and banish Electra, and finally when Electra learns from Orestes' own lips that he is her brother, this Orestes is still far from being the avenger of her dreams. On the contrary, he is still the weak young man from Corinth, the stranger who wants only to belong somewhere, to give himself the place-bound, space-creating solidity of thingness.

> Try to understand. I want to be a man who belongs somewhere, a man among men. Look, even a slave passing by, tired and surly, carrying a heavy load, dragging his steps and looking down at his feet so as not to fall—he's *in* his city like a leaf in the foliage or a tree in the forest. Argos is all around him, weighty and warm and full of itself. I want to be that slave, Electra. I want to pull the town up around myself and snuggle into it like a quilt. I won't go away.[34]

He wants to make this city *his* city; he dreams of making it dependent upon him: "My arms can defend the city, and I have gold to take care of your needy." [35] Then, just before the end of the first scene of the second act, right in the middle of the play, the turning point looms. Orestes, who up to now has desired the Good, who has been indirectly in the service of Jupiter, becomes uncertain. The first indication of an open crisis is when he asks Jupiter for a sign to tell him where to turn in his search for the Good: to Jupiter or to Electra. It is no surprise when the spectacular sign which Jupiter conjures up fails to convince him. The flash of light by which Jupiter, in the best Neoplatonic tradition, lets the Good shine visibly around the altar stone has no relevance for Orestes. This is something absolutely foreign to him; this is the good of the people of Argos, not *his* good.

His road, which he now sees plainly for the first time, though still only in an imaginary way, is a road which leads down into the slums of Argos, a road at the end of which an action waits—nothing but a possibility as yet: "Listen. All these people trembling in their dark rooms, surrounded by their dead loved ones—suppose I assume all their crimes. Suppose I want to earn the name of 'remorse-stealer' and that I store up in myself all their contrition." [36] It is remarkable and significant that the moment Orestes begins to become an avenger and savior, Electra, who up to then has been the driving element, falls behind. Up to now Orestes and Electra have side-stepped one another in their expectations and desires. Now, when a possibility emerges of their going hand in hand, when Orestes' will begins to coincide with Electra's, her will shifts; she who urged revenge becomes god-fearing, while the god-fearing Orestes surrenders to blasphemy.

Certainly there is also an element of dramatic structure involved here, but we can see how closely this technical requirement coincides with Sartre's specific ideas and how excellently it serves the purpose of rendering formally and dramatically that unbridgeable aloneness in which Roquentin and the autodidact found themselves.

After this exchange of roles, events in the second half of *Les Mouches* take their inexorable course, "like the cogs of a machine," as Electra rightly predicted. Aegisthus too feels his end approaching, senses the ineluctable advance of freedom threatening him, the lover of order. Jupiter brings home to him that this love of order is his deepest passion: "We have the same passion. You love order, Aegisthus." [37] This order has helped Aegisthus to overcome his aloneness with himself and to erect a structure that will allow him to forget his humanness, his existence: "I have established order. O terrible and godlike passion!" [38] Now he will be struck down by a dagger in the hand of a man whom he could not include in this structure of order which fetters freedom—a man who is aware of being a man, of being free. Jupiter himself is powerless against such a man: "Once freedom has exploded in a man's soul, the gods are powerless against him" (*ibid.*). But this by no means implies that such a man could not be tempted. He too is exposed to the danger of becoming structured; he too feels the urge to surrender to a reality that will enfold and support him, protecting him against the nothingness of his own soul and against the freedom to which he is condemned. Orestes will in fact resist the temptation, but its strength can be seen from the fact that Electra succumbs to it. Even before Orestes begins to prepare for the second murder, the murder of his mother, she irrevocably falls back, and Orestes soon has to recognize that his "We are free, Electra" is invalid and cannot be valid because there is no such thing as freedom with somebody else. There is no "we" in being free; there is just a solitary confrontation with action in each particular situation of making a choice.

Act III takes brother and sister in opposite directions: Electra into the arms of the goddess of vengeance and then through redeeming penitence to the feet of Jupiter; Orestes to freedom.[39] Yet Orestes does not take this road without first being tempted by Jupiter, and this temptation is a curious reversal of a Biblical event: the temptation of Jesus in the wilderness. As in the Bible (and indeed already in *La Nausée*) there are three temptations. First Jupiter appeals to the pair through their fraternal feelings, their love, relying now on clumsy sympathy, now on a well-aimed attack on Orestes' freedom. Orestes, he says, professes to love Electra, this Electra who must now suffer through his fault, yet at the same time maintains that he is free in his action and regrets nothing.

Orestes resists the attack, the temptation to remorse: "I love her more than myself. But her suffering comes from within herself. She alone can rid herself of it. She is free." [40] Electra is free, as absolutely free as he is himself. Essentially, therefore, he can do nothing for her, cannot take her choice upon himself.

The second temptation, Jupiter's offer of a throne and royal rank for them both, also finds Orestes on the alert. He knows that this would require them to adopt the guilt-atonement mentality, that their rule would inevitably bear the trappings of mourning.

Now Jupiter gets ready for the third temptation: he allows Orestes to glimpse the divine order of the cosmos, the meaning of a creation against which Orestes, a mere worm when measured against the universe, has sinned. Again Orestes replies with his proud, self-aware *no*: "You are king of the gods, Jupiter, king of the rocks and the stars, king of the waves of the sea. But you are not the king of men." [41] For him—and here existentialism shows its face—there is no such thing as Beauty and Good against which action must be measured, no order of which he forms a part. His action was a free choice, and he alone bears the responsibility for it. He will not evade this responsibility by transmuting it into a relation of guilt under the rule of norms.

This is what makes him the savior of Argos—not a savior like Christ, who creates a connection between heaven and earth, but a savior by virtue of his exemplary reminder of the one thing that according to Sartre "defines" man: his being free ("I *am* my freedom" [p. 111]), his being condemned to free choice, for which there can be no excuses and which provides no possibility, if one is to remain authentic, for getting rid of qualms of conscience by referring to norms and thus keeping conscience more or less quiescent, as the inhabitants of Argos regularly did under Aegisthus.

This, then, is Orestes' message to the people at the end of the play, when he goes out to the mob clamoring for his death: "A crime which the perpetrator can't stand by is nobody's crime any more, is it?" [42] A crime which the perpetrator disowns is an anonymous, almost forgivable crime, more of a misfortune. Orestes will stand by his crime, will freely assume responsibility for it, without relying on norms or guilt-atonement mentality of any kind.

In this way he frees Argos of the avenging flies. As he leaves the city and makes his exit, he draws them after him like rats following the Pied Piper. [43] Will the inhabitants of Argos profit by his act of redemption? Will they even understand his exemplary return to responsible freedom, let alone be able to emulate and complete it? [44] Probably not, but Orestes can do nothing more for them, as he could do nothing more for Electra, for every man is free, free, too, to choose nonfreedom.

## chapter 4

## Death and Existence

*Huis clos* (No Exit) —
*Morts sans sépulture* (The Victors)

Man's freedom is given yet always threatened, being the freedom of a being which is being and nothingness, constantly tossed back and forth between its own two poles, the thingness and the nothingness of the soul. We have become familiar with several of the dangers that threaten it, both great and small: the mirror in which Roquentin saw himself becoming something, or Brunet's commitment, almost as binding as law, from which he for so long derived the security and consistency of thingness. But in addition to these subjective dangers there are also objective ones: a danger from outside arising from another's freedom, and another one inexorably associated with the existential condition: death. Although these two dangers already appear in the works we have discussed, the first is definitively formulated in *Huis clos* (1944; No Exit, 1946) and the second is most clearly profiled in *Morts sans sépulture* (1946; The Victors, 1949).

### Another Person's Existence (Huis clos)

This is not to say that the death theme does not occur in *Huis clos*. (It is perhaps no accident that in this play the two themes meet.) Here, however, the death theme serves almost as a peg on which to hang a straight presentation of the true essence of existence (something Sartre attempts again in *Les Jeux sont faits*). The three people who keep an utterly ghastly assignation behind locked doors symbolize life, and symbolize it with a stark, almost classic sharpness which life itself can never match. As if to underline these "ideal" conditions, the form of this play is almost without exception purely horizontal. There is only one act, and this alone practically precludes any sustained build-up of dramatic tension.[1] Moreover, the proportions assigned to the individual scenes show that Sartre was not concerned with a rising curve of tension. (In the Gallimard edition the first scene takes up five pages, the second scene half a page, the third three pages, the fourth two, and the fifth seventy-three.[2]) Thus the division into scenes does not reflect a harmonic build-up, nor does it represent a calculated use of tension. *Huis clos* is epic theater, a play which developes on one level.[3] Its first few scenes, with their slight element of tension, are more like an opening chord, a kind of dramatic preface, which after some initial hesitation fixes the character of the "heroes," casting them into stationary, paradoxically lonely togetherness, into what Sartre means to be an image of hell and at the same time the idea of the constellation of existence.

Inès, Garcin, Estelle, the three "heroes"—if they can be called that—are in fact dead. Thrown together in a hotel room for all eternity, they find each other to be hell—"Hell is other people," as Sartre puts it. There are two women and one man, hence no reassuring balanced constellation can ever develop. Here the triangle, as always, is a source of internal tension that could be its own perpetual source of renewal. But in this case it is a diabolical trinity, not tension in the sense of fulfillment and mutual relationship but in the sense of constantly self-renewing frustration.

Even on earth Garcin, the coward and informer; Estelle,

the love-starved child-murderer; and Inès, the lesbian intriguer, have been other people's hell. Now they are each others' hangmen, sabotaging every attempt at self-justification, every attempt to find a modus vivendi in death. For there is no longer any question of anything else. The idealistic tension present (though sometimes intermittently) is obviously no longer possible here; it has yielded to the deeper need, outside all space, to attain an idealless, purely practical possibility of living. But this attempt meets an obstacle in the presence of another and, most of all, of a third person. Even if it were conceivable that Garcin as a man should relegate Estelle as a woman in need of love to a condition of mere thingness and thus relate himself by an act of possession, by creating an interpersonal balance, however unauthentic, the other thing Garcin seeks in Estelle is much harder to attain, and the presence of Inès does its share to frustrate it completely.

Garcin wants to create via Estelle a sort of lying mirror of himself, a mirror for his soul. He is seeking in her a partner whose lies will hide the inescapable fact of his manifest cowardice: "If there were one soul, one single soul, who would say positively, with full conviction, that I didn't run away, that I *can't have run away*, that I'm brave and decent, I . . . I'm sure I'd be saved." [4] Estelle is quite willing to take on this task, hoping in this way to bind Garcin to her and at the same time to become an object in his arms. Garcin could thus find in her a compliant mirror of his soul, even though it would take all the *mauvaise foi* he can command to trust such a mirror. But things never reach this point because Inès, the third partner, is still there. She, the authentic other person, is an inextinguishable mirror of events, before which fraudulent self-justification through lies cannot hold its ground. Relentlessly she exposes the relationship: "She needs a man, believe me, a man's arm around her waist, the smell of a man, a man's desire in a man's eyes. That's all. Ha! She'd tell you you're God almighty if she thought it would please you." [5] Actually these words are quite unnecessary, for this other mirror which Inès holds up to Garcin is more inescapable and, above all, more reliable than words: the mirror of her look. This look is an expression of a freedom which, he realizes, damns him; hence it is much more than a mirror, more precious and also more dangerous. For this look tells him that he is seen and, even more important, that somebody is there whose actions and thought escape him, who in turn has made him, Garcin, an object.

The situation is infernal. This is a game from which there is no exit, from which one cannot even will a way out. Garcin will soon sense this, for when he realizes that in the presence of Inès he cannot make Estelle a mirror of his self-justification, he hammers wildly on the door, demanding to be let out. Yet when the door opens he does not go out into the hall; he is incapable of doing so because he is caught up again in the game of "life." What life's hell revealed to him now seems to be his last chance. Inès' look, her self-assured judgment have given him hope that he may find here a more reliable source of self-justification, that with her he can make a pact on a higher, more intellectual plane.

He therefore tries to convince Inès that he is not a coward. But his attempt is useless; in fact it sets him back even further, because Inès catches him in the vise of her merciless dialectic. Garcin believes that his dreams of heroism represented his will and hence his own reality, and that he should be judged according to them. But Inès, the proponent of Sartre's viewpoint, contradicts him: "Actions alone decide what one wanted." [6] It is easy to transfer what one wants to the realm of dreams and to dream of a heroism which is just wish fulfillment and which ultimately simply provides an excuse for weakness ("everything is permitted the hero" [*ibid.*]). She also rejects the excuse that he died too young, that he was not given time for *his* action. There is no such thing as a complete life in which the goal has been achieved, because life is by definition being related to the future, being open. Thus, like man himself, it excludes by its very nature all finality, all completeness, so long as it is still life: "One always dies too soon or too late" (*ibid.*). Death rules who this man was, you add up the total, and the answer is his life, is this man: "You are your life and nothing else" (*ibid.*). a line under life at one certain point, and if you want to know

Thus Inès stands for the straight Sartrean philosophy of

life. Man is completely responsible for what he achieves in life (though the word "achieves" is not quite the right one). There are no excuses. He is what he has made of himself. Death reveals this more plainly than insight into life can, even at the moment of dying, for if dying really *were* dying, it would already be the state of being dead. Between life and death there is no in between, no kind of transition making it possible to draw boundary lines.

Thus once again and more inescapably than ever before, Garcin has to face the fact of his cowardice. Only an attempt at revenge is left to him: to love Estelle in the presence of and despite Inès. But Inès spits the poison of her words between them, focusing upon them a brutal spotlight of intellectual acuity which leaves them no chance of sinking into the oblivion of their love—just as the light which burns incessantly in their hotel room will never allow them to sink into darkness and sleep.

Estelle makes one last, desperate attempt to break out of the hellish circle. She attacks Inès with a paper knife, stabbing her in the breast again and again. It is useless: they are all dead already. Knife, poison, rope are of no avail. Condemned to live together forever, they can do nothing but resume their places in the vicious circle of their deadness, their "ideal life." The curtain falls on the words, "Well, let's get on with it."

### Morts sans sépulture

*Huis clos* dealt with being dead as the inescapable counterpart of already having lived, and this dead state became an "ideal" symbol of life. The very title *Morts sans sépulture* announces a move in the opposite direction. This play wants to show life which is already a dead state: its heroes are dead although they are still unburied.

These "unburied dead" are members of the Resistance awaiting death and execution in an attic. Their names are Canoris, Sorbier, François, Lucie, and Henri. Henri is the one who comes to grips with the problems of the situation most profoundly and plainly, and in this respect he is closest to the central heroes of *La Nausée* and *Les Chemins de la liberté*. Like Mathieu and Roquentin, Henri has reached the "existentialist" age, that is, he is between thirty and forty; to be more precise, he has just passed thirty and is thus at the beginning of the great crisis.

Lucie is woman as the true existential alternative to the reality of man, called to authenticity as he is, called upon to recognize choice and freedom. She will be more consistent than Anny in *La Nausée*, will follow the road to authenticity farther than Electra in *Les Mouches*, but she will not go all the way either. Here Sartre shows himself to be a good psychologist. Although he formally recognizes the same existential reality in woman as in man, in the end he always concedes to woman the charm of formal inconsistency and hence also the comforting warmth of human consistency. Canoris in *Morts sans sépulture*, on the contrary, is consistent to the last; right to the very end he judges and acts according to the exigency of the moment. And it is certainly significant that Sartre makes this "authentic" member of the Resistance a Greek, that is to say, a man whose commitment has little to do with national interests, who demonstrates membership in the Resistance almost *à l'état pur*.

Sorbier's role is not a bad one either: he will be the only one to master dying, though at the price of authenticity. François, still a youth, is actually the only one of the heroes to have picked a truly unrewarding role, and if one is at all familiar with the structure of Sartre's works, this is by no means surprising. The young typesetter in *La Mort dans l'âme* collapsed and committed suicide out of despair. François will be liquidated by his own comrades because he is "too young" to hold out.

Why does Sartre deny this young man his chance for authenticity? Here we must refer back to the introduction, though now we can be a little more specific. Sartre is less interested in man in his practical reality than in what he formally is, and this can best be brought out in heroes who come closest to what man is in essence, through people whose accidental human side, so to speak, is silent. Hence Sartre's purest incarnation of what existence is will more often than not be one who has reached the full maturity of his manhood, a man who, like that venturer into the beyond, Dante, has arrived at "the middle of life's way," suspended between youth and age, in whom the developmental factors of rise or decline are at their lowest effectiveness, the phase where man—if only for a brief span—is "pure" man. (We shall see that Camus, who is much more interested in man as practical reality, chooses slightly older heroes, placing them in their early forties.) [7]

### The Action

This group of Resistance fighters is doomed to death, though a delayed death (the reprieve theme). Their death is confronting a numerically smaller group of militiamen who force each of the partisans to choose between cowardice and torture, calling them out in turn for interrogation, torturing them, and venting their brutal sadism on them—especially on Lucie. This delay gives the prisoners time to think about the whole of their existence, to take a trial balance of their ebbing lives, now rapidly moving toward their final total. Their reflections are punctuated by the shouted commands of their captors, establishing a very powerful dramatic rhythm. These are moments when meaning is suspended and an unobstructed view of essence opens up. Up to now these men, like Brunet in *L'Age de raison*, have been able to define themselves in terms of a mission and a task. Now this justification is gone. Henri has to admit: "Now there's no one left to give me orders and nothing to justify me." [8]

Henri is the one to express this, because of the whole group he is the one who most keenly feels the lack of firm ground under his feet and who most needs it. For him the Resistance was not merely a momentary necessity, a purely rational commitment: it was a quest. Like Roquentin in *La Nausée*, he wanted to be purged of his existence; he was seeking exoneration of a feeling of guilt that was equated with his existence: "For thirty years I've felt guilty. Guilty because I was alive" (*ibid.*). This feeling of guilt now reaches its climax; it has found an entirely concrete explanation. Their Resistance assignment has failed, and in reprisal the Germans have set fire to houses, and women and children have been burned to death.

Canoris sees this quite differently. He acts and thinks "authentically." Henri sets his sights much too high; he is not modest; he wants to get more out of a situation than it can actually yield. The time for planning, for projecting oneself into the future, is past, and since commitment and projecting oneself into the future are life, and these possibilities have now been taken away from them, he considers himself and the others already dead: "As far as I'm concerned, we died a long time ago, at the exact moment when we stopped being useful" (*ibid.*). The play's title shows the importance Sartre attaches to Canoris' viewpoint.

This categorical attitude is not maintained for long, however, because even in the first act a decisive change occurs in their situation, a change which brings them back into the dialectic of life. Their leader, Jean, is caught and put in the same cell with them. The militiamen have not been able to identify him and will probably have to release him if he does not give in under torture. This gives the prisoners a new hold on life. Now they are again oriented toward success; their endurance and even their death become meaningful, and there is a chance of giving wholeness to existence.

This is a piece of extraordinary luck, and both Sorbier and Henri take it as such, but it is also a great danger. They already felt the end of their lives in their hands; they were already dead. Yet now their lives are going to be summed up all over again to decide whether they will go down in history as cowards, indeed, whether they *are* cowards. When Sorbier becomes aware of this risk, he is panic-stricken and begs the others to "shut him up," to free him from the possibility of failure (p. 210), for he feels that if they come for him a second time he will not be able to hold out. But he manages to "save" himself after all. When the militiamen take him out a second time, already looking forward to seeing this coward break (Act II, Scene 6), he succeeds in tricking them. Pretending he is about to betray his leader, he points with his finger as though to indicate where he is. Having diverted their attention, he jumps from the window with a shout of triumph, to find death in suicide: "Sorbier [*shouting*]: 'Hey, you up there. Henri! Canoris! I didn't talk.' [*The militiaman try to grab him. He jumps.*] 'Good night!' " [9] This, however, is not the end of the play, but only the end of the second of its four acts. Structurally it is the point at which Mathieu in *La Mort dans l'âme* breaks through to his great revenge and to the freedom of terror. And this is something to give us pause.

Sorbier's action, which looks so successful, is unauthentic. He has, so to speak, balanced accounts by ruling the final line under his life himself, but this solution, this suicide, was a lie, a flight from what is.

Lucie, one of the great tragic figures anticipated in Anny and Electra, acts quite differently. She is completely human, an idealistic, loving woman who by thinking of her lover, Jean, has found the strength to endure imprisonment and torture. Lucie lived for Jean; she draws life and courage from mentally following his footsteps, which, she says, may even now be taking him through the streets of Grenoble. When Jean is brought in and she is taken off for interrogation, she is sure that when she comes back, having held out under torture, "there will be nothing but love in my eyes." [10] But this love, appealing as it is, will not stand the crushing test of existential thinking or—in terms of the actual facts—of physical torture. It does not help Jean, left behind in the cell, to clutch at the words with which Lucie has assured him of her love and tell himself: "She's thinking only of me. It's to protect me that she's enduring torture and shame." [11] Essentially there can be no such thing as an assurance of love, a promise of love, representing a dependable bond, because the essence of human existence precludes any such continuity. Every moment brings a new decision. When Lucie is brought back, she no longer knows what this word "love" is supposed to mean. In the absolute, naked reality of a moment the structure of this concept has been shattered. Desperately alone, at the mercy of the brutal power of ruthlessly sadistic men, she has been stripped of everything, reduced to the naked shame of existing. Ideal-oriented, as always, she clutches at the one "escape" open to her. She no longer sees Jean. She has just one thing in mind—to hold out until death and thus make the humiliation inflicted upon her meaningful.

Yet even this will lead nowhere—a calvary without redemption. To achieve the goal, further sacrifices will be necessary, the first of which will be that of her younger brother François. They had taken him along, although he was really too young for the work. Now they find out how wrong they were. François is afraid. Moreover, he feels a growing hatred of Jean, their leader, who is with them but does not share their fate and whose life they are trying to save by refusing to talk. It is soon clear to all of them that François will not be able to hold out, and they draw the ghastly conclusion. Henri strangles him in the name of them all, just as Canoris speaks for them all when he asks François's forgiveness for what they are doing, for what they are forced to do because the lives of sixty of their comrades in the Resistance depend on their leader, Jean. The burden of this political murder lies heavy on all of them, especially on Lucie. Cradling her brother's body in her lap, she is a symbol of superhuman, dehumanized grief. All of them now long increasingly for death to obliterate their shame and bring them the final victory of justification.

Yet once again Sartre violently reverses the dramatic development to bring it to a climax as masterful as his finales always are. We are in the fourth and last act. Because they have held out, Jean has regained his freedom and is probably already back in action. Now the militiamen prepare their final assault on free will. They offer to let the prisoners off lightly if they will talk. Henri and Lucie already see ultimate triumph within their grasp and dream of the glory of a death chosen despite the spiritual weakening of the enemy. But now comes the turn in events, a turn for which they are quite unprepared. Canoris, who is unmoved by dreams, who freely decides what to do in response to the call of the moment, wants them to talk, to lead the Germans down a false trail in exchange for a chance of life and the possibility of continuing their work. Lucie and Henri resist for a long time. Then, when a warm rain begins to fall outside, releasing the fragrance of the earth after a long drought, Lucie, overwhelmed by the warmth of life, yields to the spell of the earth, and her frantic tension toward the goal to be attained dissolves in sobbing.

They talk—or rather Canoris talks for all of them. But to no purpose. They lose their gamble for final victory, which seemed so close, and gain nothing. One of the militiamen breaks the agreement for his own amusement and on his own authority puts the prisoners up against the wall and shoots them.

Thus death emerges as what it is for Sartre: something that no longer has anything to do with the case, that makes no difference to life and existence, that neither adds nor subtracts anything. "You die into the bargain," says Sartre in another context, and this is exactly what this unexpected, typically Sartrean ending implies. This death is not in keeping with life, does not round it out. It simply occurs, putting "paid" to the account. And in the final reckoning Lucie was a great human being, an almost tragic figure, who by her very weakening, by opening herself to the warm fragrance of the earth and of life, gives proof of her profound humanity. Henri was an idealist, that is, one who gets off the right track. And Canoris, the least human of them all, was an authentic man.

# chapter 5

# Existence and Structure

*La Putain respectueuse*
(The Respectful Prostitute) —
*Les Mains sales* (Dirty Hands) —
*Les Séquestrés d'Altona*
(The Condemned of Altona)

### Theory and Practice [1]

In the preceding chapters we have been able to show over and over again that Sartre's literary works can be properly understood only by extricating their purely formal content, the abstract essence at their core. This was quite all right so long as the subject matter was purely fictitious, so long as it depicted nonhistorical, legendary, or imaginary events, as was the case in *La Nausée*, *Les Mouches*, several of the novellas in *Le Mur*, and *Huis clos*. Even an engagement which by its very nature extended into practical life was then still a noncommittal one, exemplifying something abstract, a theoretical concept. Things have become more difficult when the subject matter was drawn from historical events, as it was in *Les Chemins de la liberté* and *Morts san sépulture*. Certainly Sartre manages to "bracket out" their historicity to a great extent by centering the second and third volumes of *Les Chemins de la liberté* on one specific moment and then making this moment absolute, in one case by singling out a week of "reprieve" (*Le Sursis*) and then making the act fail its target, in the other case by deliberately

63

making the plot of *La Mort dans l'ame* begin after the war is already lost, so that the ostensibly historical action becomes a mere manifesto of individuality.

Nevertheless it is significant that the problem of theory and practice, of "pure" and historical action, emerges in Sartre's novels and plays exactly at the end of the war, that is, between 1945 and 1946. (We should not forget that although the "non-historical" *L'Age de raison* was published simultaneously with *Le Sursis* in 1945, it was written earlier.[2]) While Sartre was still able in *Le Sursis* and *Morts sans sépulture* to bypass this problem, to raise a particular point in time to the timelessness of a situation which was in the last analysis to be interpreted abstractly, the matter was considerably more difficult in *La Mort dans l'âme*, and "*La Dernière Chance*" shows that *Les Chemins de la liberté* foundered partly on the rock of this problem.

Sartre, who until the war had given no thought to engagement, the abstract Sartre who still very much dominates *Les Mouches*, who could be charged with dilettantism in his Resistance activity,[3] obviously became more and more entangled in the tentacles of this problem after the war ended. Metaphorically speaking, he is no longer Orestes accomplishing "de-redemption" in the one-time abstract engagement of a single deed. He becomes a man, an oriented, historical man. Or at least the abstract Sartre enters into a dialectic with this part of himself which is now demanding to be heard.

This has not always made for clarity. Sartre now takes a position, tries to save his existentialism as a humanism (1946), although he withdrew some of the remarks he made in the subsequent discussion on the grounds that the hall had been overcrowded and he could not think clearly.[4] In 1947, in an important essay entitled "Qu'est-ce que la littérature?" he said that a writer cannot as a matter of principle belong to the Communist Party because this means giving up his freedom of thought, his supreme principle (*Situations II*, Paris 1948, p. 280). If he thus distanced himself from the Communist Party in practice, this also suggests how much he now felt the need for engagement in party politics.[5] So it is not at all surprising that a year later, in February 1948, Sartre, together with David Rousset and Gérard Rosenthal, founded his own party, the "Rassemblement Démocratique Révolutionnaire," an intellectual yet (abstractly) social variant of Communism. As might have been expected, nothing came of it. Sartre is not a practical man. Neither did he become one over the years, for his intellectual fellow-traveling affiliation with the Communist Party, lasting from 1952 to 1956, was on the one hand marked by utter servility in furnishing excuses for dubious Communist actions, while on the other it never became concrete enough to make him a genuine, card-carrying member. After the Hungarian revolt he did in fact dissociate himself from what he expressly called "this crime," but he placed the responsibility for it on the erroneous reactionary line which the Hungarian Communists had taken up to then. (Even among the Communists this earned him nothing but "a reputation for being naive." [6])

Sartre's significance lies elsewhere, and if we want to do justice to his literary works, we cannot and should not look at him from this point of view. To what extent this problem of theory and practice may have helped to determine the structure of his works is, however, another question, one which we shall now pursue.

### La Putain respectueuse

*The Respectful Prostitute*, written in 1946, is certainly one of the plays in which this problem assumed structural significance. This play deals with a contemporary problem, race relations in the American South, and draws its material, at least peripherally, from this theme. Anyone who has read Sartre's numerous statements on social injustice in the United States, as, for instance, in *Les Temps Modernes*, will realize that the theme of *La Putain respectueuse* was not chosen at random. On the other hand, we should not go so far as to take this for a topical play with political intent. If we do, Sartre comes off very badly and, moreover, we do him an injustice, for the element of political engagement in *La Putain* is extremely weak and unconvincing.[7]

By putting it into this perspective at all, we close ourselves to the timeless validity of this play, we lose its value. Even if the secondary theme of political engagement enters in, *La Putain* is first and foremost a specifically esthetic product. What distinguishes it from the earlier plays is that Sartre's consideration of the claims of practical, worldly reality now begin to co-determine the esthetic mode. For there is no denying that in the esthetics and structure of *La Putain* something new is emerging. We might call it the beginning of a development that will gain greater scope in *Les Jeux sont faits, Les Mains sales, Le Diable et le bon Dieu, Nékrassov,* and *Les Séquestrés d'Altona.* The new element is a dialogue with the great social and political structures which man, as a historical being, confronts. Thus the dialogue between existence and structure which we have found in just about every work of Sartre's enters a new phase, one by no means without its perils for the writer. It was already forcefully anticipated in *Morts sans sépulture,* inasmuch as Sartre there dealt for the first time with the "social" reality of a group.[8]

*La Putain* leads deeper into this treacherous thicket of social structures. Whereas Henri, Lucie, Sorbier, Canoris, and François, notwithstanding their membership in a group, decide and think each for himself, Lizzie, the respectful prostitute, is quite a social reality, an ascertainable magnitude which the other can include in his calculations, of which he can to a certain extent dispose, a human being who does not suspect how close she is to the very brink of unbelievably superior freedom. For Fred, the spoiled Senator's son, is much more unfree than Lizzie; the mesh of the structure in which he is entangled is much closer. Unlike Lizzie, Fred will never have a chance of authenticity—any more than the Senator himself will. Not only is he a social product: behind him stand the powerful ideologies of racism and democracy (though the latter, to be sure, appears only as a caricature of true democracy). Thus Lizzie deserves to be mentioned in the title as the heroine of the play, and the attributes applied to her are apt. For she is a prostitute, body and soul, a whore not in the sense of erotic tumescence or sophisticated seductiveness, but in the sense of utterly uncomplicated availability to any man who needs her. She is a prostitute as other women are mothers. She confronts the big Negro who stumbles into her room on the run from the police with the same goodwill and feminine helpfulness that she displays toward the effete Fred, who, having spent the night with her, is now behaving like a miserable repentant sinner.

The respectful prostitute now gets a genuine chance to move forward to true authenticity, as she confronts Fred, who has by now pulled himself together and become "the boss" again. He now broaches the purpose for which he has come: to persuade her to perjure herself for the sake of his cousin Thomas. He wants her to accuse the Negro who has sought refuge in her room and swear that he and another Negro tried to rape her and that Fred's cousin intervened and killed one of them in self-defense. Lizzie, however, has no intention of agreeing, not only because she has just promised the Negro to tell the truth, but also as a matter of principle, because to her a man's life is a man's life, regardless of the color of his skin. Even when Fred offers her five hundred dollars she sticks to her free, responsible choice. Not even the police, who bring all kinds of pressure to bear on her as a prostitute in violation of the law, can persuade her to sign their prepared statement: "I'd rather go to jail. I don't want to lie." [9]

Thus Lizzie rises to astounding greatness in authentic action, an action which she determines herself in complete freedom and which reveals the great potentialities of her freeness. But then comes the great temptation. The Senator appears in person. As a diplomat he recognizes immediately that Lizzie is vulnerable at one point only: in her deep yet calculable defenseless femininity. He tells her that the mother of poor Thomas who committed the murder will never get over it if her son is convicted, and she is an old lady with white hair. If Lizzie could save Thomas for her sake, she would have a place in her heart forever. Thus he appeals to two powerful components of her femininity: her sympathetic helpfulness and her desire for human contact, and it is easy enough to recognize in the latter the profound need for orientation that we have already encountered in Orestes and many other heroes. Lizzie is threatened in her freedom. All it takes to rob her of her priceless possession and make her for the first time truly poor is a masterpiece of fancy rhetoric by the glib Senator, a display of his powerful, structure-conscious thinking. Her hope of making a place for herself in the mother's heart, of being able to count on the reassurance of figuring in somebody's thoughts, soon proves to be an illusion. When the Senator hands her an envelope the next day, she assumes that it is a letter, but it contains nothing but a hundred dollar bill.

This twist is not very original, but it is not the end of the play. Sartre again proves himself a master of the dramatic end effect; above all he knows how to give his plays an almost unsurpassable aspect of unity, designed to be at the same time unlimited openness—a veritable mirror of the dialectic of being and nothingness. He makes the Negro seek refuge again in Lizzie's room, as he did at the opening of the play. Lizzie hides him in the closet, then in the bathroom when she hears somebody coming. It is Fred, here this time not on a diplomatic mission but for Lizzie's own sake. The previous night's experience has left him restless. He senses an opportunity to find something to hold on to in a person to whom he can give sexual pleasure. He wants to have Lizzie to himself, to know that on three evenings a week she will be waiting for him at nightfall. He wants to assign her a place in the cosmos of things he controls. He also wants to get rid of the disturbing element in the previous night's experience.

Things happen fast. At the last minute events take an unexpected turn again and again (as they do in *Morts sans sépulture*). Fred hears a sound in the bathroom. Lizzie tries to distract him, but Fred forces the door open. Seeing the Negro, he draws his gun. The Negro escapes, but Fred goes after him, and Lizzie hears two shots. She sits down at the table with her back to the audience and picks up the gun, which Fred on his return has carelessly thrown down. She covers Fred with it but does not dare to shoot, so that he can say in triumph—and not entirely without justification (though not before he has had a bad scare): "A girl like you *can't* shoot at a man like me." [10]

Thus social conditioning is stronger than freedom; the structure strangles the human being. Lizzie gives up; she has made a mess of what may be her last chance. Fred, however, has succeeded in getting rid of the nothingness about to open up before him. He has overcome the existentiality of existence through the structure of an order.[11] The experience of love will never disturb him again. Lizzie will be his mistress; she is now an object whose cheek he can pat with jocular self-consciousness: "Fred (*patting her cheek*): 'Now everything's in order again.' (*A pause*) 'My name's Fred.' (*Curtain*)."

### Les Mains sales

If the "anti-American" tone of *La Putain respectueuse* earned Sartre the approval of the East and an indulgent smile from the English-speaking world, *Les Mains sales* reversed the situation— and with much more clear-cut reactions. In a way this was tragic for Sartre. Although the tone of *La Putain respectueuse* may well have been intentional, in the case of *Les Mains sales* he had done nothing to deserve the indignation that his play aroused in the Communist world. From Sartre's own point of view the play's success on Broadway was also undeserved. In *Les Mains sales* Sartre wanted to present an abstract problem, but meanwhile he had become so involved in contemporary politics that without fully realizing what he was doing he struck while the iron was hot and in the creative fervor of working and shaping his material overlooked the fact that this "iron" was by no means something casually dreamed up; it touched upon political structures which in themselves—one might almost say, as a way of doing things—were incompatible with his concepts of freedom and existence.

This was tragic because in practice Sartre was, after all, very much attached to this particular sociopolitical structure. Forced to stand by helplessly while Communist propaganda attacked him as the scum of Western decadence, he cannot have derived much comfort from the enthusiasm which *Les Mains sales* generated on Broadway. To make matters worse, it was produced under the provocative title of *Red Gloves* instead of *Dirty Hands*, which underlined its allegedly anti-Communist tone. Sartre protested; in 1954 he went so far as to make a formal protest against the Vienna production on the grounds that it would "increase tension between the East and the West." [12] But the play continued to succeed and in book form still follows *The Little World of Don Camillo, The Plague*, and *Bonjour Tristesse* on the best-seller list of world literature—a thorn in the flesh of the Communists and an unintentional vexation to Sartre himself.

His intention was to exemplify an idea already familiar to us: the dead-end problem in executing a plan, that is, the disjunction between intention and performance. To resolve upon a murder and to execute it are two completely separate decisions, each of which necessitates a choice in its own particular context: this is the gist of what Sartre was trying to say. But the specific setting in which he presented this problem transformed the play into an attack on powerful structures of collective thinking and behavior, on the structure of bourgeois values on the one hand and those of Communism on the other. Here we have a hero, Hugo, who seems so determined by the social structure of his bourgeois background that free, absolute action is just as much beyond his reach as true engagement. Hugo is a hero of the type of Roquentin and Mathieu, but his actions take place in a much more binding context—a historical one.

The geographical setting is not specified: the action is set derer, the man who is to be assassinated by order of the Party, is so strongly reminiscent of Leon Trotsky, murdered in exile in in an imaginary Balkan monarchy at the end of World War II, but the figure who shares the spotlight with Hugo, Hoe-Mexico, that the plot was inevitably taken to be historical—which it certainly is to some extent, though perhaps against Sartre's will. To the Stalinists this internal Communist dispute, in the course of which Hoederer is killed, unmistakably represented the Trotsky case, especially in view of the Party's attempt, in the play as in real life, to pass the murder off as a "crime of passion," as a deluded and, moreover, nonpolitical gesture by an individual.

This is what had attracted Sartre as a dramatist, but only as an abstract case. How sound his judgment was, esthetically speaking, is demonstrated by the play itself, which falls logically into place as one of the high points of his literary work. This play has almost the quality of a thriller with a clearly defined narrative frame and a core plot which gains in suspense by reflecting the main action. Hugo stands before Olga, who is hearing his "confession" on behalf of the Party. This confession, a flashback presenting the core plot, will decide whether Hugo is to live or die, whether he can be of any further use to the Party, whether he will have to be liquidated or not. The Party representatives will be back at midnight to hear from Olga's lips the verdict which Hugo must in effect pronounce himself: "salvageable" or "not salvageable." But the specifically, almost typically Sartrean twist is that Hugo's effort to prove that he is salvageable misses precisely what the Party wants of him. This is the existential perfection of the *quid pro quo* comedy, the game of mistaken identities, a game which, as the encounter between Orestes and Electra in *Les Mouches* has already demonstrated, favors the existential thesis of man's unbridgeable isolation.

For Hugo the purpose of this examination of conscience is to stand his own test, to "save" his action by showing it to have been done on Party orders and in obedience to the ideology of Communism, and thus to prove himself salvageable in the eyes of the Party. This plunges us once again into a typically Sartrean problem. To Hugo, the son of rich bourgeois parents, the intellectual in need of communication, engagement in the Party was purely an attempt to justify himself in his own eyes; this would also liberate him from the structure of a bourgeois ideology which is an outgrowth of social conditions. Yet the way he went about it again merely expressed his social conditioning: he chose the bourgeois luxury of idealistic action. This was why he asked the Party for a particularly dangerous, one might almost say exalted, assignment, why he was eager to undertake the assassination of the Communist leader Hoederer, whom the Party now wanted to be rid of. He did not suspect how difficult this assignment would prove for him.

For Hoederer is the convinced Communist who acts authentically. He is everything that Brunet in *La Mort dans l'âme* is, and more besides. He knows how to sacrifice outward consistency of action to inner loyalty to the Party. He acts completely independently, relying upon himself alone, in response to the reality of a situation. Precisely for this reason it falls to the intellectual, irresolute Hugo to liquidate him on behalf of the Party. Hugo has gone to work for Hoederer as his secretary and from the first behaves in such a suspicious, hesitant way that it is not difficult for Hoederer to guess what he has in mind. In an almost comic scene, which is nevertheless full of chilling tension, Hoederer's two bodyguards demand to search Hugo's room and finally proceed to do so in Hoederer's presence. Hugo almost collapses from fear and nervousness. Jessica, Hugo's wife, has managed at the last minute to hide his revolver, of whose existence he has only just informed her, in her clothing. Hugo still thinks it is in the suitcase, which the guards in the end search thoroughly (Act III, Scenes 2–3). All through this scene Hoederer has remained in sovereign control of himself, has magnanimously waived his right to have the room searched, expecting that in return for his generosity they will permit it. To Hugo's dismay Jessica does permit it; moreover, impressed by Hoederer's masculinity, she hints plainly that the door of her bedroom is open to him (Act III, Scene 4).

Hoederer is also completely self-possessed in his conversations with Hugo, the intellectual whose face betrays his dream of "action," who, for all his "sincerity," remains the very personification of *mauvaise foi*, who, precisely because of his sincere aspirations, constantly objectifies and analyzes himself and his actions, thus depriving them of authenticity. Thus he seeks, for example, to lose himself in the Party, but as Hoederer reminds him, this self-forgetting is an imperative never absent from his mind, not an authentically experienced reality (Act III, Scene 4). Hoederer, however, is reality, and Hugo envies and admires him for this. Hoederer is tangible, concrete presence, which gives things solidity. Even the coffee pot and cups acquire a spatial reality when he touches them, whereas Hugo himself never manages to create anything but lies, even in his own room (Act IV, Scene 1).

Hugo would like to acquire this solidity himself, just as Orestes wanted to assume the burden of a crime in order to acquire substantiality, but Hugo is neither an Orestes nor a Hoederer. He is not disoriented; he has a past to sustain him, has been through the "bourgeois malady of youth" (Act IV, Scene 3), and since then has been aspiring to unachievable ideals. Orestes and Hoederer were either one thing or the other: the former made the transition from stranger to redeemer, the latter from child to man, without any intermediate stages: "Youth? I don't know what it is. I went directly from childhood to manhood." [13]

Hugo dreams of purity. He sets store by the whiteness of his hands. For him everything is a question of principles, of ideas. But Hoederer has dirty hands (*Les Mains sales*); he has plunged them up to the elbows in blood and filth (Act V, Scene 3). Hugo will never be so unquestioningly at one with himself; he will never be capable of this horizontal way of acting.

While Hugo did indeed kill Hoederer, it was largely as a result of circumstances and chance. The Party leaders, on whose orders he was working for Hoederer, had let him know plainly that they were not prepared to wait much longer. But he actually made up his mind when, entering Hoederer's office unexpectedly, he found him kissing Jessica. What happened next was just revenge, not unlike Mathieu's action in *La Mort dans l'âme*—revenge against the other person's strength: "You see, Hoederer, I'm looking you in the eyes and aiming, and my hand isn't shaking, and I don't give a damn what's in your head." [14] In this way he exploited the situation to deceive himself. Now he sits facing Olga, and all he has to do is liquidate his action. To him it seems like an assassination without an assassin. His answer to Olga's question about the decisive motive—"I killed him because I opened the door"; and a little later: "It wasn't me that killed him; it was chance."[15]—shows that Hugo has remained unauthentic, that he simply allowed himself to drift. He makes one last attempt to justify himself to

Olga, claiming that the assignment was, after all, carried out, which is all that matters. He is not aware that a confession of personal failure is exactly what the Party wants from him. Not until he sees how satisfied Olga is with his confession and learns what the Party has in mind for him does he begin to see how matters stand. The true meaning of Olga's word "salvageable" ("*récupérable*") dawns upon him. The Party has changed its policy and adopted Hoederer's political position and therefore wants the assassination to go down in history as nonpolitical—exactly what Hugo's confession shows it ultimately to have been.

Just as an unexpected happy ending seems imminent, Sartre, as he so often does, gives the plot a decisive final twist. Hugo, idealistic to the end, suddenly sees a chance to give his action substance, to elevate it above the level of a lie to that of a political mistake which Hoederer a martyr to his convictions.

> A man like Hoederer doesn't die by accident. He dies for his ideas, for his political program. He is responsible for his death. If I openly assume responsibility for my crime, if I claim the name Raskolnikoff and if I'm willing to pay the necessary price, then he will have had the death he deserves.[16]

Only now will he really kill Hoederer—and himself too. Kicking the door open, he shouts to the Party representatives: "Not salvageable." On these words the curtain falls.

### Les Séquestrés d'Altona

The disagreeable experiences connected with *Les Mains sales* made Sartre cautious. Although he did not break off his dialogue with power structures or renounce the historical type of plot that stems from it, he began to avoid contemporary actuality, at least so far as subject matter goes. The setting of *Le Diable et le bon Dieu* (to which we shall return later) is remote from contemporary politics—sixteenth-century Germany—and although *Les Séquestrés d'Altona* deals with postwar Germany and its beginning reconstruction, according to Sartre himself it was aimed at the French officers who had

ordered the torture of Algerian prisoners.[17] Yet anyone looking
for any overt expression of this theme, even indirectly, will feel
cheated; there are only a few vague analogies to hint at it. Although it might be even more plausible to see the play as a formulation of the German problem in the 1950's, the numerous
points of coincidence with other Sartrean themes show that in
the last analysis it is merely an extension of his familiar mode of
thought to a new situation, to a powerful structure which he has
not hitherto treated: the structure of generations within the
family.

Characteristically this is, to be sure, a motherless family—
characteristically because Sartre, as he says in *Les Mots*, regarded his mother as an older sister or a servant who counted
for nothing in the household, but also because this makes it
easier to portray the three generations of Germans that Sartre
was concerned with. The first of these is the patriarchal,
authoritarian father. (Sartre never knew his own father, and in
*Les Mots* he congratulates himself on this. His father image is
derived from his patriarchal grandfather Karl Schweitzer,
whom he calls "a kind of Heavenly Father.") Then come the
elder son, Frantz, representing the generation that fought in
World War II (accompanied by a female character, Frantz's
sister Léni, incestuously in love with her brother). Finally
there is the younger son, Werner, representing the generation
which was too young for the war and which is now working
for Germany's new prosperity. (Werner's wife, Johanna, is
the woman of alien blood who does not fit into the narrow
family structure.) Thus the basic dramatic constellation of
characters and situation is clearly defined. It has a symbolic
quality, and its structure is reminiscent of certain groupings of
Biblical characters: Isaac and his sons Esau and Jacob, for instance, particularly since here again it is the younger son who is
to inherit his father's property, while the older one is deprived
of his birthright.

Yet this clear definition, familiar to us from other plays of
Sartre's, becomes blurred as the play develops. Although *Les
Séquestrés* at first seems an almost classical five-act play, it soon
proves to be quite obscure—the most obscure of all Sartre's

dramas. Obscurity is, of course, not necessarily a disadvantage in literature, but in this case it seems to be due simply to Sartre's having tried to crowd in too many themes instead of confining himself to a dramatic exemplification of one single problem, as he did in *Huis clos, Morts sans sépulture*, and *Les Mouches*.[18] Perhaps his mistake begins even with his decision to make it a five-act play, because this rhythmic pattern, which normally presupposes a regular curve of tension, conflicted with his "metaphysical" point of departure, with his horizontality.[19] ( $\_-\;\overline{\;}\;-\_$ )

It may be objected that *Les Mouches*, having three acts, necessarily falls into this same pattern ( $\_-\_$ ). This is true, but it should not be forgotten that here Sartre breaks the rhythm internally by dividing the second act into two scenes or *tableaux*, so that the play falls into two halves and the continuous pattern is broken:

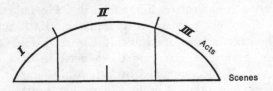

Thus the thematic construction of *Les Mouches* was just as clear and ultimately horizontal as that of *Les Séquestrés*.

But in addition to the generation problem, *Les Séquestrés* has other central themes: the problem of "the other person" (*Huis clos*), that of engagement through one single action (*Les Mouches*), the problem of madness which erects a wall between two partners in love (*La Chambre*), the problem of love between brother and sister (barely suggested in *Les Mouches*), the problem of the guilt-atonement pattern of thinking, and finally the problem of the pervasive national and social structure. Here Sartre disregards (or does not sufficiently respect) the first law of classical literature: the law of internal unity demanding that the medium center entirely upon one basic theme. This is a disturbing element in *Les Séquestrés* and

makes it a nonclassical but nevertheless great play. Gabriel
Marcel is not entirely wrong in considering its last scene, between the father and his eldest son, the best thing Sartre has
ever written.[20] And it is not surprising that Gabriel Marcel of
all people should like this play, since here more than anywhere
else Sartre engages in a dialogue with the structures of social
life—one might almost say shows himself already hopelessly
involved in them. Here for the first time he turns the spotlight
on the very crux of social life: the structure of a family.

The structure that emerges is an imposing—and suffo-
catingly tight—one. The von Gerlach family of Hamburg
industrial magnates has fallen into—or has let the paterfamilias
impose upon it—a strict order.[21] For one thing, they own a
sumptuously furnished though forbidding house in Altona surrounded by a parklike garden shutting out the outside world.
Moreover, the family is also subject to a rigorous, rigid internal
order under the sole authority of the father. The latter might
be called the Aegisthus of this "miniature Argos," an Aegisthus
who is ultimaltely even more inflexible and authoritarian—and
more terrible too because more methodical.

We sense this at the very beginning of the play, even before this despot appears. Léni, Werner, and Johanna are sitting,
tongue-tied, waiting for the father, who has summoned this
family council. Léni knows why he is keeping them waiting
and why he will appear with absolutely military punctuality:
he wants to give them time to be afraid. Johanna makes the
cruel discovery that Werner, the husband she loves, becomes a
new man in the aura of this father whose anticipated presence
alone annihilates him, a man quite different from the one she
met and fell in love with in Hamburg three years ago. That
Werner was free, open, happy; he was true existential reality,
with which she, being equally free, could communicate intel-
lectually. But here, in thralldom to his father, Werner seems to
be turning into an unfree object, a satellite of somebody else
who pushes him up against the wall and makes him a func-
tioning part of himself, so that Léni can say in all seriousness at
the end of the scene: "It's ten past three, Werner. You can get
up." [22]

And in fact at this moment the father enters. He has called his important family council because he feels himself close to death. He announces bluntly what they all know already: that he has cancer and has not much time left. He now wants to resign his position as head of the firm in favor of his son Werner, and above all he wants to force him by the terms of the will to accommodate himself so fully to the structures which he, the father, has erected that Werner will have practically no freedom, will simply be a continuation of his father. For to be king of the biggest shipbuilding concern in Europe entails, first, living sequestered in the family villa (hence the title of the play) and, second, taking charge of the other son, always referred to as dead in official family parlance but actually living shut up in a room at the top of the house. It means in fact being doubly sequestered, confined and at the same time chained to the existence of one even more rigorously confined.[23] It is characteristic of the von Gerlach's family way of life that the supposedly dead elder brother cannot even be mentioned. The father's glance and his will keep them all in a state bordering on paralysis.

The only character who retains any freedom of movement is the outsider, Johanna. Johanna has not yet been domesticated. Thus she introduces a dialectical element of uncertainty into this rigid structure, although she herself is to some extent caught up in its mechanism. And so it is she who dares to speak the truth, well known to them all, and to remind them that Frantz, the elder brother, is still there. She knows that something happened in 1946 and a charge was brought against him. He was said to have fled to Argentina, and in 1956 a death certificate was obtained from there for this Frantz who has actually been living upstairs since the end of the war, divorced from the passage of time. Johanna refuses to let Werner and herself be caught in this tight net, and her attempts to see Frantz are the key to the action of the play.

She conducts a kind of inquiry to get to the bottom of the whole mystery, and first of all to shed some light on the reasons for it. She learns something from the father himself, who wants to use her for his own ends. She learns, for instance that

Frantz made his way back from Poland to Germany on foot in 1946, when the war trials were taking place in Nuremberg. Frantz, who besides fighting in the war had ordered the torture and execution of prisoners in Poland, could not refrain from identifying with Goering, who had been sentenced to death by hanging in Nuremberg: "I *am* Goering. If they hang him, they'll be hanging me." [24] This experience produced in Frantz, who had gone unpunished, a compelling desire to see the balance between guilt and atonement set straight, and at the same time a need to lie his own personal guilt out of existence. He shut himself up in a room and became a dead rather than a living symbol of the phenomenon known as collective guilt, which consists essentially in exempting oneself from personal responsibility through a notion of a suprapersonal interrelation of guilt and atonement. (We have already seen something of the sort in *Les Mouches*.) Obsessed by this collective guilt for which restitution has to be made, Frantz will opt out of time, will cease to be a man who develops and constantly changes, and will know nothing of the reconstruction of Germany.

Johanna now intrudes upon this make-believe world of Frantz, not without yielding slightly to its seductions herself.[25] But Léni jealously makes sure that the awakening love between Johanna and Frantz cannot attain a tranquil equilibrium (cf. the theme of *Huis clos*). She tears down the new fabric of lies growing up between them and in her jealousy exposes the truth which Frantz is keeping from Johanna: that he ordered the torture and execution of Polish prisoners. She also confronts him with the truth of Germany's revival by giving him a newspaper. She knows that this means his death, but she prefers this to losing him.

Having read the newspaper, Frantz stands there, pale, his face twitching. He looks to Johanna for support, but Léni frustrates him by throwing up the truth about Frantz's guilt, from which Johanna recoils. Frantz stands alone, his lies shattered. There remains only the liquidation of his life and before that the stock-taking. He asks to see his father. It is thirteen years since they have seen one another, and they meet now for an accounting which Gabriel Marcel is justified in calling one of the greatest scenes Sartre ever wrote (Act V, Scene 1), a scene which, like many others in Sartre, retrospectively illuminates the meaning of the whole play.

We are given the final key to the story by Frantz himself when he suddenly sees everything with the unexpected clarity that comes from being close to death: "Well played! You played Johanna off against Léni and then Léni against Johanna. Mate in three movies." [26] Johanna, as well as Léni, has been manipulated by the father; both of them have been puppets in his hand. The father, aware of his own imminent death, has checkmated his son in three moves, forced him to join him in death as his father's satellite. The first move was to get Johanna admitted to Frantz's room, the second to exploit Léni's jealousy of Johanna. Now there remains only "the black king": death.

Though Frantz now understands the game, he cannot defend himself. He is too little himself, too much his father, too much a pawn in his father's game, to be able to go his own way. But at least he can take the opportunity to make a kind of testament, an attempt to present father and son in their true light, the light of their respective responsibility and freedom. Now everything he has repressed breaks forth. It all began years ago when a young Polish rabbi escaped from the nearby concentration camp (for which his father had donated the land) and Frantz hid him. The father informed on his own son in return for a promise that he would not be punished, thus saving his life. The S.S. men came, knocked the rabbi down, and strangled him before Frantz's eyes. Frantz stood by, helpless, because four men were holding the rabbi down while others finished him off. He was incapable of lifting his little finger. It was like rape; Hitler was raping him, and yet at the same time he was somehow participating. He had turned into Hitler's mistress: "The rabbi was bleeding, and I discovered at the heart of my helplessness a sort of assent." [27] An "assent" had come into being in his heart, some kind of mysterious, lascivious delight in power. His father, who had prevented him from risking his life for a rabbi by his own free choice, was responsible for his being tempted by this delight in power, but he himself had freely acquiesced, driven by an impulse of which he may have been quite unconscious at the time.[28] He attacked the rabbi, thus activating the intoxication with power to which he was to yield as the "hangman of Smolensk." At that moment he turned himself over to his father, became an object in his hand—and hence in Hitler's hand too.

Even now, summing things up, he will not be able—will not in fact even try—to divorce himself from his father's existence as his own man, going his own way in freedom. "You will have been my origin and my destiny to the very end," [29] he says to his father, admitting that his existence is absolutely determined—something that existence can ultimately never be, no matter how adverse the circumstances. Yet at the same time these words are a harsh indictment of the father and of the generation that fathered those who are directly responsible, yet failed to initiate them into the freedom of being forced to choose. The father regarded Frantz less as a son or a human being than as a thing at his beck and call, whose destiny he controlled, whose decision to risk his life by helping a rabbi he thwarted. This father can say: "Frantz, there has never been anyone but me." And he is right, not absolutely but practically, for he has acted—and events have turned out—as if he had been right. And so, as the last link in the long chain of his interference with the sacrosanct existence of another, of his son, he decides that they will go to their deaths together: "I made you. I shall destroy you. My death will envelop yours, and in the end I shall be the only one to die."

In the closing scene, depicted only through the grief-stricken reactions of the survivors, father and son meet death in a fast Porsche which crashes from the Teufelsbrücke into the river at more than a hundred miles an hour. And indeed it is truly only the father's death, for the son's death, like his whole life, which has been directed by his father, was not freely chosen.

Thus, despite the many differences, the ending of this play is not unlike that of Les Mouches. Those who are responsible make their exit, leave Argos (or Altona or Germany, as the case may be). Will this other Argos they have left behind understand its freedom, which is responsibility?

## chapter 6

# Existence and Love

*Les Jeux sont faits*
(The Chips Are Down) —
*Le Diable et le bon Dieu*
(The Devil and the Good Lord)

The dialogue with the phenomenon of structure which we have traced in the foregoing chapters suggested an analysis of the concept and reality of love, taking love to mean that which enables man to build and maintain an enduring bridge between himself and the other, whether the other is represented by another person, by values, or by God. Love is thus a peculiarly fundamental example of structure, of the erection of an enduring context of relationship. It is the positive complement to the problem of "the other" as Sartre sees it, the bridge to the Thou. Thus if love existed, that is to say, if love as a structure proved under existential analysis to be a reality, then the existentiality of existence would be overcome at one point—and hence once and for all.

So it is not surprising that we find this theme throughout Sartre's works: in *La Nausée* and *Les Chemins de la liberté* as in *Les Mouches*, *Huis clos*, and *Morts sans sépulture*, in *La Putain respectueuse* as in *Les Mains sales* and *Les Séquestrés d'Altona*. Yet in all these works love seems to be rather a secondary aspect of events, a powerful and significant phenomenon, to be sure, yet not one that can seriously affect the unbridgeable loneliness of existence. Either it represents an obviously false action—*mauvaise foi*—or it breaks down, as it does in the case of Lucie, Anny, and Electra. Not until *Les Jeux sont faits* (1947) and *Le Diable et le bon Dieu* (1951) does love become a sustaining dramatic element, and between these two formulations of it we shall discern a path leading, like the path which leads from *Morts sans sépulture* (1946) to *Les Séquestrés d'Altona* (1959), from stark alternative to true dialogue.

### Les Jeux sont faits

The plot of this classic scenario (which was made into a film in 1947) is as clear and straightforward as its theme. There is no doubt that Sartre is here concerned not just with the phenomenon of love but with existence pure and simple and—as in everything he wrote after 1945—with the phenomenon of social structure. But among these themes love is the focus of dramatic interest, a love born in the beyond, in the realm of the dead, where the lovers, reduced to their souls, have come to know and love one another as pure forms. They are Eve, the dead wife of a rich businessman, poisoned by her husband so that he may be free to love and marry her younger sister Lucette and inherit her property, and Pierre, the active Communist, who led a conspiracy against the Regent but was shot down from an ambush by Lucien, a young comrade, the day before the decisive day of action. (The shooting was an act of revenge. Pierre had refused to take Lucien back into his unit because the boy had failed to hold out under torture by the militia.)

Thus both Pierre and Eve have reached the land of shades. Unlike Dante among others, Sartre ascribes no specific geographical location to this realm; it exists within the world of the living, unseen by them—a pure existence freed from its bodily limitations. These dead are now unrestrictedly what human existence really is in the face of tangible reality: they are literally nothing. When they try to look at themselves in the mirror, they no longer see themselves as objects but as what they are in a more essential sense: as nothing. (This shows once again how close Sartre's concept of nothingness can come to the Christian concept of soul.) And it is quite understandable that it should be considerably easier for this personal nothingness to find the loving way to the other nothing, the Thou of true partnership, because there is nothing to prevent these souls from loving each other, from understanding each other as nothingness, from becoming absorbed in one another undisturbed by the eyes of a third person and free from the danger of being made into objects.

But these "souls" who here come to know each other as nothingness divorced from love remember that they once possessed in their bodies a possibility of expressing love in a more heartfelt, tangible, concrete way, of experiencing, instead of merely knowing, the loving presence of the other. Eve, with whose shade Pierre, himself a shade, dances in time to the music, used to be flesh and blood. How perfect, they think, would have been their love and happiness if their whole human reality had been able to chime in. It is clear now that their souls were destined for each other, but it was not granted to them to meet while they were alive. They do not suspect that in the beyond, thoughts of this kind are carefully recorded, and that they are automatically invoking Paragraph 140, which states:

> If, as a result of an error for which the Administration is wholly responsible, a man and woman destined for one another did not meet during their lifetime, they may request and be granted permission to return to earth on certain conditions in order to realize the love and live the common life of which they have been unduly deprived.[1]

So the two soon find themselves back in the little shop where they were entered on the roll of the dead and shown the way to the absolute freedom of death, and the old lady in charge there verifies from her books that they were in fact destined for one another: "You were authentically destined for one another. But the Births Department made a mistake." [2] So they fall under Paragraph 140, and the Platonic myth of the souls destined for one another for eternity, which meet in love in the flesh, is renewed—and perhaps answered—in a remarkable way. They are allowed to return to life, at first only for a test period of twenty-four hours. If they succeed in keeping their love intact, if they still love one another without reservations when this time is up, they win the right to a new human existence. Sartre's intention is clear. What Pierre and Eve are about to attempt will decide in an exemplary manner whether love is in fact possible and whether it can last.

The two of them already feel a slight uncertainty when the old woman reminds them again of the condition: if at 10.30 A.M. the following day there is the least distrust between them, they have lost. Then a workman asks them to look after his little daughter because since his death his wife has been living with a man who beats the child, and they promise to take care of this. The lights go out, and they find themselves back where death overtook them, at liberty to resume their lives. Pierre gets up from the pavement where he was shot down. Eve opens her eyes in her bedroom to see her husband bending over the bed, obviously disappointed that she is not dead. For Pierre and Eve the adventure which is to decide about life and death has begun. They are soon to learn how dangerous this adventure is, how unavailing are their efforts to love each other forever in the flesh, amid all the structures which life erects around people. And this realization is what the play is all about.

Eve quickly discovers that besides her love for Pierre other things also make demands on her and often influence her thinking more decisively: her attempt to protect her younger sister from an unhappy love affair, for one, for she knows now that her husband only wants to marry Lucette for the sake of her money. Pierre is in a similar situation. Having been able to go anywhere unseen, he has discovered that the Regent has long been informed of their conspiracy. He therefore tries to warn his comrades and prevent their putting their plan into action, without, of course, being able to tell them where he got this new information.

Serious as are the difficulties they both encounter, they

face even greater ones in their personal relations with each other. Eve's husband belongs to the government party and is head of the militia against which Pierre is fighting. She hates force and terror. Moreover, her high social position separates her from Pierre, who is a foreman in a foundry. Although both of them have the best will in the world, they are soon forced to admit that their love is impossible. They have nothing in common; their love is not a bond that unites closely enough even to diminish the other ties that conflict with it. They both bear the stamp of the conditions under which they grew up; they have become part of a social and ideological structure from which they cannot free themselves.

So that their return to life shall not have been completely in vain, they want at least to do what the workman asked: go and see his little daughter and place her in good hands. This they manage to do, and their success unexpectedly brings them something else: the hope of realizing their love after all and then being able to adopt the little girl.

> Eve and Pierre laughed and then looked at each other:
> "At least we'll have succeeded in that," said Eve.
> She thought for a moment and added:
> "Pierre, we'll keep her if everything works out all right."
> "It'll work out," Pierre assured her.[3]

Obviously they owe this hope, which represents opportunity, to the fact that they have set themselves a common aim, united in a shared experience. Thus they have not yet proved that love is possible, because any such proof would have to be derived from love itself, not from love in the service of others or love saved by some other factor.

It will soon become clear that they have again dissembled toward one another. Pierre takes Eve to his simple apartment, and Eve needs all the courage she can muster to agree to wait there while Pierre goes to see his comrades. Again she manages to pull herself together, as she has so often done before; she even manages to wave quite cheerfully to Pierre from the window as he leaves. But then she is overwhelmed by terrible depression. She will regain control of herself but only when she has made the room in which she is waiting *her* room. She brings flowers, buys new curtains, a tablecloth, a new lampshade: in brief, she does not rest until the room has acquired a new look, *her* look, has been so changed in structure that she can live in it.

When Pierre comes back he is disappointed for two reasons: first because his comrades have refused to listen to him and think he is a traitor because they have seen him with the wife of a militiaman, and second because he is annoyed that Eve has changed his room around. They are both discouraged, and when one of Pierre's comrades comes to the door and warns him that the others are going to take their revenge, they are content to wait for death. They are disillusioned. It is now clear that Pierre came back for the sake of the rebellion, not for love, and that Eve came back chiefly for the sake of Lucette. She too has to admit to herself that her love seems to have been more or less a pretext.

Yet precisely this genuine, disinterested admission of failure, this silence of meaning in the face of expected death, finally brings them together, gives them the chance to overcome death in love, not of course forever but for a few moments. They now have nothing but each other, and they love one another, give themselves to one another, exist entirely for one another. Each experiences the other as the freedom of self-giving. They are not subject and object, thing and possessor. They are both the freedom of a choice. And this love is stronger than death. The former comrades come to the door but go away again. They are powerless against the strength of two people who love one another in freedom.

Meantime evening has fallen, the moment when aim-directed day draws to a close, when it is relatively easy to free oneself from the fetters of its thought structures and habits and to be free. Then a new day comes, and with it the question: "Pierre, what are we going to do with this new life?" "Whatever we like. We don't owe anything to anybody now." [4]

This is Pierre's answer, but the structure of life will relentlessly contradict it, will separate them again inexorably. It is useless for Pierre to draw Eve to him and say: "We are alone in the world." [5] They are not alone in the world, and the nervous haste with which Pierre speaks these words shows all too plainly that he is eager to be back with his comrades, that it is there that he seeks life's meaning. Eve is as brave as ever: " 'Go, then . . .' she whispered. 'Go, Pierre. That's the most beautiful proof of love I can give you.' " [6] But like all fine words, her "most beautiful proof of love" is a lie. At heart she agrees so readily only because she too wants to get away to see Lucette. She tells Pierre to telephone her there.

It is now purely a question of time, for they have only an hour left. Pierre meets his comrades and tries to convince them. By the time he succeeds it is too late. Lucien, who has already killed Pierre once, betrays the secret meeting and himself ambushes Pierre. At the very last minute, at twenty-five past ten, Pierre telephonse Eve to tell her of his decision: he is going to stay with his comrades. To no avail she shouts into the receiver: "You can't. . . . It's impossible. You're going to get killed. It's absurd. Remember I love you, Pierre. . . . It was to love each other that we came back." [7] Again Pierre insists that he loves Eve, but the other is stronger. Punctually to the very second, Lucien shoots him through the window of the telephone booth, and the grenades of the militia explode in the shed where Pierre had met his comrades. Eve, who has heard everything, falls dead, as though she herself had been shot.

And so the attempt of Pierre and Eve has failed: love has been proved possible but not as an ideal which people possess inalienably when they love, not as something inherent in existence, not as a fateful predestination for one another, but rather as something that has to be created anew every minute, something noncontinuous which man must perpetually realize afresh, something which always demands man's freedom, his free choice, if it is really to be what it is. Pierre and Eve found this freedom in the face of what they had become and of their objectization only when, confronting death and their own failure, they broke through to the honesty of mutual love, which is its own meaning. Otherwise they show themselves to be unfree, to be "in bad faith," to be unsalvageably yet guiltily determined and thus incapable of authentic love. As soon as they give up the intimacy of a loving isolation, as soon as they expose themselves to the light of day, they lose their freedom. Under the Medusa stare (first anticipated, then actually experienced) of others they become things, people expected to act in a certain way, to be what the Medusa stare turns them into: a foreman who is the leader of a resistance group and a woman married to the head of the militia.

### Le Diable et le bon Dieu

Sartre's attitude to love as stated in *Les Jeux sont faits* is formulated unambiguously and clearly. It has something of the either/or element that dominates his work up to and including *Les Mains sales*. This attitude is largely consistent with the one that emerges from his theoretical works such as *L'Etre et le néant*: love can meet the existential claim (which here reveals itself to be a kind of ideality) only when time falls silent, so to speak, when in the act of love, in its isolated, one-time consummation, the desire to love coincides with loving, making love completely at one with itself, making it horizontal (which in this case means undifferentiated). In the long run, however, this "ideal" of an idealless love which is purely itself falters; it comes into conflict with the real structures of life and thus becomes a more or less forced will to live with which loving cannot keep pace.

Sartre's second position turns out to be quite different. It leads us into the period when his thinking moves into a powerful attempt to cope with the phenomenon of structure, an attempt which necessarily pushes this phenomenon out of absolute horizontality, despite the constant effort of his thinking to retain contact with this plane, to remain ultimately horizontal and existentialist.

*Le Diable et le bon Dieu* is not of course intended to be exclusively an analysis of the phenomenon of love. On the contrary it was, in Sartre's own words, "exclusively dedicated to man's relation to God or, if you prefer, man's relation to the absolute." [8] In practice, however (and perhaps not entirely by chance), this amounted to a continuation of his discussion of the phenomenon of love and led to his taking up a position no longer apodictic but dialectical toward the Thou as a potential means of overcoming the unbridgeable isolation of human existence.

### The Construction

The outward form of *Le Diable et le bon Dieu* already suggests this dialectical structure. Like *Les Mouches*, this play has three acts, so that we might expect a continuous tension, relating, like an arch, every element to every other one. However, the eleven scenes into which it is divided are numbered consecutively, so that the serial principle and, as we shall see, the principle of succession outweigh the principle of inner tension. A brief survey of the ordering of the scenes will in fact show that the interplay of this order with the division into acts produces a kind of dialectical movement: a progression of thesis, antithesis, and synthesis. The structure thus reminds us in a way of the quatrains and tercets of the sonnet, which was also originally a dialectical form:

ACT I
First Scene
Second Scene
Third Scene

ACT II
Fourth Scene
Fifth Scene
Sixth Scene

ACT III
Seventh Scene
Eighth and Ninth Scenes
Tenth Scene
Eleventh Scene

It is curious, to say the least, that Sartre should have combined the eighth and ninth scenes. If he had not done so, the "dialectical" progression of $3/3/2 + 2$ (as compared to the sonnet's 4/4/3 + 3) would have been broken; a composition scheme giving Act III five instead of four scenes would have suggested tension, and Act III would have lost its character of synthesis.

Whether Sartre was aware of this is another question. The facts, however, are there, and they correspond to what we find in the content. For the subject matter too shows a remarkable combination of continuity of tension and dialectical progression. On the one hand, the whole play is pervaded by a crescendo of tension centering on the phenomenon of love; on the other hand, it shows the strict dialectical progression of an analysis in the course of which the hero Goetz attacks first evil (Act I), then good (Act II), and finally finds a solution in a remarkable synthesis.

### Content and Structure

Goetz has for the time being dedicated himself to evil. He has broken his oath of loyalty to his brother Conrad, and in return the Archbishop, now his ally, has promised him Conrad's lands. But this is merely a symptom of a deep-rooted passion which compels him to do evil always and on principle, to terrorize and bewilder his fellow men, to make fools of them and, in short, always to do the unexpected. This applies also to his relationship with Catherine, his mistress for as long as the siege of Worms may last. He loves her in his own way, loves in her the woman who does not want him, whom he took by force, and he can continue to love her only so long as she manages to keep alive his illusion that she does not love him, that she is even scheming to murder him.

When *Le Diable et le bon Dieu* opens, their relationship has reached a crisis. Catherine has long been in thrall to Goetz. She returns his love, and it is only a question of time until she betrays herself. When Goetz has to decide whether to go to live on the lands of his brother Conrad, now dead, or to take Worms, that time has come. Catherine is now afraid of losing Goetz, and at the same time she hopes for something he can never grant her: that he may take her with him to his castle. In her distress she forgets the rules by which she is playing and lets him know that she belongs to him. She begs him to keep on treating her as a thing: "I want to be your brothel." [9] But this is exactly what Goetz is not looking for in her—and here he shows himself a true Sartrean hero. He draws the logical conclusion, presses a purse of money into her hand, and sends her away (end of Act I, Scene 3).

In the meantime, however, the day of a new love dawns, a love which for Goetz begins in the same spirit of deliberate contrariness but which is to take him further despite himself. "Try, then, to love your neighbor" is the challenge of Heinrich, the priest who presents him with the key to Worms. Goetz accepts the challenge, true to his principle of doing the opposite of what is expected of him: "And why shouldn't I love him, if I took it into my head?" [10] He takes a bet that he will succeed in doing good and in loving his neighbor.

So now (in Act II) Goetz will do good. He gives away his lands to needy peasants, washes the feet of his serfs, calls his servants "brother," and if somebody strikes him on the left cheek he does not strike back. He enacts in fact an unmistakable parody of Christianity—a parody which sometimes becomes quite coarse, as when, having been cursed and beaten, he throws himself to the ground, crying: "Help, you angels! Help me to conquer myself!" or when he responds to threats by praying: "O Lord, deliver me from this abominable desire to laugh!" [11] Goetz's aim is nothing less than to re-create the communion of the early Christians; he wants all men to be brothers, united in Paradise regained, in the "Cité du Soleil" (p. 135, City of the Sun), where love reigns unconstrained.

These plans are a satirically emphasized antithesis to what we encountered in the first act—an antithesis which contains quite concrete allusions to Christian writers. For instance a leper whom Goetz kisses says: "Someone else who wants to try that business of a kiss for the leper." [12] This is certainly an allusion to François Mauriac, author of Le Baiser au lépreux, and later there are even more obvious digs at the Claudel of Le Soulier de satin.[13]

Yet the second act is not just stark antithesis. A hint

emerges of something like an answer to the question implicit in the figure of Catherine, an answer in which a second, nobler figure will elevate the love of the first act to a higher plane so that it grows into a first, slowly maturing fruit of the dialectical play between good and evil, between the devil and the good Lord.

For Hilda, the noblest female character Sartre ever created, is already a promise of the synthesis to come.[14] She encompasses the secret of love; she is love. A rich woman, she had intended to take the veil, but just as unquestioningly cast her lot with the common people when they were threatened by famine. She is the woman born for love, to whom all hearts respond—including that of Goetz. "Do not be my enemy," he begs her (p. 181), and this is the first plea ever to cross his lips. He too is attracted by the purity of a love without problems, which is purely itself, which brings hope and human warmth, which always finds the right word, always finds the good without really trying to and, above all, without meaning to serve God or an idea. Hilda can say of herself: "I suffer in everybody; I am struck on every cheek; I die every death." [15] Hilda is, as it were, a second Eve, a second Catherine, who has shared the pain of the wounds and sins of the original Catherine and even been wounded by them too.

And so Hilda sends Goetz back to Catherine. He goes off in search of this woman, now said to be dead. He finds her on the steps of the church, begging to be carried up to the altar, that she may die there as a sinner received in mercy. The people shout that she is unworthy of this, that she is damned, but Goetz and Hilda are not deterred. Again Hilda is the mediator, finding the right words to make the crowd draw back in silence. The dying woman is carried into the church. She asks for a priest, but Heinrich says that he is no longer a priest, and Nasty, who once said that all men are priests, simply shrugs his shoulders. Goetz dismisses them all, including Hilda. He is going to make a final try at good in the spirit of Christianity: he will try to become Catherine's redeemer. He goes up into the pulpit and beseeches Jesus on the cross to give him His wounds, the stigmata. But nothing happens, and Goetz draws his conclusions: "My god, I'm stupid! Heaven helps those who help themselves." [16] Drawing his knife, he stabs himself in the palms and the side and approaches Catherine. Now she will believe that he can bring her redemption: "Do not be afraid any more, my love. I touch your forehead, your eyes and your mouth with the blood of our Lord Jesus" (*ibid.*).

And indeed Catherine is at peace, though her peace comes from faith in man, not God, from faith in Goetz, which is now at last possible for her: "Your blood, Goetz, your blood. You have given it for me" (*ibid.*). She dies, and her death marks the end of the first two acts, of the antithetical opposition of good and evil, because the power of this blood on his hands has revealed to Goetz the possibility of a synthesis between good and evil. He has seen the crowd draw back in awe, and this means that he can make himself its master again and hurt it through good just as he had hurt it through evil. "Don't harm them," Hilda, his good spirit, warns him, but Goetz no longer hears her. He has eyes for one thing only: the chance to make people his possessions: "They're mine. At last!" The curtain falls on the second act.

The third act opens quite logically in a model center for ideological indoctrination. Goetz has founded the *Cité du Soleil* and peopled it with men and women whose actions and thinking he can control totally through his authority as a prophet, as a man of God, and as one who bears the stigmata. A peasant woman is given the task of teaching the inhabitants the alphabet of love, the catechism of nonviolence. But Hilda disturbs this reality of constructive love. "Sister . . . you are disturbing us," [17] says the teacher, and in fact Hilda's simple, unquestioning personification of love is a disturbing element in this milieu. In the face of Hilda's horizontal humanness the *Cité du Soleil* reveals itself as nothing but a structure which will in fact soon collapse, which will not withstand the serious assault of reality. When the angry peasants find no sympathy in the *Cité du Soleil* for their warlike plans (the time is the period of the peasants' revolt), they massacre the Utopians and put their carefully erected structure of meaning to fire and the sword.

Yet this is still not the end of Goetz or of the synthesis, for this third act, the act of synthesis, is in itself dialectically structured, and it is Hilda who holds the key to this dialectic. She takes Goetz still further. While herself remaining pure existential reality, she lures him on to unity, to the Thou, prompts him to overcome the either/or, to get rid of the duality of his two beings in a new identity—an identity of love, of a We: "You are light and *you are not* me. That's unbearable. I don't understand why there must be two of us, and I would like to become you but stay myself too." [18] Goetz has come an unbelievably long way since the first act, as a trivial little incident shows. In the first act he refers to Catherine as his *"animal domestique"* before whom a banker can speak freely (p. 79). When, in the third act, the question arises whether Hilda may stay while Nasty makes his report, Goetz's reason for not finding her presence disturbing is quite a different one: "She is I. Speak or go away." [19]

Between Hilda and Goetz there exists a kind of brotherhood: they are the first We in Sartre's literary works.

GOETZ: We're making the decision together?
HILDA: Yes. Together.
GOETZ: And we'll bear the consequences together?
HILDA: Together, no matter what may happen.[20]

Here love becomes a free dialogue between two people who accept each other as end, who no longer seek to make the other a thing, a means, but accept and encourage him for his own sake.

Thus this We does not rob Goetz and Hilda of their ability to live according to the exigencies of the moment. It will not save Goetz from having to follow his road to the end. He will carry on the *"comédie du Bien"* to its conclusion, will finally realize that it is impossible to keep peace among men, and above all will recognize that what he wanted to obtain through good was basically what he wanted to attain through evil: "I used to ravish souls through torture; now I ravish them through Good." [21]

In the end he will stand alone, having neither good nor evil as his goal, free as Orestes, free as Hilda, and their love will consist in hating one common enemy: *"S'aimer, c'est haïr le même ennemi."* [22]

And so for the first time in Sartre two free people find a common way. The tragedy of Roquentin and Anny is not repeated, and there even seems to be a positive counterpart for the third central character of *La Nausée* the autodidact, because a third person, Nasty the ideologist, is also drawn into the community of aloneness: "My god, Hilda, this man is as alone as I am." [23]

The practical solution Goetz finds at the end of the play is also surprisingly positive. Having hitherto more or less played at good and evil, he decides to give up his sandbox constructivity and from now on become constructive by conviction. He will volunteer to lead Nasty's army, to give orders and to inspire terror, because that is the way it has to be: "I'll terrorize them because I have no other way of loving them. I'll give them orders because I have no other way of obeying. I'll remain alone with this empty sky above my head because I have no other way of being with them all. There's this war to be fought and I'll fight it." [24]

# chapter 7

# Perspectives

Sartre and Simone de Beauvoir —
*Les Mots* (The Words)

A comparison of *Les Jeux sont faits* and *Le Diable et le bon Dieu*, like a comparison of *La Putain respectueuse*, *Les Mains sales*, and *Les Séquestrés d'Altona*, shows that Sartre's thinking entered a new phase about 1950: what might be called its constructive phase. The dialogue with the great sociopolitical and religious structures of thought, begun already in *La Putain*, obviously caused Sartre to become somewhat constructive himself—though this did not do his literary work much good. The true Sartre is and remains the one who stands forth clearly at the end of *Les Séquestrés*, in *Saint-Genêt, Comédien et martyr* too and, last but not least, in *Les Mots*—the horizontal Sartre concerned only with the ultimate statement of being, the abstract Sartre of *L'Etre et le néant*.

Nevertheless, when he wrote *Le Diable et le bon Dieu*, Sartre was sincerely trying to go beyond the rigid either/or point of view. In an interview at that time he said:

Long before I planned to write an ethics I was convinced that true morality, like true existence, can only be conceived as existence with and for the Thou. I believe quite simply that I must now try to explain these relations to the Thou philosophically and dialectically. It is essential to show to what extent this relation is impossible in a society whose economic and political structure as such obstructs it. Today the problem consists in the fact that man is regarded, as Kant already demanded, not as a means but as an end. Here lies the ideal of relationship with a Thou.[1]

Apparently Sartre soon relinquished this briefly envisaged point of view, in contrast to Simone de Beauvoir, his companion of many years, for whom the Thou had played an important role from the first and whose works specifically take this constructivity, this sustaining "answering" element in human intercourse, as their point of departure. This provides an occasion for taking a quick look at Simone de Beauvoir's works in the hope that the comparison may enable us to grasp Sartre's position more clearly and possibly even to find an answer to the question why he, unlike Simone de Beauvoir, hesitates to formulate a constructive ethics of this kind, although he certainly practices one.

### Simone de Beauvoir

However justifiable it may be, on biographical grounds alone, to speak of Simone de Beauvoir and Sartre in the same breath, this should not lead us to overlook the fact that fundamentally they follow very different paths. In Simone de Beauvoir's work we encounter quite different characteristics: an omnipresent orientation toward the future, toward a way out, toward implicit positing of meaning, but also a deeper sense of the spirit of "communion," a reciprocity of giving and taking, of bestowing and receiving, such as we find in Sartre only in *Le Diable et le bon Dieu* and even there only by intimation, hidden and distorted by parodistic tendencies. Whereas for Sartre existence— the existence of things as well as people—has its ground in itself alone, and all the concatenations of necessity merely cover up its true nature, Simone de Beauvoir can for example state, in *Pyrrhus et Cinéas* (1944, p. 96), without characterizing the attitude as false or ill-chosen: "We need another person in order that our existence may become grounded and necessary." In *Pour une morale de l'ambiguité* (1947) she says: "To complete itself, my liberty needs to flow into an open future. It is other men who open the future to me." A decisive and positive significance for our existence is thus attributed to the other; it is through him that we can give our existence necessity.

Hence, Simone de Beauvoir's works are characterized *not* by Sartre's calmness of epic existence, *not* by Sartre's plateau-like being-in-itself of the individual, but by a kinetic relatedness to a variegated, differentiated abundance of things; *not* by Sartre's world that exists as a phenomenon that can be mastered only by the trial-and-error method of acquiring experience (and at best it is only apparently mastered), but by a world that is essentially a challenge to be conquered and that indeed can only be summoned into being by man.

Of Françoise in *L'Invitée* (She Came to Stay) she writes: "When she wasn't there, this smell of dust, this semidarkness, this desolate solitude—all this did not exist for anybody; it did not exist at all. . . . It had to be made to exist, that deserted room full of darkness." [2] That which *is* not for something else counts as wholly nonexistent, as we see. For Françoise (and we may say for Simone de Beauvoir too), being taken into a relationship, being seen, existing for something, is the very condition of existence. This is a position that takes us very far from Sartre, and the passages previously quoted show that it is not to be taken purely as a statement by a fictional character. Here the subjectivism of thought as represented by Sartre, a subjectivism which nonetheless never questions the objective reality of the world, seems to yield to the subjectivism of a perceiving consciousness. So central is this being taken into a relationship that it claims for itself the status of an act of creation. And this represents such a radical divergence from Sartre that we would be justified in speaking of "vertical" as opposed to "horizontal" existentialism (although it would be necessary to determine whether the former is not an internal contradiction which Sartre avoided). But let us not anticipate. Let us allow Simone de Beauvoir—or rather the reality of her work—to speak.

The dialogic structure of her novels offers further proof that they are predominantly vertical and constructive, that they seek above all to establish relationships. In Sartre, on the other hand, dialogue moves gradually to the fore as his work progresses, especially in *La Mort dans l'âme*, a work whose subject matter is also dialectically conceived, but it never becomes a sustaining element.

The first of Simone de Beauvoir's novels to show this dialogic structure is *L'Invitée*, the work in which she is still relatively close to Sartre.[3] Yet the differences are already obvious. *L'Invitée* was written at almost the same time as *Huis clos* (in 1943, one year earlier, to be precise), and it too deals with a trio, a man and two women. Apart from this, however, the similarity is confined to a few themes. The whole setting and the starting point are different and bespeak a different basic methaphysical conception, already adumbrated in the formal aspects of the novel. Whereas the three characters in *Huis clos* are all completely independent and every attempt at relating them fails, Simone de Beauvoir presupposes the possibility of relationship as one of the premises of the novel. From the first she places Françoise and Pierre in the structured I-Thou relationship of a couple—a couple which represents mutual fulfillment and freedom in a free, loving exchange.[4]

What fails, however, is their attempt to build up from this basic structure, to introduce a third person, Xavière, into the circuit of connectedness as a loosely attached satellite, so to speak. This obviously fails in the first place because Xavière is one of the most fascinating female characters Simone de Beauvoir ever created, quite authentically "other," [5] a figure standing absolutely for herself ("She was absolute separateness" [6]), an existence which in turn makes the couple an object, relegates it to the thingness of being seen. But it also fails because Françoise approaches this task of including a third partner with a false attitude. In contrast to her free relationship with Pierre, she seeks possession; she wants to do with Xavière what she is in the habit of doing with things: "What particularly enchanted

her was to have attached this sad little existence to her life . . .
nothing ever gave Françoise such intense joy as this kind of
possession." [7] And a little farther on: "Xavière's gestures, her
face, her very life needed Françoise in order to exist." Yet such
a desire to possess was bound to falter under Xavière's Medusa
look, under the passionate love of freedom that brings her close
to Mathieu.

It is this *mauvaise foi*, this guilt, that finally leads Françoise
to choose the self-deception of killing. She poisons Xavière because Xavière, with her awareness of freedom, resists being
made dependent upon her. She kills Xavière because Xavière is
a consciousness which threatens and disillusions her own creative, relationship-positing consciousness. Françoise has acted
quite consistently. She constructs, establishes connections, and
sacrifices her conscience to this structure, to preserving what
she has already attained. For in this respect too she is vertical;
she is a magnitude within a given context; she is woman, and
she cannot postulate an absolute killing, as Orestes does, but
already foresees the consequences of having committed a crime
as a guilt to be borne.

Thematically, then, this work has much in common with
Sartre. Yet it is as though Electra were now the spokesman instead of Orestes—woman as Sartre too usually shows her. This
is existentialism as seen by a woman, by Simone de Beauvoir:
less hard, less consistent, more human, but also less fascinating.
Something that appears in Sartre really only by mistake (except
for *Le Diable et le bon Dieu*)—a desire to construct, to establish connections—is here a fully accepted basic principle. Simone de Beauvoir's point of departure is indeed not so much a
purely formal as a practical one: the practical face of existentialism.

If the ending of *L'Invitée* is still structurally close to Sartre,
the endings of Simone de Beauvoir's later works show how
important it was to her to make the concluding note a positive,
constructive one. Occasionally the note becomes almost inspirational, for instance in her only play, *Les Bouches inutiles*
(The Useless Mouths). Here a besieged Flemish town refuses
to rid itself of its useless mouths; instead it stands up for human

solidarity and musters its last reserves of strength to break the siege. Similarly in *Le Sang des autres* (The Blood of Others) it is brought home to the leader of a Resistance group that all his decisions provoke retaliations and that in the end he has even caused the death of the wife he loves. Nonetheless he takes this curse of responsible action upon himself and finds in it his justification for existence.

Simone de Beauvoir's interest in her subject obviously begins exactly where Sartre's leaves off. She is less interested in the phenomenon of action than in its consequences, in what becomes of the deed and the doer of it. She is development- rather than phenomenon-oriented. This is particularly obvious in *Les Mandarins* (1945; The Mandarins), the odyssey of a group of leftist intellectuals ("mandarin" is a slightly ironical term for intellectual) in which life structures in the biographical sense are readily identifiable.[8] Robert Dubreuilh has much in common with Sartre: he is a famous writer, has founded a political party, and is publisher of a newspaper. Henri Perron has much in common with Camus: he too is a writer; he wants to avoid party affiliation yet utilize every opportunity of helping the needy. And finally Anne Dubreuilh has many of Simone de Beauvoir's own features. Anyone who has read this prize-winning work, which seeks to present the history of intellectual France from immediately after the liberation to 1948, knows that in the sphere of love and politics the constellations are constantly shifting and there is steady, uninterrupted development oriented toward the future and the way out.

Why can Simone de Beauvoir allow herself to pursue these practical and historical structures with impunity when this was quite obviously deleterious to Sartre's literary work? Why is it not equally damaging to *Les Mandarins*? Why does it not strike us as a breach of style, as is the case with *La Nausée*, when the book ends positively, when Anny says to herself: "Since my heart keeps on beating, it is going to have to beat for something, for somebody"[9]? To a certain extent the answer is already given. Constructivity is a ground element of Simone de Beauvoir's literary and intellectual cosmos but not of Sartre's. Yet if literature seeks to be great, if it seeks to convince, its formal reality must be appropriate to the metaphysical structure of the thought that is the underlying origin of the created work. Through his dialogue with structure as well as through his personal involvement in contemporary political problems, Sartre was sidetracked into a constructivity which was accidental and nonessential, which was inappropriate to the ground element of his thinking and hence to one of the ground elements of his writing. Thus the constructivity that is unexceptionable (except where it becomes inspirational) in the work of Simone de Beauvoir entails for Sartre a danger of losing his way, of promoting the disintegration of his own work. For form—which in this case means constructivity—is not an autonomous component of literature. If literature is to be great, its form must be directly related to its content.

Thus Sartre's introduction of dialectical forms in *Le Diable et le bon Dieu* was esthetically as well as ontologically inconsistent, and the same is true of the classical five-act structure of *Les Séquestrés*, despite the fact that in both cases the thematic subject prompted the decision to treat it in that particular way.

Sartre had got himself into an esthetic corner. He was able to master the situation esthetically and ontologically only by turning the tables, so to speak, and describing how he got into the fix. This he does in *Les Mots*.

### Les Mots

Although it is perhaps going too far to call *Les Mots* (1964) a work of art in the strict sense, it is still more than straightforward autobiography whose aim is objectivity. As the title suggests, Sartre is concerned in *Les Mots* with one single phenomenon, and the division of the book into two parts, "Reading" and "Writing," is sufficient indication that he has compressed and telescoped the autobiographical reality under aspects that retrospectively posit his literary—and in Sartre this is tantamount to ontological—consciousness. This division into two distinct parts is most promising. Sartre has found his way back to the either/or—and this in his autobiography, of all places, where historicity and development would normally be the aim. Yet in this work of art (and we use the term advisedly) the "journey" element (also latent in, say, *La Nausée*) is by no means absent. Here, however, the journey consists of two steps only; moreover, like *La Nausée*, it is the story of a divagation.

Here we have again the "best" Sartre, in some ways the Sartre of *La Nausée* and *Les Mouches*, a Sartre who, although obliged as an artist to condense and shape reality into an edifice, retains beneath the framework of this construction the internally identical world of one single divagation. In this context *Les Mots* becomes particularly interesting because, as well as being an example of this paradox of a literature of existence, it also seeks to recount the history of the paradox. In this "biography of childhood" Sartre is not really concerned with what we call life but, as the title already suggests, with Sartre confronting what was to become for him life's content, with an interesting special case of existence and engagement.

Little Poulou, as he was nicknamed, was in fact actually born into the whole problem of existence and engagement. He is descended on his mother's side from a family almost disastrously linked to engagement, especially spiritual engagement: the Schweitzers. In a genealogy of spiritual engagement written with great humor, Sartre traces this chain back to his great-grandfather, a primary schoolteacher—that is to say, an idealist—who later became a grocer. Seeking a kind of compensation through his sons for the engagement he had abandoned, he wanted to make them pastors. Karl Schweitzer, Sartre's grandfather, escaped and chose a more moderate form of "priestly" engagement: he became a high schoolteacher. Only the youngest son, Louis, lacked the strength of will to resist his father; he became a pastor and "even carried obedience so far as to beget in his turn another pastor," the famous Albert Schweitzer.

Yet Sartre is not so narrowly bound to this imposing line as to lack scope for an awakening awareness of the existentiality of his existence. It is not his father who oppresses him with the presence of a family destiny, but his grandfather, Karl Schweitzer, who, because of the early death of Jean-Paul's father, in many ways assumed the role of a father. His mother, on the contrary, who is hardly more to him than an older sister, is not a true Schweitzer. Like her own mother, she is a Catholic, thus introducing in her own way a new form of spiritual engagement, though one lacking in vigor and conviction, for her Catholicism is merely an opposition to Protestantism.

On his father's side, however, the existential predominates, characteristically in the form of speechless existence. (Here the literary invention already begins, the constructivity in the spirit of the theme of *Les Mots*.) The day after his wedding the grandfather, a country doctor, discovered that his father-in-law had no money: "Outraged, Dr. Sartre went for forty years *without speaking to* his wife. At table he expressed himself by signs; she ended by calling him 'my boarder.' Nevertheless he shared her bed and from time to time, *without a word*, made her pregnant." [10] The children of this wordless marriage, Jean-Baptiste, Joseph, and Hélène, ran true to form. Hélène was married late in life to a cavalry officer who went mad. Joseph did his military service with the Zouaves, then came to live with his parents, but he never had any regular occupation: "Caught between the stubborn silence of the one and the shouting of the other, he became a stutterer and spent his life struggling with words" (*ibid*). The last son, Jean-Paul's father, Jean-Baptiste, wanted to go to sea. As a naval officer, already sick with a mortal fever, he met Anne-Marie Schweitzer in 1904 and, as Sartre puts it, "took possession of this big, forlorn girl, married her, hastily gave her a child—myself—and sought refuge in death" (*ibid*).

So Jean-Paul grew up without a father, and looking back from adulthood, he sees this as his chance of freedom (p. 11): he was able to go *his own* way. The young Poulou does in fact go his own way to a certain extent, but the world into which it takes him is the world of his grandfather, the world of idealism. This produces the remarkable mixture of a perspective which actually is already existential and idealism. While other children are discovering and investigating the immediacy of material and personal things, Poulou's road leads directly into abstraction, into the world of words. When his mother read to him she would disappear, and Poulou would be in exile. The book would speak, and

> Out of it came sentences which frightened me. They were real centipedes; they swarmed with syllables and letters, dragged out their diphthongs, set the double consonants vibrating. Singing, nasal, broken by pauses and sighs, rich in unknown words, they were enchanted with themselves and their own meanderings without paying any heed to me.[11]

He takes possession of this world, as another child might take possession of the garden or the nearby woods: "I never scratched up the soil or searched for birds' nests. I did not botanize or throw stones at birds. But books were my birds and my nests, my domestic animals, my cowshed and my countryside. The library was the world caught in a mirror. . . ."[12] Words are to him like things: "Sentences resisted me as if they had been things" (*ibid*). Indeed, words and ideas are for him the true things, reality, from which he starts: "A Platonist by avocation, I went from knowledge to its subject. I found more reality in the idea than in the thing, because it gave itself to me first and because it gave itself as a thing."[13] Nevertheless all this is subject to a point of view which leads away from the conqueror of things, away from the Platonist, and announces the future existentialist. For these words and ideas are to the little Poulou to some extent what the world will be to the big Jean-Paul: something that confronts him without his being correlated with it, something toward which he feels no eros but which presents itself to him in his position of exile (p. 34) as an autonomous existence which may, at best, invite identification but never invites development. Here that either/or thinking that will always be characteristic of Sartre is already predominant. Words are objects to him, something that confronts him, or else reading triggers a state in which he is no longer himself, in which he becomes what is read: "In the course of time I came to enjoy that click of the trigger which snapped me out of myself."[14] Hence it is also characteristic that the image he chooses in speaking of his relation to ideas and things is not one of climbing but one of being above or being on a level with. He is God the Father or creature: "The Universe rose in tiers at my feet, and every thing humbly‚begged for a name. To bestow it was to create the thing and simultaneously to take it."[15] Progress, likewise, was for him not something that leads ahead, not something that concerned him dialectically, but something that had led to him without directly concerning him: "My grandfather believes in Progress, and so do I: Progress, that long, uphill road which leads to me." [16]

This ordered world of ideas cracks for the first time the day Poulou encounters the phenomenon of social injustice. He experiences this injustice as a disorder, a disproportion. Mlle. Marie-Louise gives him private tuition, and she is recognized to be a good teacher. Why, then, must she complain about her hard life? Why is she not rewarded according to her deserts? Poulou draws the conclusion: "The order of the world hid intolerable disorders." [17] This recognition of social distinction is the beginning of self-criticism and of his realization that as a child he is a fraud, putting on an act for the grown-ups, doing everything with a view to making himself important in their eyes, getting them to affirm his value (p. 67). His actions divorce themselves from the context of an order, from the context of his total personality; they attain an existence of their own as gesture: "I felt my actions changing into gestures" (*ibid*). He feels *de trop* in the adult world: "My own reason for existing was giving way; I was suddenly discovering that I didn't really count, and I was ashamed of my anomalous presence in this well-ordered world." [18] Things, and also *true* people, those convinced of their justification for existing and of their task, were real; yet he was essentially *nothing*: "The pebbles in the Luxembourg Gardens, M. Simonnot, the chestnut trees, Karlémami were beings. I wasn't. I possessed neither inertia nor depth nor impenetrability. I was *nothing*: an ineffaceable transparency." [19]

Religion could have saved him, could have given him a meaning, a justification for existing: "God would have got me out of my difficulties; I would have been a signed masterpiece. Sure of playing my part in the concert of the universe, I would have waited patiently for Him to reveal to me his designs and my necessity. I had a presentiment of religion. I hoped for it; it was the remedy." [20] He was taught that the Almighty had created him for His own glory: "That was more than I dared to dream of. But later I did not recognize the God my soul was waiting for in the fashionable God I was taught about. I needed a Creator and I was given a Boss. The two were really one, but this I didn't know" (*ibid*). No sooner had God been made accessible to him than He was sentenced to death: "Since He did not take root in my heart, He vegetated within me for a time and then died."[21] Poulou therefore chooses a substitute for religion: first magic and loss of self in an imaginary meaning (pp. 101–102). But when he leaves the movie theater, the victories he has lived vanish, and he finds himself back in the street, just as *surnuméraire* as ever.

Now, however (in Part II: "Writing"), a more substantial fraud offers itself: the spirituality of writing. From reading, from experiencing the word that offers itself to him, he goes on to the creating of words, to the revenge of the man who in his books wins victories which the world cannot give him. And here he immediately discovers a great mission of redemption. "My brothers, I decided, were quite simply asking me to consecrate my pen to their redemption." [22]

No doubt there is a note of irony here, but we need only think back to the end of *La Nausée* to realize that Sartre had in fact considered this kind of redemptive function of literature and at least played with its possibilities. Writing was for him a form of constructivity and hence of faith: "I would erect cathedrals of words under the blue eye of the word 'heaven.' I would build for the ages." [23] And so he betrayed his intuitive knowledge of the existentiality of his existence and despite himself produced fruits of faith: "I grew, like a weed, in the humus of Catholicity. My roots sucked up its juices, and I turned them into sap. This was the origin of the lucid blindness from which I suffered for thirty years." [24] When we recall that in this book, published in 1964, Sartre says that he has been cured for about ten years (p. 211), it is obvious that when he speaks of that "malady," that wrong turning, he means his whole literary production with the single exceptions of *Les Séquestrés d'Altona* and *Les Mots* itself.

But are *Les Séquestres* and *Les Mots* really exceptions? Has Sartre been cured of writing? Fortunately not, one might say, and Sartre himself contradicts his own statement before the end of the book. To write means to construct, to build; thus it automatically means to believe. No matter how hard one tries to combat constructivity, to revert to horizontality, to destroy meaning, it is useless, because literature—great literature at any rate—arises anew out of itself. The elimination of meaning becomes new meaning; the demolition of structures becomes new, as it were negative, structure.

Jean-Paul Sartre knows this, of course. He knows that for him "literature of existence" is a paradox, even when it pretends to be autobiographical. *Les Mots* not only liquidates the ideality of writing; willy-nilly it produces in itself new ideality, being itself writing. And at the end of the book, much as in *La Nausée*, this new ideality shines forth, weak, distorted, almost negated, and yet penetrating and unmistakable. Sartre tells himself that despite the fact that literature is inherently a "wrong direction" he will continue to write.

> No matter. I write, I shall keep on writing books. *They are necessary*. They *serve some purpose*, after all. Culture does not save anything or anybody; it does not justify. *But* it is a *product* of man: he projects himself into it and recognizes himself in it. That critical mirror is the only thing that offers him his image.[25]

Thus, despite everything, the Sartre of *Les Mots* is not so far from the Sartre of nausea. While he no longer cherishes any illusions, no longer wants to write "a book to make man ashamed of his existence," he still wants his writing to provide a *"miroir critique,"* and this is not so very different from the solution he dimly perceives at the end of *La Nausée*. Sartre himself obviously has not the least intention of fooling himself on this score, for self-knowledge is not far behind: "Moreover, this old ruined edifice, my imposture, is also my character. One gets rid of a neurosis; one does not get cured of oneself" (*ibid*). And is this really self-knowledge? Is it not rather that this time, in contrast to *La Nausée*, one last inspiration follows the vertical structure of meaning and its sole aim is to wipe out with a final stroke of the pen the suggested constructivity, to make it look false, to present it as an incurable malady? Sartre is capable of this, and the present writer is almost sure that here he is playing some such structural trick. After all, we have already seen how skillfully he uses the technique of the double switch at the end of his plays.

Thus horizontality has the last word, but this word is like the silent period at the end of a sentence: horizontal to be sure, seemingly resting within itself, and yet a conclusion which is quite incapable of canceling out what has gone before but on the contrary confirms it as the nothing which throws it into relief. The writer Sartre has become a writer against his will.

## chapter 8

# From Sartre to Camus

*L'Envers et l'endroit —*
*Entre Plotin et Saint Augustin*

### Sartre and Camus

Camus once jokingly proposed that he and Sartre should jointly
state in a paid advertisement that they had nothing in common
and declined to be responsible for each other's debts.[1] This was
an understandable reaction on Camus's part to inevitably being
taken for an existentialist, even after he had written *Le Mythe
de Sisyhpe*, one object of which was to refute the so-called existentialists. Yet the amount of positive truth contained in such a
statement would not have been very great, for despite all their
differences Sartre and Camus have much in common. They are
children of the same century—Sartre was only four years older
than Camus. They lived for many years in the same city, Paris.
They were both close to the Communist Party. (Camus was
even formally a member of it for a time.) They were both
writers and philosophers. But besides all this they are linked by
something more profound which makes them brothers—though
dissimilar ones—in spirit: a certain radical sense of what existence is for twentieth-century man, an endeavor not to dwell on
fractional aspects such as society, religion, political action,

111

nature, regionalism, family, and what not, but to go after the essence of existence itself and seek a fundamental solution for the problems it poses.[2]

However different the solutions they propose, their kinship is not to be underestimated, for if we were to apply a counter-proof and seek a writer more compatible with Sartre than Camus or a writer of comparable stature more akin to Camus than Sartre, we should have some difficulty finding one.[3] Their kinship, however, is in approach rather than content, and this is where it clearly ends. To appreciate this we need only go a step further and ask ourselves what existence is for Sartre and for Camus. A deep and unbridgeable gulf then appears between the two writers, and it no longer seems surprising that the two friends should have broken for good in the famous "Sartre-Camus quarrel" of August 1952.[4]

Actually Sartre and Camus are two entirely distinct thinkers; their thinking is differently oriented and different in kind right down to its substructures. This is fully evident in the dynamics of their creativity, where we again have a clear basis for comparison. Both writers successfully attempted four main genres: the philosophical treatise, the novel and short story, the drama, and the essay. Taken as a whole, their work is marked by persistent traits which give it the character of a journey. Yet these journeys take them in entirely different directions. Sartre's road throughout his work is one of successive, partly overlapping phases, each marked by an early, abrupt rise to a climax followed by a slow subsiding. These phases are all formally as well as philosophically defined. Each of them opens with a philosophical treatise.

First comes the epic and phenomenological phase. Announced by *L'Imagination* (1936), it rockets to a climax with *La Nausée*, falls again in the novellas of *Le Mur* (1939), and slowly draws to a close in the three volumes of *Les Chemins de la liberté*.[5] Then comes the specifically existentialist dramatic phase, the strongest within the total work. It issues its impressive philosophical manifesto in *L'Etre et le néant*, rises steeply to a literary peak with the simultaneously published *Les Mouches*, sinks slightly to *Morts sans sépulture*, and then gives way to a second dramatic phase, which has in turn been announced by the new philosophical impetus of *L'Existentialisme est un humanisme* (1946). This second dramatic phase, which might be called the humanistic-existentialist or socio-existentialist one, begins somewhat weakly with *La Putain respectueuse* (1946), reaches its climax with *Les Jeux sont faits* (1947) and *Les Mains sales* (1948), and falls again in *Le Diable et le bon Dieu* (1951), *Nékrassov* (1955), and *Les Séquestrés d'Altona* (1959). Whether the *Critique de la raison dialectique* (1960) introduced a fourth phase—an analytical or autobiographical one—whose climax would be *Les Mots*, remains to be seen.[6]

In general, then, it is to be noted that Sartre's literary work is precipitated and determined by its intellectual component, that this intellectual component acts as "ignition" (Sartre himself speaks in *Les Mots* of an "internal combustion engine"), giving a powerful initial thrust followed by a relatively quick drop, thus making it a remarkable image of what Sartre in fact sees as the characteristic quality of being: an image of viscosity, of shifting, unfixable moving toward. This can be schematically shown as follows:

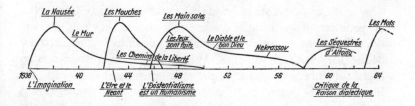

The work of Camus presents itself in quite another way. This is a journey in the human sense of the word, a journey on which we encounter both the one and the other, light and shade, death and life, sense and absurdity, in the kaleidoscopic shifts of what world and himself mean and can mean to man. This is not an abstract, formal journey but a *real* search which knows no formal philosophical either/or discipline but is always both *"envers"* (reverse) and *"endroit"* (obverse), always *"sic et non,"* to use Abelard's phrase.

Hence in Camus's work we find no phases like those in Sartre. At most we might speak of thematically unified periods, but even then we would have to make the reservation that each of them already encompasses the whole. Thus Camus's work has been seen—and certain theoretical statements of his own corroborate this—as falling into three parts: the absurd (*Caligula*, *L'Etranger*, *Le Malentendu*, and *Le Mythe de Sisyphe*), revolt (*La Peste*, *L'Etat de siège*, *Les Justes*, and *L'Homme révolté*), and an incipient final phase leading perhaps toward the goal of love or, less pretentiously, loyalty. Although there is certainly much to say for this sensible and practical division, there is also much against it. We need only think of the late *La Chute*, which negated all speculations about a relatively logical conversion to love, or of the early *L'Envers et l'endroit*, the penultimate chapter of which is entitled "Amour de vivre." We must remember that throughout Camus's works the sun of a joyous oneness with the world and the moment breaks through again and again. Camus's journey is always arrival as well; hence it does not run parallel to the changes of genre in his work. The play *Caligula* and the lyrical essay *Noces* stand beside the novel *L'Etranger* just as *Le Malentendu*, *L'Etat de siège* and *Les Justes* stand beside *La Peste*. Obviously Camus has no problem of genre in the sense of a choice between alternatives. Here, as in his subject matter, he replaces the Sartrean "either/or" with "both/and." What may perhaps be seen is an increasing preponderance of the epic genre, and if Camus, unlike Sartre, is particularly at home in this epic genre, this is probably because it is ideal-oriented—the genre of being on the way.

### L'Envers et l'endroit

Thus, what links Camus and Sartre is to a great extent their oppositeness—a quite exemplary polarity. An early essay, *L'Envers et l'endroit* (1937), which might be said to contain all Camus in embryo, will show this in its full literary significance. This essay which, like others by Camus, stands midway between the epic and the lyric and hence must not be regarded in any way as a theoretical treatise, in fact lends itself admirably to the comparison, since the title of one of its chapters is exactly the same as the title of one of Sartre's novels—"*La Mort dans l'âme*." [7] Moreover, the chapter that bears this title is thematically very close to *La Nausée*. Thus a basis for comparison exists, but—characteristically—this is just about all the two works have in common. To be sure, the first-person narrative form resembles the diary form of *La Nausée*, and it could also be claimed the title *L'Envers et l'endroit* is related to Sartre's title *L'Etre et le néant*. But anyone who takes the trouble to look more closely will soon change his mind, even if he begins to read the essay at the very point where for a moment, in the chapter title "La Mort dans l'Ame," there is absolute identity of expression. [8] For this very "*mort dans l'âme*" means something quite different and has a different significance. It stands in a context which leads onward; it is a stage in a journey, a stage which even in itself does not live up to its title since it too, like the whole, knows light and shade, death and the sun of life. In *La Nausée* and *La Mort dans l'âme*, Sartre confines himself, as usual, to one thing: to the negative, in which the essence of existence nonetheless shines forth. Camus, on the contrary, dwells briefly on *ennui*, nothingness, death, and *angst*, only to turn back immediately to the lovable world.

The narrator does indeed falter. The ground gives under his feet when he gets to the unknown city of Prague. He experiences the existence of others as an existence that eludes his grasp, that is independent of his own presence, alien to him in language and movement.

> Around me a million human beings who had lived up to now, and nothing in their eixstence was known to me. They were living. I was thousands of kilometers away from my homeland. I did not understand their language. They were all walking fast. And overtaking me, they all broke away from me. I lost my footing. [9]

But he reacts to this with more intense, systematic constructivity, with a pioneer spirit. By means of a rigid program of activity he gains a footing in the city and soon, like some gratuitous, undeserved grace, his very *angst*, nothingness itself, becomes the way to meaning.

> And yet it is in this way that his travels bring him illumination. A great discord develops between himself and things. This less substantial heart is more easily penetrated by the music of the world. And in this great bareness the smallest isolated tree becomes the most tender and fragile of images.[10]

Yet too much importance should not be attached to this passage. It stands alongside others which seem to contradict it but in fact merely suggest that the opposition has to be understood in the light of a more comprehensive unity. The experience of meaning just referred to is not a sure way to meaning but rather an ecstatic surrender to meaning which does not end the basic situation of being in exile. Even so, it is obvious how far from Sartre we are here. Even where Sartre seems to be seeking peaks of meaning and ideality, he is actually only leveling them and forcing them to appear before the mercilessly rigorous tribunal of his either/or thinking. For Camus, on the contrary, meaning is the only desirable thing. "At the darkest point of our nihilism I looked only for reasons to go beyond it," he says in *L'Eté*.[11] And this is actually the case. He makes connections, constructs, is perpetually meaning-oriented. For him the search for meaning is what the question of being, of ultimate truth and human dignity, is for Sartre. At the very beginning of *Le Mythe de Sisyphe* Camus formulates this in an unmistakable refutation of existentialism: "To decide whether life is worth living or not is to reply to the fundamental question of philosophy." [12] And a little further on he states no less dogmatically: "I therefore believe that the meaning of life is the most pressing of all questions."

Camus is not the least bit interested in the ontological question: "I have never known anyone to die for the ontological argument" (*ibid*). He is interested not in being, not in the existentiality of existence, but in the meaning of being, the meaning of existence. For him literature as such means from the outset a search for meaning, an attempt at redemption, precisely that which for Sartre became literature only by mistake and, in a way, against his will.[13] He does not stop at the cognitive value of what is experienced; he is not interested in the existentiality of existence as it intuitively dawns upon him in Prague, but only in the vacuum of meaning into which he plunges, in absurdity as the impossibility of seeing oneself in context, and this only as a low point to be overcome. Literal "not being at home" in Prague is thus a symbolic anticipation of what Camus was to attempt in Le Mythe de Sisyphe, a symbol of the estrangement of man and background, man and environment, of the slipping away of meaning, of going into exile.

It is significant that Camus should bring this notion of exile, which of course occurs in Sartre too, strongly into the foreground. This reveals the dynamics of the structure of his thought. Whereas for Sartre exile is something static and horizontal, an ontic fact, for Camus it is still charged with the dynamics of its sense of "having fallen out of" (which is its etymological sense too). It is a magnitude which itself stands in the context of rising and falling. This becomes clear if we pursue the interpretation of the narrator's situation in Prague—and Camus himself encourages us to do so when he says: "A novel is never anything but a philosophy translated into images." [14] Feeling oneself a stranger in Prague, in fact, presupposes a having been at home, a memory of the familiarité of a meaning —even though this has been lost. And if we take the metaphor of L'Envers et l'endroit completely seriously on this point, the absurdity is thus already overcome, and the possibility of ascent, the presence of something higher, is basically there, even before the new meaning of a sun-drenched city, the Mediterranean Vicenza, presents itself to the narrator. It is only necessary to find a link back to the lost feeling of being at home.

Thus, what may earlier have struck us as a contradiction can quite well be conceived as consistency. In Prague the narrator already achieves an ecstatic sense of being lifted out of exile. In recueillement, in opening himself to the transparency of the unauthentic world around him, he experiences the simplicity of the lost paradise, the at-homeness only attainable now as an image, as a reflection: "Yes, simply to grasp the transparency and simplicity of the lost paradises: in an image." [15] This ecstatic surrender to lost meaning does not negate the absurd, but it is a source of strength. More than that even, it gives meaning to absurdity itself, makes it the *tertium movens* in a dialectic which continuously leads back to its beginning, apparently without progress, to the rock which waits again for Sisyphus at the foot of the hill, to an absurdity which has now paradoxically assumed the character of meaning.

A look at Camus's outline for *L'Envers et l'endroit* may help us to grasp this structure of meaning:

FIRST PART. *Les vieilles gens* (The Old People)
   Chapter I.   *La mère et le fils* (Mother and Son)
   Chapter II.   *Le quartier pauvre* (The Poor Section of Town)
   Chapter III.   *L'absurde* (The Absurd)

SECOND PART. *Redécouverte d'une vie* (Rediscovery of a Life)
   (subdivisions not indicated)

THIRD PART
   I.   *Avec la mère* (With the Mother)
   II.   *Le Monde. Ma comédie vous servira* (The World. My Play-Acting Will Serve You) [16]

It is not difficult to recognize where the analogies with his actual treatment of the theme are to be sought. Death, old age, and poverty play the role of Prague, the mother that of the lost home, and life the role of Vicenza. In both cases the absurd as the exile situation precipitated by the experience of meaninglessness is the *tertium movens* that initiates the rediscovery of the pure values of life and that finally leads to synthesis, to the Yes, to absurdity. "*Ma comédie vous servira*" (my play-acting will serve you).

The meaning that shines forth in this synthesis, then, is that of a world-immanent usefulness, the "*vivez comme si . . .*" (live as if . . .) solution of which Camus speaks in the closing lines of *L'Envers et l'endroit*, the play-acting of *"il faut imaginer Sisyphe heureux"* (one must imagine Sisyphus happy) with which *Le Mythe de Sisyphe* ends.[17] It is a practical meaning with no pretensions to ultimate truth: "After all, I'm not sure I'm right" (p. 49). But beyond this, this solution is also nourished by a mythical truth, a faith which will of course never be realized but whose strengths, divorced from their source, are enduring. A hint of what this faith may be is revealed in the capitalization of the words *"Le Monde."* It is a faith in which the Mediterranean Camus, the "Greek" Camus, reveals himself in full contrast with the "northern" Sartre. But it is also a faith which bears entirely concrete traces of a philosophical system to which the young Camus seems just as indebted as the young artre was to the phenomenology of Husserl.[18]

### Entre Plotin et Saint Augustin

It really did not take the publication of Camus's philosophical dissertation *Entre Plotin et Saint Augustin* to prove that Neoplatonism had left its mark on him or, alternatively, that he had found in Neoplatonism a system which seemed made for a Mediterranean man and for which he was bound to feel a natural elective affinity. *L'Envers et l'endroit*, *Noces*, *L'Eté*, and *L'Etranger* too amply prove this to anyone who reads them with his eyes open.[19] *Entre Plotin et Saint Augustin* offers the additional advantage of unassailable documentary evidence; it provides plain evidence that Camus came to grips with Neoplatonism very early. Moreover, since it reveals his view of Neoplatonism, it is a precious key to the understanding of his thought and, equally important, of his works. *L'Envers et l'endroit* is linked to Neoplatonism, and especially to Plotinus, by more than just a few technical terms. The title can be read not only as "The *Reverse* and the Obverse" but also as "The *Place (endroit)* and Its Reverse," and this title alone plainly suggests Neoplatonism, although it should be added that Camus's position is never identical with that of Plotinus.[20]

What attracts Camus to this leading representative of Neoplatonism is the thrust toward profound, paradoxical unity in his thought and his system. While Gnostics such as Basilidius and Marcion proceed from the ugliness of the world as World and Flesh, thus measuring human existence by its level of spirituality and degree of knowledge (gnosis),[21] the fascination of Plotinus lies in a construction which unites thinking and feeling in a *raison mystique* which is not unlike Pascal's "*coeur*." For Plotinus there exists between the perceptible and the intelligible world something ultimate and, so to speak, fluid, which preserves the unity of the whole: the World Soul, which as the third hypostasis of the One is eminently *The* One (comparable in this respect to the Holy Spirit in the Christian doctrine of the Trinity). Bodies also have their part in this World Soul as forms, insofar as they can make transparent their own soul, and hence the World Soul, and thus ultimately make the One transparent in the part.

Understandably enough, this was an attractive doctrine to Camus the "Greek." He loves in Plotinus the "*amoureux du monde*," the man in love with the world, the "thinking poet" and "feeling philosopher."

> Meditation of a solitary in love with the world insofar as it is nothing but a crystal reflecting divinity, thought penetrated through and through by the soundless rhythm of the stars, yet disturbed about the God who orders them, Plotinus thinks as an artist and feels as a philosopher, thanks to a mind drenched with light and facing a world in which intelligence breathes.[22]

He quotes Plotinus' words: "No, I repeat, to despise the world, the gods, and all the beauties it contains is not to become a good man." [23] Plotinus is the man who is able to see the reverse of things in things themselves, who recognizes in them the traces of the lost paradise: "It is not appearance that Plotinus seeks but rather that reverse side of things that is his lost paradise." [24]

Not by chance have we come back to our starting point: the title of the essay. The one essential deviation is that Camus gives a completely different, many-layered, and sometimes contradictory significance to this "reverse side" of things, which for him can no longer be the transcendental Beyond of ideas or of the One. This "reverse side" is, on the one hand, transitoriness and death in contrast to the "place," the "obverse," of life. But it is also "the smile of heaven" as against "the eye and voice of the one we have to love."

> One man contemplates and the other digs his grave. How shall we separate them? Men and their absurdity? But here is the smile of heaven. The light swells and soon it is summer! But here are the eyes and the voice of those whom I must love. I hold on to the world with all my gestures and to men with all my pity and gratitude. I don't want to choose between this obverse and this reverse side of this world. I don't like anyone to make such choices.[25]

The reverse side is that which is irresistibly enticing in the world or which lies like a shadow over everything that seems to be world in the ideal sense, usually the promise of an ideal world of this kind or an appeal to it, and which nevertheless conflicts with the world as place, indeed is its reverse side, the one which brings death in its train [26] and can make man forget his duties as a man.[27]

What Plotinus was able to see as fulfillment and return to the One has to remain for Camus within the limits set by his atheism.[28] It can be affirmed only as long as it remains within the sphere of the internal world, the sphere of the world soul, so long as the source to which he finds his way back is the world as its own reverse side, the Algerian beaches, the eternal value of a silence which fills him in Vicenza, the pagan feeling of oneness with the rhythm of "World." "This inward silence which accompanies me is born of the slow course which leads one day into the next." [29] Here place and reverse are inseparably linked; the one makes the other transparent. Here the world can be ideal world itself, while in gloomy, northern Prague its other, dualistic, deadly reverse side made itself felt, the side that made it impossible to take possession of the "right side": "In Prague I suffocated between walls. Here I was face to face with the world and, projecting myself around me, I peopled the universe with forms in my own likeness." [30]

Thus when Camus experiences in Vicenza an ecstasy comparable to the "conversion" of the Neoplatonists,[31] this ecstasy cannot mean for him a return to the lost paradise; it is, rather, a mundane experience of the world's own ideal reverse side, which Camus, along with Sartre, here conceives under the heading of nothingness: "What I was touching with my finger was a bare and unattractive form of this feeling for nothingness which I bore within me." [32] Thus his ecstasy cannot be ultimate fulfillment. Its "joyless peace" and "tearless fulfillment" are rather an awareness of anxiety, which renews itself in this abandonment to the world, to become more essential: "This country took me back to the heart of myself and brought me face to face with my secret anguish." His ecstasy does not lift him out of his human limitation; it cannot do so because he does not believe in a god who could "raise" him above it or to whom he could surrender himself. It confirms precisely this human nature of his, giving it a nobility and strength which makes him capable of finding meaning not outside but within the world. "From this I drew the strength to be simultaneously brave and aware." [33]

Thus the act of finding meaning feeds on a "religion" which Camus no longer professes, whose *religio*—whose binding character—he can no longer acknowledge because he acknowledges no god above himself.[34] These are nevertheless sources of a fundamentally pantheistic religion of nature on which he continually draws and which he occasionally even professes. For example, in *Les Noces* man's union with the earth is celebrated through the image of a bride whose love is consummated: "This loving understanding between earth and man delivered from his humanness—how readily I would be converted to it if it were not already my religion!" [35] Wherever in Camus's work man finds his way to meaning, this Neoplatonic kind of nature religion without gods is involved, even in the masterfully absurd ending of the *Mythe de Sisyphe*, for in the rock which—beyond all hope—Sisyphus lifts up there still shines forth a sense of world coherence: "This universe henceforward without a master seems to him neither sterile nor futile. Every grain of that rock, every mineral gleam of that benighted mountain, in itself forms a world." [36]

The contrast between the worlds of Sartre and Camus could hardly be more radical. It extends from the fundamental dynamics of thought and creation to ethics and metaphysics. It extends to esthetics too, for Camus's esthetics is closely connected with the dynamics of his thought and with his metaphysics. We have already seen that Camus finds *his* vehicle in the novel or, more generally, in the epic genre, and this choice already comprises much of his esthetics. He wants to build, ("for the work of art too is a construction" [37]), wants to create in the most profound sense of the word, wants to construct through his thought and writing a cosmos in which the meaning of the world will be mirrored. He can best do this in the epic genre, where the orientation to ideal and unity, the "universal" character of the work, can best be realized. He would not be able to do it at all if he were to use the novel as a demonstration, if he were to create a *roman à thèse*, as Sartre did to a certain extent in *La Nausée* and *Les Chemins de la liberté*. Camus was thus acting quite consistently in rejecting *La Nausée* as not enjoyable.[38] "Thinking means primarily wanting to create a world," he once said in discussing questions connected with the esthetics of the novel.[39] In his novels—or perhaps one should say in his *récits*—Camus seeks not exemplary reality but immediate cosmic reality, which, enfolded in its own unbreached unity, is a whole,[40] nowhere dissolved into theory or reference to something else, but permanently integrated in an image, a reality in which everything is determined from inside, from within the work itself. For him literature is mimesis ("creation is the great mime" [41]), and this it can be to Camus the "Neoplatonist" because for him there is no better way of teaching than through the image, the *"apparence sensible"* [42] which becomes in its transparency an intimation of true essence.

In this way the novel becomes an "instrument of knowing" [43] for Camus too—though of a knowledge not to be shaped as knowledge, plain or encoded, but as reality in the full sense of the word, as esthetic cosmos which man can encounter as he encounters the world, that is, without understanding, but which he truly encounters only when he knows what the wordless language of this cosmos is.

Camus's literary works, then, in contrast to Sartre's, are realities, completely self-contained and esthetically determined; no ulterior philosophical meaning can be read out of them; they themselves *are* metaphysical meaning. They are practical, not formal, existence. And the first outward sign that no *écrivain à thèse* is at work here is that it seems impossible to classify the works of Camus under comprehensive thematic labels, as we were able to do with Sartre's. This is not to say that Camus entirely dispenses with the thematic element. He has never written a "pure" novel in either sense. *L'Etranger, La Peste, La Chute,* and *L'Exil et le royaume* are all thematic propositions *as well*, propositions which at once expose the novel or novella to a reduction to definitions and thus to the danger of narrowing their perspective. But these titles, thematic pointers as they are, still indicate only one side of the poetic cosmos they designate.

# chapter 9

# Creation and Transparency

*L'Etranger* (The Stranger)

"*Aujourd'hui, maman est morte*" (Today Mother died). So begins one of the most gripping, convincing, and best constructed novels in world literature, in which even the lowliest stylistic device, the most insignificant turn of phrase, is an integral part in the cosmos of a work which seeks to be at once created and mimed reality. And within this cosmos, posited by words, lives, as a kind of literary Logos, a mysteriously contradictory creation, a man who *is* only in the word: the Stranger.

### The "Prologue"

"*Aujourd'hui, maman est morte.*" This is our first glimpse of this stranger. This is the word pronounced by the Stranger: disconnected, abrupt, almost brutal—brutal as the reality of what he holds in his hands, abrupt and disconnected as the telegram informing him of his mother's death. The Stranger tries to escape from this phenomenon of death, which affects him so immediately, into the reassuring orientation of fixation in time. Dizzily he reaches out, as if trying to grasp the blow which has transformed what was for him "place" into the darkness of its "reverse side," which has disoriented him, deprived him of *his* place within the shelter of a mother, albeit a long repudiated one. This is why he says: "*Today* Mother died." But this "today" eludes him; perhaps it is a "yesterday," and even at that only *perhaps*. The telegram itself admits of no certainty. (This is the meaning of "*cela ne veut rien dire*".)

For a man just informed of his mother's death to be concerned only about whether she died today or yesterday certainly sounds callous and lacking in shame; it sounds like aloofness and indifference. But apart from the fact that it really is important for the Stranger to know when the funeral (which is mentioned in the telegram) is to be held, our impression of shamelessness will be dispelled as inapplicable to the Stranger if we trace out the conceptual and formal development, the total structure of what may be called the "prologue."

In fact the first six paragraphs of the novel (up to "*deux heures de route*") follow a rhythm which unites them in a sort of epic "prologue," not a theoretical prologue but an immediate introduction somewhat in the manner of the *Chanson de Roland*,[1] a kind of prelude presenting the stylistic devices in a particularly dense and complex form not unlike the brilliant opening chapter of Flaubert's *Un Coeur simple*. In both cases the "prologue" comprises just a few paragraphs: eight in *Un Coeur simple* and six in *L'Etranger*. The only difference is that Flaubert rounds his off into a chapter, while Camus lets the movement flow on so that the reader is hardly aware of the inner coherence of these paragraphs. In both cases the story begins abruptly, almost brutally, carrying the reader *in medias res*, giving him no time to adjust himself gradually to the mood but immediately confronting him with a massive facticity which receives historical weight from an initial fixing of the time. "For half a century the bourgeois inhabitants of Pont-l'Evêque envied Mme. Aubain her servant Félicité," is the way Flaubert put it.

"*Aujourd'hui, maman est morte*" is Camus's beginning,

and the content of this statement immediately removes him far from Flaubert, with whom the external form of the "prologue" linked him. Its internal form will confirm this radical difference, for Camus's technique is not that of the perpective-creating camera which, after a brief opening shot of the hero, shifts to a series of images (or paragraphs) stressing the overwhelming presence of the concrete, of the environment, compensating for the close focus by detail and range of impressions (*Un Coeur simple*, paragraphs 1–5), and then reverting, in a fore-shortening formal countermovement, to the heroine, this one a heroine living in concreteness. Camus is not concerned with perspective, nor with the general and the concrete. What he is after is not an image, not a zeroing in on factual reality, but the inseparable togetherness of the place and the reverse side of being. He is concerned with a pure, transparent event, so to speak, like a crystal in which the authentic, the reverse side, the internal, is prismatically refracted. Hence the internal will never appear as such, but always as something reflected in the outer, sensible world, a hypostasis, as it were, of what Soul is. The internal becomes scrutable, tangible. It is a quality of a way of acting which extends into the formal sphere, which makes itself felt in the frequency of certain types of words, and in syntax and the use of tenses.

So far as narrative technique is concerned, this requires a curious combination of subjectivity and objectivity, of indirectness and immediacy. Happenings are narrated not by a third person but by the one who experiences them, yet always in such a way that the happening is still on the brink of becoming object. Whereas in *La Nausée* the diary form presupposes the consciousness of having already experienced, the distance of knowing oneself to be in a confrontation, the Stranger as narrator always stands near the center of events, allowing himself only the precise distance necessary for writing about them.

So *L'Etranger* begins on the day the telegram has arrived. Indeed the Stranger first speaks of his distress at the news of his mother's death without having distanced himself from it at all (*"j'ai reçu; cela ne veut rien dire"*—I received; that has no meaning). Still proceeding from the immediacy of the experience, he projects into the future what he now intends to do (paragraph 2, sentences 2–3.) Only after this does he take his distance in time (*"j'ai demandé deux jours de congé"*—I requested two days' leave) and then only just enough to permit the retrospective perfect tense. For when in the same paragraph the Stranger says that his employer will certainly offer his condolences "the day after tomorrow," after the funeral, this fixes the time of narration as immediately after the event. This fictitious time of writing then moves along imperceptibly with the story, always keeping just enough distance to permit the story to reflect this internal quality shining forth in the immediate indirectness of the events.[2]

This internal quality appears first as restlessness and perplexity (in paragraph 1 "perhaps" occurs twice, as well as "I don't know"), frantically seeking something to hold on to (the numerous designations of time). It sets itself a program (paragraph 2, sentences 1–3) and in this way finds a bridge to the relative security of distance-maintaining isolation (paragraph 2, sentence 4: the perfect tense). Yet this perfect tense as a helpless reaction to the strangeness of a happening should not conceal the fact that the Stranger's disquiet has not by any means left him. The tension will have to fall in several more drops before the even level of indifference toward the event, the absolute balance between the action and its narrator, is restored. One step is extreme, tension-betraying negation (paragraph 2, sentences 4–7: five negative particles), another the restrictive adverbial phrases indicating uncertainty (paragraph 2, sentences 8–12: *en somme, plutôt, sans doute, pour le moment, un peu, au contraire*).[3] Another is the over-mechanical paratactical stringing together of sentences which reflects the negative tension of soullessness (paragraph 3, sentences 1–3)—negative chiefly because in this stringing together the time sequence is not respected. Thus the Stranger first speaks of getting into the bus at two o'clock and then narrates events which immediately preceded this. One might almost call this a shying away from the subsequent hypotactical phase (paragraph 3, sentences 4–5 or 6[4]) in which the memory of disagreeable, disturbing associations surfaces. He had to go to see Emmanuel to borrow a black tie and armband. Emmanuel owned these articles because an uncle of his had died a few months earlier. Then comes the rush to the bus, the falling asleep during the journey (paragraph 4), and the disturbingly stiff encounter with the director of the old people's home where his mother died—a reflection of the Stranger's awkwardness (paragraph 5). This awkwardness, this dull feeling of guilt again find expression in hypotactical constructions (sentences 4, 9, 11). Finally there is the moment of coming to himself, as the question rises up why he put his mother in the old people's home and almost stopped going to see her (paragraph 6) and—as a counterpart to the brutal start of the "prologue"—the realization that it was "a little bit" because his mother had got used to the old people's home and used to cry when he came to see her, but also because visiting her meant giving up his Sunday, "not to mention the effort of rushing for the bus, having to buy tickets and then taking two hours to get there." [5]

But we should not take these instances of "shamelessness" too seriously. We should bear in mind that, here at any rate, they make a point, being entries and final chord in an excellently orchestrated overture.[6] It is worth reading these passages aloud to discover the reaction they produce in a listener with normal sensitivity. His reaction is a smile of complicity and delight in the masterful extravagance of this outrageousness which, after all, merely states frankly something that might occur to anybody, although most people probably—though not necessarily—would refrain from saying it. Thus there is an element of humor too, a harmless humor which can discover the reflection of the sun, of smilingly accepted humanness, even in the Slough of Despond.[7]

### The Stranger

Thus the reality of the Stranger will elude us if we consider him merely indifferent in the sense of being uninvolved, of not caring about things.[8] For good reason Camus himself would not accept the word *impassibilité* applied to the Stranger by his critics and proposed instead the word *bienveillance* or good-will, which, however, is not entirely apt either.[9] The fact is that the Stranger is not a documentary figure exemplifying either of these notions; he is a human cosmos: living, autonomous Creation in the full sense of the word. He lacks much that one would expect of a healthily "normal" man, but this does not alter the fact that he is a person standing over against man, one with whom the reader must come to grips, who does not fit into his preconceived ideas.

Thus the Stranger is certainly not *the* indifferent man for whom he has often been taken.[10] Indeed we must ask ourselves whether it is proper at all to define his relation to things and events as indifferent. The "prologue" offered no suggestion of it, but now, as we follow the Stranger in the monotonous rhythm of the perfect tense, which reduces everything to the same level, as we experience objects with him in the apparent aloofness of mere confrontation—the little whitewashed mortuary chapel, the walnut-colored coffin with shiny screws, not yet completely screwed in, the Arab nurse in her white robe and bright headdress—now we might well take this sober objectivity, this bracketing out of the internal and of all that affects the soul, for indifference.

Yet if we read on carefully, we shall be forced to question this, for, as the concierge prepares to open the coffin lid so that the Stranger may see his mother for the last time, this man who seems so unconcerned intervenes and holds the concierge back as he approaches the coffin: "I stopped him as he was approaching the coffin." More than that: he now becomes uncertain. He is embarrassed at having done something he should not have done because it offends convention. So not only does the Stranger think; he even feels the presence of thought in the other. When the concierge asks him why he does not want to see his mother one last time or (as the Stranger thinks it) why he does not want to have the coffin lid opened, he replies, "I don't know," and this is probably the pure truth. It is therefore useless to speculate about the motives that prompted the Stranger's intervention: whether it was his feeling that the dead woman now belongs to the earth, the fear of destroying his own picture of his mother, or perhaps even consideration for the concierge, who has obviously forgotten to open the coffin and inarticulately, almost apologetically, explains why he has to unscrew the lid ("*je dois*"). Camus offers no explanation, and this is certainly more than a trick to maintain the tension of uncertainty; it is a sign that the Stranger has no deliberate motive at all.

This brings us to what really defines the Stranger—not in terms of irrefutable fact but in terms of a basic dimension which will soon reveal its instability. The Stranger is neither unconcerned nor indifferent; he is alien to everything going on around him insofar as it is anything more than World pure and simple. He feels social, structured, coherent, and explicitly related activity to be a reality essentially alien to him because it is something more than, or, more accurately, something other than, that which simply *is*. At any given moment the Stranger merely is what he does; he *is* this, and it would be impossible to break down this identity with one's own actions into subject, cause, and effect. Up to now he has never been able to experience what confronts him as something connected with him, something that concerns and fixes him, except through embarrassment and a still undefinable feeling of having been caught doing something wrong, which is a first step to guilt. Far from meaning that he is soulless, this merely means that in him the internal is not yet differentiated as the explicitly internal.

He finds it impossible, for instance, to follow the concierge's attempt to tell him that the nurse has an ulcer on her face: "As I didn't understand, I looked at the nurse, and I saw that she had a bandage round her head below the eyes." [11] When his reactions are supposed to provide some kind of internal answer, they become mistakes which promptly turn into the undifferentiated surrender to the objective typical of the Stranger. Thus the cloth the nurse wears over her mouth becomes for him the "absolute" answer to what the concierge really wanted to say.

The Stranger is in fact incapable of putting things in their proper place, and in this he may be compared with the "naïve" Perceval of Chrétien de Troyes's Holy Grail novel. To borrow a term from psychology, he is maladjusted, nonstructured. He stands outside connected thought which posits and recognizes relationships. He is what he is, he sees and hears what he sees and hears, neither more nor less. His internal soul and the soul of what confronts him are inseparably integrated with appearance and action; they are their unspoken transparency. Thus, if one experience has a stronger internal quality for him than some other experience, it is only as an image which he help-lessly confronts, which, as we have just seen, he avoids either by not relating it until later or else, as we shall now see, by treating it with shy respect and hiding it in a string of syn-tactical clauses so as to protect it from the assault of brutal causal thinking.

> Then there was the church and the villagers on the sidewalks, the red geraniums on the graves in the cemetery, Perez's fainting spell (he looked like a limp marionette), *the blood-colored earth* rolling over Mother's coffin, *the white flesh of the roots tangled up in it*, more people, voices, the village, the wait outside a café, the incessant throbbing of the engine, and my happiness when the bus entered the nest of lights of Algiers and *I thought that I was about to go to bed and sleep for twelve hours.*[12]

This sentence marks the end of the first chapter and also of the account of the funeral. It is itself like a burial of all he has experienced, like a timid slamming closed and sealing off of the whole essence of the funeral, the earth-to-earth, the mingling of the blood-red earth and white root flesh as image and reality of what is happening to his mother. It is a fleeting image which barely suggests the emotion behind it, and the Stranger has given himself over to it in spite of himself, as it were, for he immediately flees, through a hasty, closely packed sequence of events, into the sheltering at-homeness of the city, and finally into sleep and forgetfulness.

### The Stranger and the Others

The Stranger is certainly not soulless; he is merely absolutely horizontal. Everything structured, every kind of connection, is alien to him. He is—and here he is a perfect though unintentional illustration of what Sartre regards as existentiality—immediacy of action created anew from moment to moment. This is why he sees nothing wrong in going swimming with an old friend, Marie, the day after the funeral, or, prompted by the natural momentary logic of flirtation, in inviting her to a movie and then taking her back home with him. And when he has managed somehow or other to get through the following day, a Sunday, he says: "I thought that at least I'd got through another Sunday and that Mother was buried now and I would be going back to work and that all in all nothing had changed." [13] Thus, although the Stranger obviously has trouble with Sundays, apparently his mother's funeral too has somewhat disturbed the routine of unproblematical peace with himself and the world. Now, however, he will step back into the usual rhythm of his daily life. The round of work, eating, seeing friends and acquaintances, swimming, sunbathing, and sleeping will absorb him again; he will be able to be World again. He will have dealings with people again too, both at work and in his free time, and it is curious how little difficulty this causes him, how easily he can cope with it, provided certain requirements are met.

Obviously he enjoys his casually polite contact with his employer,[14] whereas he had found it difficult to ask this same employer for time off, and had even mentioned apologetically that it was not his fault that his mother had died. Conversely his employer will later encounter passive resistance when he makes Meursault the flattering offer of a transfer to a newly opened branch in Paris while maintaining his connection with the head office in Algeria. The minute his employer sends for him, Meursault withdraws into himself, overcome by that feeling of having been caught doing something wrong that always overwhelms him when authority addresses him very personally and explicitly, exceeding its function as World. So far as his employer's plans are concerned, it's "all the same" to him (p. 63). The Stranger simply cannot enter into an explicit, willed relationship with anything. He is not—or not yet—capable of becoming divided in himself, of being one thing and wanting the other. He is immediate internal unity which feels unbearably threatened by the mere idea of possibly stepping out of itself.

He behaves in a similar way toward his friend Marie and his neighbors Raymond and Salamano. Here he is by no means shy and anxious, as might perhaps have been expected—though only so long as the "no obligations" rule of the game is observed. Marie is for him a sensuous and carnal partner; she is flesh and color, a piece of world which he loves as he loves to wash his hands at midday and dry them on a fresh white towel. For him this love is not something intrinsically internal, not something that binds them. It is a particularly intensive and gripping ritual of being at one with World.[15] Their acts of love are therefore never precipitated by an internal feeling but by sensuous impressions which for the Stranger are also soul because of the way lovable World shines forth in Marie. So we should not find it surprising that the color of the dress Marie is wearing becomes for Meursault an immediate reason for making love to her: "I wanted her very much because she was wearing a lovely red and white striped dress and leather sandals."[16] Let us make no mistake: what is involved here is not what we understand by the term "sensual," but a relationship of World to World encompassing the spiritual and the physical in one unbreakable totality.[17]

As soon as Marie attempts to take this unity apart, to draw Meursault out of being World into the differentiation of an express commitment to her, the Stranger cannot help letting her down, and she has to recognize that the word "love" means nothing to him, and that it is therefore "all the same" to him whether or not he loves her and she loves him. Only when this word has died away, when Marie again offers herself to him as lovable World, as being, akin to sun, sea, and shore, does he again become what is generally known as love.[18] "She looked sad. But while we were getting lunch ready she laughed again for no reason at all and that made me kiss her."[19] For him loving is an immediate outpouring of the sensuous. And so, when Marie comes to see him in the evening in order to ask him if he will marry her, the only answer he can give is that it is "all the same" to him (p. 64)—another instance of his "shameless" behavior which, as usual, denotes not indifference but an absolute incapacity to break out of the unity of his thoughts, actions, and feelings. If Marie wants him to marry her, he will do her the favor, but it has no significance. This is not something he can want, because it is not World. For the same reason it is "all the same" to him whether Raymond needs him as a witness or not. He will do it if he has to, but to accept this action as a postulate is beyond him (p. 58).

It almost looks as though the Stranger were revealing himself to be a Satrean existentialist, a man for whom existence precedes essence, who cannot opt for good because for him good does not exist *a priori*. This, however, would be a hasty conclusion; it would be to forget that there is nothing in Sartre that corresponds to the Stranger's being World, and that this being World is the real key to understanding him. The total structure of *L'Etranger* centers on this theme, and it is worth examining the structure analytically, for here, as in so many cases, only the formal element, that which can be measured and counted, provides reliable access to the content; in fact, correctly understood, it can even be taken as a transposition of the content.

### Crisis

Taking the external construction as our point of departure, we are struck first by the division of the work into two parts, by its dualistic structure. This is certainly not without significance for the author of *L'Envers et l'endroit*, in which the two types of city he chose—dark, northern Prague and bright, Mediterranean Vicenza—revealed his affinity for dualistic Neoplatonic thinking, for the contrast of light and darkness, good and evil. On the other hand, it soon becomes evident that these two parts of *L'Etranger* do not represent two absolutely separate realities any more than Prague and Vicenza do in *L'Envers et l'endroit* but that they are linked at their point of intersection by a crisis in the first reality through which the second reality announces itself.

This crisis has its prehistory, which can again be read off from the structural pattern. The first thing we notice is that all chapters in the first part with the exception of the last (the chapter leading up to the open crisis) follow the same rhythm, a rhythm which is still recognizable, though broken, at the beginning of the last chapter. Each of these chapters, in fact, begins with the Stranger opening himself to the world, with an awakening, with a "today," or with work that implies openness toward the world:

> *Aujourd'hui, maman est morte.* (*Today* Mother died.) (Chapter I)
> *En* me reveillant. . . . (On *waking up.* . . .) (Chapter II)
> *Aujourd'hui j'ai beaucoup* travaillé *au bureau.* (*Today* I *worked* hard at the office.) (Chapter III)
> *J'ai bien* travaillé *toute la semaine.* ( I *worked* hard all week.) (Chapter IV)
> *Raymond m'a telephoné* au bureau. (Raymond telephoned me *at the office.*) (Chapter V)

Thus the chapters begin with an extroversion in harmony with nature, with a morninglike opening of the self. And each of these chapters closes with a dying away: Chapters I, II, IV, and V with evening and going to bed, Chapter III with an analogous tiredness. Apparently the Stranger is in perfect harmony with cosmic happening; he *is* cosmos, and everything is alien to him, even his own activity, whenever it seeks to be more than a natural expression of this feeling that he is cosmos.

Nevertheless there are already signs of crisis. One is his uncertainty and his tendency to apologize at the beginning of the story, that is, immediately after his mother's death. Another, as we shall show, is a barely suggested crack in the Stranger's mental-physical integrity in Chapters IV and V. Finally, in Chapter VI, there is the open cleavage within himself, the gathering of the crisis. Thus at the end of Chapter IV we read for the first time that the Stranger thinks of his mother, and he thinks of her because through the thin wall he can hear his neighbor Salamano crying for his lost dog.[20] To be sure, he shakes off this thought, but the effort throws his mental-physical unity so much off balance that he goes to bed without eating anything. Then, at the end of Chapter V, the Stranger is back where he was at the end of the "prologue," perhaps even a little farther ahead, because he tells Salamano that he put his mother in the old people's home only because she would have been bored at home and he could not afford a nurse for her. Thus, thoughts arise in him which in the middle chapters of the first part seemed to have been overcome but which were actually only repressed. His confrontation with grief as sensuous reality, with grief as image, precipitated by Salamano and his lost dog, once more uncovers the impact of the funeral upon him, and this so effectively that his unproblematical oneness with himself and the world is partly lost, until finally, on Sunday morning (opening of Chapter VI), he gets "completely out of kilter," feels empty, has a headache, so that Marie suggests, though in fun, that he has *"une tête d'enterrement."*

The signs of crisis multiply, extending now to the intellectual sphere. For the first time the Stranger thinks about the future, and again it is an image that produces this crisis, this inner cleavage: the picture of marital harmony presented by Raymond and his wife. "Perhaps for the first time I *really thought* I would get married." [21] Thinking thus separates itself from the context of his total personality and becomes explicit as thinking.

The sun will do the rest. Just as it did on the day of his mother's funeral, it will stab him mercilessly with its knives, finally driving him to murder,[22] driving him into the illusion that he can call down by force the night of oneness with himself and with the world, make everything quiet, and in this silence regain himself as a protected world.

The effect of this murder, however, is quite different. Instead of finding night and oneness with things, he has destroyed the balance of the day, *"l'équilibre du jour,"* shut himself off from the silence of the beach, where he was happy. Desperate, he fires four more shots at the body, shots which refuse to recognize what has happened, but these shots are "like four sharp knocks at the door of misfortune" (p. 90). This is already the knocking at the door of the prison, where we shall find the Stranger in the second part of the book.

### Tension and Release

The second part has a different structure from the first, corresponding to the reality expressed in it.[23] The number of chapters is already an indication of this: there are five, whereas the first part has six. This numerical relationship reveals the principle of tension, whereas the dominant principle in the first part is seriality, balance (which, however, is not achieved smoothly). The Stranger's unity is in fact impaired now, if not destroyed; now it can only reveal itself to him as tension and demand. So it comes as no surprise that the chapter openings in the second part show no consistent rhythm—another structural indication of the Stranger's separation from the ground that sustains him. What these chapters have in common is, first, the tension of his lost oneness, and, second, something that is essentially only a metaphor for the same thing: the state of being in prison, always a favorite image for not being at-one, for having been cast out of the at-home of oneness.[24] Camus even underlines this image structurally by ending each chapter with an explicit reference to the state of imprisonment.

But, as we have already said, being in prison is also a measure of tension, a pledge of differentiation. This is the place of contemplation. The Stranger will now try to regain his lost unity by discipline of thought, though at first without realizing it. And turning again to our analysis of structural focal points, which has worked before, we find that they contain hints of his success. Just as the chapter endings of the first part reflected a growing split in his unity, those of the second show his groping progress back to the shelter of night.

Whereas the first chapter of the second part ends with the words "Then they would turn me over to the gendarmes again," the end of the second chapter reads: "No one can imagine what *evenings* are like in prison." At the end of Chapter III night has drawn on, bringing an enigmatic identification of sleep and prison. It seems to the Stranger "as if the familiar paths traced in the summer skies could lead just as well to prisons as to *innocent sleep*." Through this night the Stranger finds his way back to himself. In the night of contemplation he finds his way from his lost guiltless oneness with nature to a reflected opening of himself. Cut off from experience, he is forced back upon the inwardness of a search which has to rely essentially on memory and imagination.

In the last chapter this circling search, which soon comes to realize that it faces an unavoidable end, the execution, comes to a crisis in an encounter with a representative of Christianity. The confrontation with the prison chaplain produces an outburst comparable to the murder. In a contrasting parallel to the destruction of the "*équilibre du jour*," the Stranger breaks the spell that holds in his inwardness: "I poured out upon him the very bottom of my heart, which leaped with joy and anger all mixed up together." [25] Although the murder had produced tension and disunity with himself, thus plunging Meursault into the verticality of differentiation and reflection, this outburst, this ecstatic proclamation of *his* cosmic truth (cf. p. 176), causes the tension to fall again just as suddenly—and yet according to plan—and to yield to the horizontality of already knowing, of finally knowing.

This knowledge takes him beyond the chaplain's "otherworldly" faith.[26] It is a knowledge that resides in the truth of night, earth, and salt, in the finally recaptured peace of feeling at one with the world. "The marvelous peace of this sleeping summer flooded into me like a rising tide." [27] The ships' sirens of "vertical" transcendence do not matter to him now: "At that moment, on the very edge of the night, ships' sirens sounded. They were announcing the start of voyages to a world which had forever ceased to concern me" (*ibid.*). He finds his way back to his mother, to the mother who has become earth: "For the first time in a long while I thought of Mother" (*ibid.*). And now, in a conscious opening of himself, he recaptures the innocent happiness of sun, beach, and girl, and the all-embracing indifference that comes from being World. "I opened myself for the first time to the gentle indifference of the world." [28]

Now he knows that he is World, and this knowledge constitutes his happiness,[29] a happiness which death cannot take away from him but which it must reinforce by bringing son and mother together [30] in a finally recovered unbroken unity.

### Structure and Meaning

Thus *L'Etranger* as a whole is a cosmos, as Camus demanded that a literary work should be. It is a re-creation, a world in which everything is related to everything else, in which, despite the hero's seeming unrelatedness, everything is integrated in a curve of all-embracing cosmic movement. It is living order, which shows itself, particularly in its numerical relationships and proportions, to be harmony, World, coherence.[31]

A diagram may clarify this:

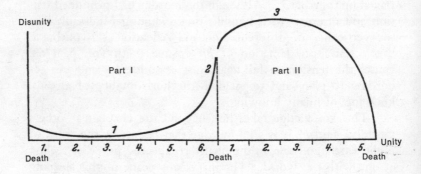

The Stranger, his oneness slightly disturbed by the unexpected death of his mother, finds his way back to almost intact unity with world, sun, water, beach, and flesh (1). But the experience of death, only repressed, is released again associatively, making him just the least bit uncertain. On a Sunday, the most difficult day of the week, the sun, in a contrasting parallel to the funeral, drives him to murder (2), thus destroying his balance. In prison the disunity reaches its climax in meditation and awareness of guilt (3), until, in a reverse counterpart to the end of Part I, the Stranger recaptures his inner unity in a violent outburst.

How far this cosmos of a literary work has taken us from Sartre need not be stressed. We only need to consider how, in this cosmos of Camus's work, death itself still appears as a "spellbound" reality which accommodates itself to the rhythm of World. Three times it intervenes—and this alone is a pledge of world order: at the beginning, in the mother's death; at the axis of the novel, in the death of the murdered Algerian; and at the end, in the imminent execution of the Stranger.

And this death is not something that supervenes *par-dessus le marché*, not something that always comes too soon or too late, as Sartre says. On the contrary, it is something so significant that it matters more than anything else. Not only has the Stranger thought about it incessantly in prison, but he has even come to the conclusion that there can be nothing on earth more important than watching an execution: the momentary, ineluctable occurrence of death. "How could I have failed to see that nothing is more important than an execution and that ultimately this is the only thing of genuine interest to a man!" [32] Not that death acquires this significance from a vertical transcendence derived from the execution. On the contrary, the Stranger is anxious to exclude the least suspicion of verticality, even geometrical verticality, from the action of execution: "Actually the machine stood on the ground. It was as simple as that." [33] And again: "One always gets exaggerated ideas about the unknown. On the contrary, I was to find that everything was simple: the machine is on the same level as the man walking toward it. He approaches it as a man would step forward to meet another person."

Imagination has no longer any chance of taking off into the vertical, of building steps, of trying its wings: "Mounting the scaffold, ascending into the open sky—that was something for the imagination to work on. But as it was, the mechanism overshadowed everything else: one was killed discreetly, with a little shame and a great deal of precision."

This, one might think, is a horizontality worthy of Sartre—but it stands in a context. Here the horizontality is a link to the sacred plane of being World; it is ultimately *religio*, a profession of faith that the world can be its own meaning.[34]

And so Meursault will not be nailed to a cross whose dominant feature is the vertical; on the contrary, he will utter his "It is finished" at ground level,[35] and he hopes there will be plenty of World, plenty of intense humanness as a demonstration of this horizontality: "So that all may be consummated, so that I may feel less alone, there was only one thing more I could wish for: that on the day of my execution there would be plenty of spectators and that they would greet me with shouts of execration." [36]

# chapter 10

# Cosmos and Drama

*Révolte dans les Asturies* — *Caligula* —
*Le Malentendu* — *L'Etat de siège* —
*Les Justes* — *L'Homme révolté*

### An Experiment

Camus's program of literature as a universe, a cosmos created
by the writer, naturally steered him most strongly toward the
epic and especially toward the totality-oriented genre of the
novel. But an extension of this conception to the drama was
quite feasible; it required merely the drawing of certain formal
conclusions, such as have been drawn in the *auto sacramental* or
in the grandiose epic drama of Paul Claudel. The drama had to
be opened to the epic; it had to sacrifice the structural principle
of dramatic tension to the principle of horizontality; it had to
force king and peasant alike into the horizontality of a single
humanity, as Calderón, for instance, did in the *Gran teatro del
mundo*, placing them between the two doors of cradle and
grave on one scenic plane common to all, or else expand the
scenic plane, as Claudel does, to allow the torrent of cosmic
happening to stream in. It is therefore more than mere chance
that such a passionate dramatist as Camus should repeatedly
show his fondness for the *auto sacramental* or that *L'Etat de
siège*, for instance, recalls the "Spanish" Claudel in more than

one respect and that a noticeable tendency to allegory links this play with the world of the *auto sacramental*.

*Révolte dans les Asturies* (1935; Revolt in Asturias), a play which Camus wrote for the "Théâtre du Travail" he founded in Algeria, already shows a distinct leaning toward the typical, the anonymous, and hence the universal. "A woman," "the pharmacist," "a spectator," and so on comprise the cast of this short four-act play which Camus calls an *"essai de création collective."* As he conceived it, this play is not meant to be performed to a homogeneous audience which is not directly involved in it, but rather to force every member of the audience to experience it from his own viewpoint. The addition of all these individual viewpoints is supposed to loosen the usual static audience-stage relationship into a totality of collective seeing, giving the play a cosmic dimension. What this amounts to in practice is that Camus takes the stage apart and arranges it around instead of in front of the audience. Whereas in classical drama the spectator experiences the action from the outside as something he confronts, here he is supposed to experience it from within as something that surrounds and threatens him, just as the cosmos does. If we visualize and compare the two systems, it becomes obvious why Sartre never undertook such a revolutionary experiment.[1]

While the static *vis à vis* of the traditional audience-stage relationship fitted Sartre's either/or thinking, here again Camus shows himself to be a dialectician oriented toward ideals and totality, a writer who certainly loves the theater dearly (he directed a theater company in Algeria as a young man) but who from the very outset cannot hide the epic writer within him.

The miners' revolt, the capture of Oviedo, the numerous news reports on the radio, which are only tenuously related to the factual unity of the plot but accent the political events—all this is epic subject matter and epic technique. Even the tragic outcome, the suppression of the rebellion, finds a triumphant counterpoise at the end of the play in the radio reports of casualties among the government troops.

### Caligula

In *Caligula* Camus takes a different yet analogous direction. Again, what he is trying to create is a whole world, but this time his stage technique does not directly contribute to it. The play itself is to be its own world, with its big cast of characters, most of whom are types. There are writers—seven of them, almost a *pléiade*—only one of whom, Scipio, emerges from anonymity. There are servants, guards, patricians. Above all, there are the two "duelists," the moody emperor Caligula, who holds the lives and freedom of his subjects in the palm of his hand, and Cherea, who with single-minded foresight organizes the revolt which will ultimately mean the liquidation of the tyrant.

This might look like an almost Sartrean confrontation of two people who represent different aspects of each other. One of them at least does indeed possess many of the traits of a Sartrean character: Caligula, this moody emperor spellbound by the absurd,[2] who kills his subjects with sadistic extravagance and forces their sons to acknowledge that in doing so he has done them a favor, who with his devilish logic is incessantly questioning people about essence and regularly turns the question into a death sentence for the one to whom it is addressed. This Caligula is the "idealist," a figure whose deadly obsession with freedom recalls Mathieu in *Les Chemins de la liberté*, for Caligula too knows only one freedom, the "philosophical" freedom of terror.[3]

We should not forget, however, that Mathieu is a much later figure than Camus's Caligula, for although *Caligula* was not published until 1944, one year before the first two volumes of *Les Chemins de la liberté*, it was written in 1938.[4] Neither should we forget that in creating his Caligula figure Camus largely followed his source, Suetonius' *Lives of the Twelve Caesars*, whereas in the opposing character, Cherea, the *homme révolté*, as he might already be called, he diverged from it, thus indicating the points he wanted to bring out. As in *Le Mythe de Sisyphe*, the predominant idea is the very opposite of existentialism: the awareness that the meaning and worth of existence are more important than existence itself: "To lose one's life is no great matter, and I shall find this courage when the time comes. But to watch the meaning of this life disappear, to watch our reason for existing vanish—that's intolerable. One can't live without a reason." [5] Cherea wants nothing to do with this *"lyrisme inhumain"* which attaches no value to his life. This abstract and at the same time perverse obsession with truth does not appeal to him. He represents the positive values of life.

Besides the thematic antithesis to Sartre and existentialism, there is also a formal, structural antithesis, for Camus is not content with opposing two positions; he does not stop at the either/or. To ensure a dialectic he introduces a third main character, a figure who stands between the two positions and has a foot in both of them, Scipio, the poet. Scipio is the man who understands both Caligula and Cherea, who is too fascinated by the absolute in Caligula to be able to side unequivocally with Cherea and rebellion. He is a "halfway man," as Camus was to call the poet in *Discours de Suède*, a man who cannot be either one thing or the other absolutely. He represents synthesis which somehow has a tinge of betrayal.

### Le Malentendu and L'Etat de siège

Although *Caligula* has some effective dramatic scenes, it is not on the whole an exciting play to see or read. *Le Malentendu* (The Misunderstanding), Camus's blackest play,[6] goes much farther in meeting this dramatic requirement. Its plot is clearly and economically constructed, thrown into relief by the poignantly tragic ending.[7] After an absence of twenty years a son returns home unrecognized. His mother and sister are living with an old deaf poet whose name, Nada (Nothing), carries a suggestion of allegory.[8] The son takes a room with them for one night. They murder him for his money and throw him in the river. The next day, when the daughter-in-law comes looking for her husband, Martha, the sister, learns that the money which she stole in the hope of finding happiness (she had planned to use it to go live at the seashore) has brought her nothing but unhappiness. *Le Malentendu* is well constructed, though one could hardly go so far as to call it a really good play in the same class as *Les Mains sales*, *Les Mouches*, or *Huis clos*. Camus himself had no great illusions on this score.[9]

In *L'Etat de siège* (State of Siege), a weaker play, Camus again seeks a cosmic formula, as he did in *Révolte dans les Asturies*, introducing a comet, choruses, anonymous figures and voices, and assigning the leading role to an allegorical character, the Plague. The play is far less convincing than the epic treatment of the phenomenon of plague that Camus had already undertaken in his *chronique*, *La Peste*. Even its production by Jean-Louis Barrault, which might have been expected to guarantee success, did not save *L'Etat de siège* from rejection by the merciless public. The quite cosmically anonymous doomsday atmosphere in which the play opens, the collective fear of the disaster foretold by a tremendous comet, the servile posture of supplication into which the people and their judges sink, the negation embodied in Nada—all this makes a very promising prologue, but Camus lacks the dramatic, epic *souffle* of a Claudel that it would take to live up to this promise, to maintain this style and breathe life into it, and he also lacks the necessary metaphysical stance.

This herald who forbids the people to believe in events has neither the farcical baroque quality nor the heavy impact that might bring him to life; esthetically and metaphysically he is *gratuit*. Again, the Diego-Victoria pair has neither the richness of the sensuous world nor visible ideal reality. To be sure, Victoria is woman, seeking the happiness of love and wanting to hold on to it.[10] To be sure, Diego is the *homme révolté* who demands happiness for everyone and refuses to be confined to *one* love because his encounter with the phenomenon of plague has filled him with compassion for all, who declares war on the totalitarian state which seems to lie hidden behind the phenomenon of plague and liberates the city of Cadiz from its tyranny.[11] All this is shadowlessly clear, yet it has no impact as experienced reality. Far from sustaining dramatic interest, it hardly even arouses any.

This failure is an inseparable interaction of formal and metaphysical shortcomings. A play plainly designed to be imbued with the spirit of the mystery plays cannot do without their metaphysical assumptions, for its form directly expresses its metaphysics. Formally the mystery play depends on a belief in one world facing another, a faith in a watching eye, an affirmation of world as creation. Only a faith of this kind could have breathed life into this play's apparent rigidity.

Thus for Camus the solution to the whole problem complex of dramatic literature lay elsewhere: in abandonment of allegory and the cosmic dimension. What he had to do was create a drama whose formal and thematic assumptions would not imply the least trace of belief in ideas, much less of theism, in which, in conformity with his metaphysics of the absurd, he could work out a completely self-contained dialectical dramatics. This he did successfully in *Les Justes*.

### *Les Justes* (The Just Assassins)

*Les Justes* (1949) is, as it were, a dramatic harnessing of all the unused or improperly applied dramatic energies latent in *Caligula*, *L'Etat de siège*, and *Le Malentendu*. The harsh, single-minded tension of *Le Malentendu* is now blended with the dialectic of *Caligula*, while the problematic theme of love and engagement suggested by the Diego-Victoria pair on *L'Etat de siège* falls into place in the economy of dramatic tension. And it is certainly no accident that in this successful play there is much that reminds us of Sartre.[12]

Here we have a group of terrorists. They are five in number, as in *Morts sans sépulture*, but in *Les Justes* this number is not an ever-fluctuating one to which a sixth, the leader, is added from time to time. On the contrary, like the number of acts, also five, it guarantees the presence of real structure, in this case that of a community.[13] Whereas in Sartre's play each man stands alone, and Jean, the leader, is the one who is unable to do anything for the others, who has no communal relationship with them, Annenkov is a leader who smooths things out, pours oil on troubled waters, although—or perhaps because—he is just as vulnerable as a man as the others. And in this little community there are considerable tensions. There is Stepan, the passionate terrorist. Once he was whipped, and the inner wounds he has borne ever since drive him to seek release in action ("*agir enfin*," p. 309), in the restless, intolerant activity of hating and destroying (p. 355). It is no wonder that this Stepan has little understanding for Yanek, the poet and idealist, who is still living essentially on his childhood faith, which has not been shattered but only rendered questionable, and who wants to restore its wholeness through the vindication of success. Yanek would despair if this vindication were denied him (p. 320). There is Voinov, still young and with the best intentions of becoming a good terrorist, who loses his nerve when the assignment is postponed. He is not liquidated like François in *Morts sans sépulture*; on the contrary, Annenkov discreetly gives him a chance to recover, to regain his nerve and to prove himself later. (The situation is of course quite different from that in *Morts sans sépulture*, where this way out would have been impossible. Nevertheless it is the writer himself who determines the setting of the play.) Finally there is Dora, who loves Yanek, the poet. She loves him as a woman longing for the happiness of "forgetting" and for *tendresse*, who is forced to fight down this natural longing so that she may support the decision that Yanek is to throw the bomb which may bring death to him.

In all of them, Yanek, Voinov, Stepan, and Dora, the human *dessous* is visible, as it is in their leader too, for he was in love for four years before dedicating himself to the Party. Yet far from disillusioning their idealism and their efforts to make something of themselves—and here we have a significant difference from Sartre—this *dessous* is a ground which, although hollow, can still sustain them, a weakness which, once overcome, becomes the secret source of strength for an absurd but nonetheless great action.[14]

For the time being this great action is nothing but a plan

they have in mind: the assassination of a grand duke in the interests of Russia and the Communist Party.[15] This reminds us of Sartre's *Les Mains sales*, which appeared a year before *Les Justes*, but the problem is posed quite differently. Camus is not interested in showing the *aporia* of action, the gap between intention and execution. On the contrary, the plot deals quite straightforwardly with the development of the plan, though with setbacks that renew the tension, and then, just as straightforwardly, with the effects of the assassin's action on himself.

Let us now trace this action in detail. The first act presents the theoretical and ideological preparation for the attempted assassination and the first arguments between Stepan and Yanek. Yanek has been selected to throw the bomb, and Stepan, obviously jealous, accuses him of not being a genuine revolutionary and not really deserving this assignment. Yanek's revolutionary activities, he says, are purely selfish, a means of self-justification. In the course of the argument, however, it already becomes clear that Stepan has his own valid reasons for being so "absolute" and that these reasons have more to do with his past experience than with revolution.

In the second act the argument is resumed after the unsuccessful—or rather the aborted—attempt. Yanek has not been able to throw the bomb because he saw that there were children in the grand duke's car, children staring blankly ahead, and the sight of them deflated his idealistic exaltation. He says he will throw the bomb only if Annenkov expressly orders him to do so after the ceremony in which the grand duke and his family are participating. He now needs an order to rely on, the moral support of having to obey. Stepan remonstrates. He assumes the role of the man who acts "philosophically," rather like the emperor in *Caligula*, for whom circumstances are not sufficient reason to betray one's essence. But we are not in a play by Sartre now. This essential, abstract viewpoint is not upheld. Right is on the side of the just (though there is no attempt to brand the other position as "wrong")—on the side of those who believe, with Dora and Yanek and ultimately with their leader Annenkov, too, that a revolution which ignores the rules of humanity contradicts itself. Yanek even goes so far as to say

that he would immediately abandon the common cause if it conflicted with honor. Since Annenkov covers Yanek and accepts
the principle of "guiltless" revolution, they decide to wait for
the next opportunity, which will probably arise two days later.

Thus the tension builds up again, now that the terroristic
act looms so close, and the whole of the third act contributes to
it, bringing home to the participants the full reality of what has
to be overcome. First there is the fear which causes Voinov to
withdraw and ask for an easier assignment, and Voinov is not
by any means the only one who feels this fear. Then there is
love, which causes Dora to make a final attempt, disavowed and
yet only waiting for an answer, to induce Yanek to yield to the
tenderness of loving and being loved, to perform the only action that has any real, perceptible meaning. And finally we hear
from Stepan's own lips his doubts in his own revolutionary mission, his suspicion that Yanek will carry the bomb "like a cross,"
and that this cross-bearing self-sacrifice will ultimately be no
more than a delayed and unauthentic fulfillment of his childhood faith.[16]

All this fails to deflect Yanek from his purpose, and the
fourth act finds him in prison after the attempt has been successfully carried out. But whether it is really a success will only
be decided now that the deed is done, as happened with Orestes
in *Les Mouches*. Yanek is now tempted by remorse, as the
grand duchess, a devout woman, comes to him in all the humanity of her grief to ask the assassin to join her in the communion
of prayer. This is a much greater temptation to the open-
hearted Yanek than the more concrete temptation, much more
easily identifiable as inimical, as appealing for mercy and re-
opening the way to life.[17] When the curtain falls on him in
prison at the end of Act IV, the outcome of the struggle he will
undergo during the long hours of the night is quite uncertain.

Act V brings the certainty of victory. His comrades have
been in doubt about him; the government newspapers have
published a report that he has made an appeal. But then Stepan
comes and tells them of Yanek's dark, earthly victory. Just
before two o'clock in the morning they took him out, dressed
all in black. The rain poured down on him until he was no more

than a clump of muddy earth, standing motionless while they read the verdict to him. Just once he moved his leg to shake some dirt off his shoes. Now almost earth himself, he made his dying an "ideal" victory, an ascent. Then he ascended into the darkness; the executioners wrapped him in a shroud, and then they heard a "terrible sound," a howling cry. With the strength of someone about to drown, Dora breaks into its immediacy: "Don't cry. No, no! Don't cry! Don't you see, this is the day of justification! At this hour something is arising which is our testimony, our testimony as revolutionaries. Yanek is no longer a murderer. A terrible sound! A terrible sound was enough to take him back to the joy of childhood." [18]

Now she longs for nothing more passionately than to bear the cross of the bomb herself: "Give me the bomb. . . . Yes, next time. I want to throw it. I want to be the first to throw it" (*ibid.*).

### Les Justes and L'Homme révolté

Thus the ending of *Les Justes* denotes the victory of that immanent idealism which the just represent, a revolutionary idealism which is not a belief in ideas but one which the hero wrests from his life despite adverse conditions. So although the ending is somewhat reminiscent of the concluding lines of *Le Mythe de Sisphe*, in *Les Justes* Camus has taken a significant step forward, a step which removes the play from the works of his first period and places it with his literature of rebellion. Although Sisyphus does indeed pick up the rock again, it is in defiance of all hope. The meaning he wrests from absurdity is nothing to build on; it is a horizontal, absurd meaning, a meaning essentially grounded in an act of understanding, not in an action. It is the meaning that comes from the superiority of knowing oneself to be absurd.

In the period of rebellion (of which we have of course already seen preliminary signs) all this is changed. An *homme révolté*, as Camus explains, is a man who says no but also a man who feels within himself the right to say no. In other words, in practice rebellion presupposes a belief in values, a consciousness, vague as it may be, that one can rebel in the name of something: "Not every value entails rebellion, but any movement of rebellion tacitly invokes a value." [19] And a little further on Camus says of the slave who rebels: "That part of himself that he wants to have respected he sets above all the rest and proclaims it preferable to everything, even to life itself." Cherea in *Caligula* knew a little of this rebellion too, but in him it went along with submitting *quand même*; in spite of his final victory over the tyrant it was crushed by the absurdity of a cosmos which to the very last was subject to Caligula's whim. Now, in 1947, when Camus receives the *Prix des Critiques* for *La Peste*, his new constructive phase vigorously announces itself, and this is in no way contradicted by the fact that *L'Homme révolté* (The Rebel) itself did not appear until 1951, for in the introductory comparison with Sartre we already established that in Camus the theoretical stance usually follows the literary formulation, and not vice versa.

In fact, whole passages of *L'Homme révolté* read like a commentary on *Les Justes*,[20] for example, the one in which Camus explains that the only kingdom that might be opposed to the kingdom of grace is the kingdom of justice, where human communion can be rediscovered among the ruins of divine communion (p. 510) or when he expatiates on the idea that the ideal form of construction without God is revolution—but a revolution undertaken in love and fruitfulness. This is what he says about revolution: "And so either it is love and fruitfulness or it is nothing. Revolution without honor, calculated revolution, which, in preferring an abstract man to the man of flesh and blood, denies the man of flesh and blood, denies the human being as many times as may be necessary, in fact puts resentment in the place of love." [21] These words confirm his striving toward a "guiltless" revolution in which "the just" would find fulfillment. They also confirm Yanek's conception of honor and revolutionary dignity.

But it is not only the thematic coincidences that entitle us to assign *Les Justes* to what Camus very early referred to as the *"série de la révolte."* [22] (And in fact he himself later upheld this classification.[23]) Quite apart from this, formal and related metaphysical criteria also place it definitively in this phase. For the phase of rebellion, like the phase of the absurd, has a formal and at the same time "metaphysical" unity. The phase of the absurd was characterized by the inflexible opposition of mutually exclusive possibilities. In *L'Etranger* there was on one side the world of the judge and the priest, on the other the world of the Stranger; in *Caligula* there were the worlds of the poet, of rebellion, and of the absurd, but each world ultimately remained confined to itself, always in opposition to the other world, never in dialogue with it. Things were much the same in *Le Malentendu* and *L'Etat de siège*. The fundamental ontological position of the world of rebellion, however, is a different one: a position of construction, of dialogue, of communion. And this difference is just as discernible in form as in subject matter. *L'Etranger* has two parts (the dualistic principle). *Caligula* has four acts (the number four, as being divisible by two, also conforms to the dualistic principle). *Le Malentendu* [24] and *L'Etat de siège*,[25] which structurally and thematically mark the transition, each have three acts. *Les Justes* attains the classical five, and its structure is accordingly that of a continuous, phenomenon-oriented curve of development:

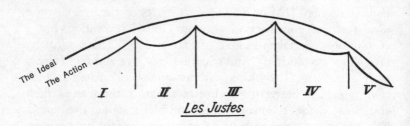

metaphysical significance, that it represents an espousal of constructivity,[26] will not be surprised to find that *La Peste* also has five parts, for this almost hopeless encounter with an enemy who has sovereign power to determine the rhythm of the battle also has its idealistic side—even without ideals.

Anyone who realizes that this form, which at first glance may appear purely external and extrinsic, also has a metaphysical significance, that it represents an espousal of constructivity,[26] will not be surprised to find that *La Peste* also has five parts, for this almost hopeless encounter with an enemy who has sovereign power to determine the rhythm of the battle also has its idealistic side—even without ideals.

# chapter 11

# "Worldness" and Heroism

*La Peste* — The Plague

Camus's heroes are linked with the world in a very special way. To a certain extent they *are* World,[1] *are* cosmos, and, as we have seen again and again, this tendency reflects the Mediterranean, "Greek" Camus, the Camus who is alive to the metaphysical in the world and in his share in it—a metaphysical element which for him of course is no longer divine, although it somehow stems from divine sources. This was particularly evident in *L'Etranger* and the early essays, and there is something of it in the sudden flash of cosmic power from the rock that Sisyphus picks up again. At his execution, Yanek in *Les Justes* was like a rain-drenched clod of earth, like a man about to sink back into the womb of earth from which he originally issued. But Yanek had nonetheless set himself apart already, striving for markedly vertical meaning; he had shaken the earth from his shoes before he ascended into death, and a cry (even though it was distorted into a howl) had set the seal on his victory. The momentary, almost unconscious rebellion which consists in shouting out "truths," as Meursault did in his encounter with the prison chaplain, had become a continuing, conscious rebellion; it had become revolution. Horizontal "worldness" of the kind demonstrated in Meursault's "ground-level" death had been superseded by the differentiation of idealistic action and the vertical death to which it leads.

*La Peste*,[2] the great literary summing up of all that Camus means by rebellion, will carry this differentiation a step farther, will give the dialogue between "worldness" and heroism a specific epic and cosmic formulation even more perfectly suited to it.

### Development and Ideality

In *La Peste* the heroes, primarily Dr. Rieux, Tarrou, and Father Paneloux, will be heroes—in a very different way, of course—in the sense that they are on the way to ideality, but in addition they are part and parcel of a cosmic destiny which forces them to develop and has an influence on their relationship to ideality, sometimes even determining it. At the same time this cosmic destiny is also the antagonist they are struggling against, the master against whom they are rebelling; it is the plague. This plague begins in spring with the appearance of dying rats, reaches its negative peak in late summer, and declines again as winter approaches. And the "heroes" too will develop in tune with this same rhythm, demonstrating a remarkable interplay of individual heroism and collective "worldness."

How carefully Camus laid out this cosmic plan for *La Peste* and the importance he attached to a continuing development can be seen from the fact that he expanded the seasonal cycle (already mentioned in the prologue) to include five seasons, so that the plague year, like *Les Justes*, falls into five parts and the numerical ratio alone tends to give the work a dialogic unity. Camus managed this by introducing a sort of Indian summer (Part III) after spring (Part I) and summer (Part II), so that the five-season cycle closes with autumn (Part IV) and winter (Part V).

Everybody participates equally in the dialogic unity of this plague year, for it is an event that affects them all equally,[3] that yokes together in a common destiny the worlds which in *L'Etranger, Caligula,* and *Le Malentendu* pass by one another unrecognized, that forces them all to pull together against an adversary who can only be combatted through menial service: service which consists for the most part in registering the casualties and consigning them to the earth.[4] This sets everybody on the same plane and brings them into a dialogue.

### The Open Dialogue: An Example

To make this clearer, let us take the example of the priest, that is to say, of a social-ideological type who in *L'Etranger* still stood completely apart and never succeeded in becoming a part of the Stranger's world. There the priest was chaplain of an institution, a chaplain who, for all his goodwill, obviously carried out his duties in a routine manner, using all the standard pastoral tricks and gestures. The priest was disturbed when he found that he was not getting anywhere and finally sensed that he was confronted by a man to whom the earth meant everything, whose only conception of a hereafter was a life in which it would be granted to him to remember his life on earth. This is a priest who finally takes refuge in a patronizing "I shall pray for you"—a statement which the Stranger takes as an uncalled-for humiliation and which provokes the crisis and his final break with Christian spirituality.

How different is Paneloux in *La Peste,* this Jesuit who, like Camus himself, has made a study of Saint Augustine! His human reality is not isolated from that of Dr. Rieux but is ready from the very first for dialogue. Not only are they both guided by the hand of another reality, a cosmic one, which forces them into development; their basic dispositions are also similar, as we see from the start. Thus, in Part I, in the spring of the cosmos of *La Peste,* Paneloux, just like Dr. Rieux, is kind, unselfish helpfulness. Together they take care of the first victim claimed by the deadly disease, the old concierge. In Part II, when the reality of the plague has become inescapable to the inhabitants of Oran but has not yet completed its hold over them, the two men's paths diverge temporarily, and they retreat to the "peak"

of their own selves. Paneloux remembers his priestly respon-
sibilities and delivers a sermon full of emphatic rhetoric and
pastoral passion in which he presents the plague as a punishment, as a call to repentance. Pouring rain, like a cosmic symbol
of verticality, accompanies this sermon, and the counterpoint in
the sound of rain and the preaching makes the people fall to
their knees.

> The rain was pouring down harder than ever outside,
> and this last sentence, uttered in an absolute silence which
> was intensified by the rattling of the rain against the stained
> glass windows, rang out with such force that after a mo-
> mentary hesitation some of the congregation slid forward
> from their seats onto their knees.[5]

Dr. Rieux for his part will later have to admit that in those early
days, when the plague summer was just beginning, he still cher-
ished dreams of heroism.

But the two men soon come together again; the common
enemy sees to that. Toward the end of the plague summer
Tarrou asks Paneloux whether he would be willing to join their
voluntary rescue team. Paneloux does so, not only helping with
the work, but walking, shoulder to shoulder with the others
in absolute solidarity, man's road into exile, into the sterility
of "collective history," into the Indian summer of humanness,
when *ennui* and a feeling of being useless undermine man's
verticality: "No doubt our love was still there, but it was, quite
simply, no good for anything. It was a heavy load, inert within
us, sterile as crime or a death sentence. It was no more now than
patience without a future and dogged waiting." [6]

But then the plague autumn arrives, an autumn of wind,
heat, and rain, a wearying autumn that takes its pick among the
people, singling out those who are not destined to enter into the
luminous brilliance of perfect world, the light of winter. The
winds howl around the cathedral, penetrating doors and windows, as Paneloux delivers his second sermon, this time in the
presence of Dr. Rieux. It is a much less orthodox sermon than
the first, and in it Paneloux asserts that man must make the

choice between believing everything and denying everything. The constructivity of his doctrinal offerings has been shattered by the death of an innocent child; the winds of heresy blow in from every direction. Paneloux has pursued solidarity with men to the point of recognizing life's absurdity, and all he can do now is opt for naked faith, for death and the cross. He does not hesitate to do so.

He is buried just before All Saints' Day, when cold winds are already announcing the winter of total humanness, and significantly the diagnosis cannot state categorically "plague." It reads "*cas douteux*," and this has a metaphorical sense too. Paneloux is a "doubtful case" also because he was not able to go all the way with Tarrou and Rieux. But let us remember how far he did go and how open the dialogue was in comparison with the priest's dialogue with the Stranger. A diagram may crystallize it.

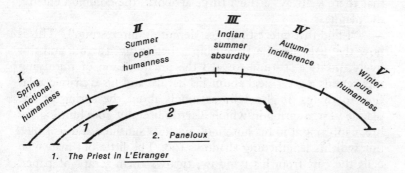

Whereas the priest in *L'Etranger* pursues the dialogue only until his solid pastoral structure begins to show slight cracks, Paneloux goes along with the others well into the autumn of humanness. Only then does he part from them, to keep on believing in spite of everything and to meet death just before All Saints'.[7] We should certainly not be justified in concluding that Paneloux lacked the crucial sense of fellowship and that this only becomes clear toward the end. For Tarrou, who is certainly one of Camus's positive heroes, will also die before the winter of pure humanness sets in.

### Tarrou and Dr. Rieux

The friendship between Tarrou and Dr. Rieux, natural as it is, has its history. These friends who are apparently in such close agreement have their differences too. Up to a point the two of them might even be said to embody a slight conflict which reflects the ethical problem of heroism as Camus sees it. This is the conflict between a horizontal heroism, as personified by Dr. Rieux, and an explicit, idealistic, vertical heroism, such as Tarrou stands for. It is thus a conflict that recalls Sartrean problems: Canoris, for example, as compared with Henri in *Morts sans sépulture*. But no sooner have we formulated this analogy than its limits become obvious and we see that in the case of Tarrou and Dr. Rieux the word "conflict" really means no more than dialogue—the history of a road the two friends, with all their differences, follow together. If we trace this road we shall see that there is always a third force at work, the common enemy, the plague.

"I find that interesting, yes, definitely interesting." [8] This is how the dialogue of a friendship is begun by Tarrou, and this lively, positive attitude toward the phenomenon of the dying rats reveals a great deal about his nature and his dynamic relation to things. It also tells us much about the spring of the plague year, a spring in which Tarrou literally goes hunting for life, capturing it in his notebook with its sunshine and its smile, but with its lengthening shadows too. The little old man who calls the cats from his window, throws them scraps of paper, and then, having fooled them, spits on them "*avec force et précision*," gloating when he hits one,[9] is described very lovingly and with delight in all the kindly, vivid detail. Tarrou confronts life very positively and openly, continually questioning it. His positiveness reveals ideological tension, whereas that of Dr. Rieux is more relaxed, more neutral. Dr. Rieux sees his ideal in a sober fulfillment of duty: "There lay certainty: in everyday work. The rest hung on threads and unimportant impulses, and there was no time for it. The main thing was to do your job properly." [10] Big words and lofty aims are not in his line; he resists everything constructed, everything explicitly constructive—even the verticality of technical language: "Rieux replied that he had not been describing a syndrome; he had described what he had seen." [11] Although Tarrou is not the opposite of Rieux in this respect, his goals are more explicit, more profound, and at the same time higher; he seeks "inner peace."

The difference persists when they set up the rescue team together and their ideals seem to draw closer in the fight against a single enemy, when Rieux "declares war on creation as it is" (p. 1320), thus joining Tarrou in his positive defensive action—in rebellion—while Tarrou "de-idealizes" his ethical ideal into the relatively flat and neutral notion of *"compréhension"* (p. 1323), thus bringing it closer to Rieux's ideal of *honnêteté* or common decency (p. 1350). Not until after the plague ecstasy and the abstraction of "collective history" will their differences come out into the open again, and then they will not harm the friendship or interfere with their following the same road. On the contrary their friendship grows, finally becoming an almost mythical consecration.

It reaches full maturity just about All Saints' Day. In effect it embraces Paneloux too, although the priest had renounced the human fulfillment of such a friendship: "Those in holy orders have no friends. They have invested everything in God." [12] Tarrou and Rieux, however, continue on their common road, and the Indian summer of the plague will soon give them plenty of time to find the appropriate name for it: to call it—casually, of course, and *sur un ton très naturel*—friendship.

Tarrou begins to talk about himself and recounts the pre-history of his undeviating if deluded idealism. His father was a public prosecutor and hence belonged to the category of people who in *L'Etranger* were still absolutely "other." Having to condemn people to death was in effect his job. For Tarrou as a boy and young man it had therefore become a terrifying sign when his father got up early, because this meant that he was going to court to condemn a man to death. One night when his father had asked to be called early, Tarrou felt that his own connivance so implicated him in the passing of the death sentence that he spent a sleepless night and left home for good the next morning. Ever since then his one concern has been to avoid passing sentence of death, always to take the side of the condemned. This is why he has fought the plague, that continual death sentence. He indulged in no great illusions, to be sure. It is impossible to abstain entirely from passing judgment; life always implies guilt and killing. But he for his part was determined to try to be an "innocent murderer." [13]

This may not sound like a very lofty aim, but it shows that Tarrou is and has been from the very first explicitly idealistic, and Rieux now knows where this tense orientation toward the ideal originated. Tarrou reveals the height of this "ambitionless ideal" when he goes on to say: "In short . . . what interests me is finding out how to become a saint." When Rieux reminds him that he does not believe in God, Tarrou elucidates: "Exactly. Whether one can be a saint without God is the only concrete problem I recognize today." [14] Rieux understands this, but he himself is not interested in this question; he is concerned with something else: "What interests me is being a man." And with a curious twist Tarrou answers: "Yes, we're after the same thing, but I'm less ambitious" (*ibid.*). For Rieux too this remark is so unexpected that he fails to grasp Tarrou's meaning. In fact he must not grasp it if his idealless ideal is to remain unjeopardized, if it is not to become explicitly an ideal.

Rieux's ideal is in fact one of natural helpfulness which cannot and should not identify itself by name and which is hence even more demanding than the ideal Tarrou has set himself. (Here we are very close to the Sartrean ideal of total commitment as a matter of course.) In the strict sense it is not even an ideal at all, not something that exists independently of Rieux's human reality, as a goal which he may approach more or less successfully. This is heroism as being, not as an ideal. It is a heroism (and here Sartre and Camus diverge again) that has its roots in an unshakable faith, a faith which almost automatically gives one the courage to begin again. (*Recommencer* —to begin again—is one of the key words of *La Peste*.) This faith, which has much in common with religious faith and is accordingly referred to as *"la foi,"* [15] believes in an immanent meaning residing in action, in a structure of meaning which is active within itself, regardless of its origin and aim. It is faith in man, the faith of Sisyphus.

Tarrou, however, is concerned with more than this, even though he pretends in his conversation with Dr. Rieux that his aim is less ambitious. What he is concerned with is a genuinely religious, transcendent consecration of his actions. It is this he is seeking when he does something that at first glance seems to denote no more than a turning toward the world: when he proposes to his friend that after his "confession" they should "do something for their friendship," namely, go swimming together in the sea to which they at last have access again. Of course he is hardly aware of being prompted by a strong urge to perform a cultic action and not at all aware that for him, the "future saint," this "plunge into the earth's baptismal font" [16] will acquire a quite different, transcendent significance. For him this will be the final catharsis, the river Lethe, on the farther bank of which the afterlife beckons.

For Tarrou is an idealist, a "saint," and saints, just like Christians, must die when innocence lies there "*avec les yeux crevés,*" as Tarrou said himself in speaking of Paneloux.[17] *La Peste's* well-wrought cosmos of meaning and symbol now calls upon Tarrou too to take the consequence of his aspirations: death, which will claim him as winter sets in. But for Dr. Rieux this plunge into the sea is simply that and nothing more: a cleansing, invigorating swim which sets the seal on friendship, a swim celebrating his newly recovered oneness with the world,[18] after which he will enter the heaven of earth, his newly recovered life, and the wintry sun of Algeria.[19]

### Symbolic Cosmos or "Real" Life

Thus the cosmos of *La Peste* shows here and there the inner coherence of a symbolic cosmos.[20] The timing of Paneloux's and Tarrou's deaths, the fact that Rieux, as the only "pure" human being among these three great heroes of the plague, is the only one to survive it, and, last but by no means least, the phenomenon of the plague itself could be adduced, along with much more, as by no means farfetched evidence that the plague symbolizes a literary cosmos. But we should not forget that this symbolic meaning emerges only sporadically and never openly, that Camus succeeded in interweaving it so imperceptibly with real life that it reveals itself only to the patient analyst. Besides Paneloux, Tarrou, and Rieux there are many other figures who together profile the plague no less distinctively, as they bob up from time to time in the stream of events, though always conforming to the cosmic development according to their individual temperaments.[21]

There is, for example, Judge Othon, the paterfamilias in his full social reality, who appears holding his little son's hand at the opening of the novel (p. 1224) and later on in that same plague spring presents an idyllic picture of almost animal harmony as he sits with his family in a restaurant. Tarrou sketches them all in his notebook: him as an owl, her as a good-natured mouse, and the children as well-trained little dogs.[22] This public prosecutor will naturally find Paneloux's first sermon "*absolument irréfutable*." For him the world is a balancing of guilt and atonement, the incorruptible order of a justice which really does prevail. But the ecstasy of the plague will seize him too and force him into the silence of essential suffering, for his son will fall ill and what remains of his social, family structure will be torn apart. His wife and little daughter will be quarantined in a hotel, and he himself will have to go to an isolation camp because there is no room for him in the hotel kept by Rambert, the journalist. This Rambert too has his history. He tried desperately to escape from the plague-stricken city, first through the official channels open to him, then unofficially through a band of smugglers. Then he came across Rieux and Tarrou, but he still did not reach a consistent position until the plague autumn (cf. p. 1381). Judge Othon has not reached this point even by All Saints' Day; he has too much leeway to make up in becoming *human*. His son is buried the next day. Tarrou brings him the news, and bats are flying around the tents in the isolation camp as the gates close behind him and he murmurs to himself: "The poor judge! . . . We ought to do something for him. But how can you help a judge?" [23]

Thus, real life is constantly acquiring symbolic meaning,

constantly revealing flashes of it, thanks to an essential transparency of events and scenes, so that reality never supersedes or
interferes with symbolism or vice versa. This is true not only of
Othon and the three great plague heroes; it also applies to the
unforgettably strange friendship between Cottard and Grand.
In fact, if we are to believe Rieux, much of the meaning of this
work is to be sought in these two unlikely heroes. These so
dissimilar friends and neighbors, who live on the same floor,
next door to one another, remind us a little of the friendship
between Meursault and Raymond. The parallel, however, does
not extend very far, and it applies chiefly to Cottard, who is a
sort of Meursault transposed to the world of the plague, a
Meursault who no longer holds meaning in his hands, who has
entirely lost his oneness with himself, who is not only continually
saying "Excuse me," but actually flees from a tobacconist's shop
when he hears that a clerk has killed an Arab on the beach. This
is a Meursault who is never given a chance of contemplation, of
finding his way back into the rhythm of the world step by step,
a Meursault no one has understood and who now carries his
guilty conscience around with him.

In Grand, the poet who wrestles with words and has come
hopelessly to grief on one single sentence, Cottard has found a
partner who complements him admirably, especially when he
loses contact with his surroundings, notably with a girl with
whom he has been speechlessly in love and for whom he has
been able to find no words when words were the only thing
that might have held her. Thus Grand too has something in
common with Meursault.

These two friends make their entrance with a macabre
humor in the early days of the plague. On the door to which
Grand leads Dr. Rieux is written in red chalk: "Come in. I've
hanged myself." Fortunately, Grand explains, he did of course
"come in" and was just in time "to get Cottard off the hook." [24]
Cottard had heard that the authorities were on his track because
of an "old story" and he wanted to escape justice. He is therefore the one man to welcome the plague, because it prevents
the authorities from following up his case. When it begins to
abate he becomes frantic, loses his mind and shoots from his

window at the people in the street, and the police finally have to overpower him. His friend and neighbor Grand, however, though deeply shocked by these events, goes back to work. Unobtrusively, quietly, and with humility, he does his duty. He has but one ideal: to polish a single sentence to perfection in the hope of making it an "ideal" sentence. In a way it is a ludicrous ideal which can never be taken seriously, an ideal which just about sums up Dr. Rieux's idea of heroism.

> Yes, if it's true that men insist on setting up examples and models which they call heroes, and if there absolutely has to be one in this story, the narrator would like to nominate this insignificant, unobtrusive hero who had nothing to his credit but a little goodness of heart and an apparently ridiculous ideal.[25]

Yet Grand's "heroism" will not readily be recognized for what it is. On the contrary, Grand, along with Cottard and many others, offers living proof that *La Peste* seeks to be not only a symbolic cosmos but life pure and simple, a reality in which the anonymity of modern heroism holds good but which nevertheless as a construct of life also represents a doctrine of life, a legible interpretation of it. What it has to teach us about men can ultimately be discerned in each of the heroes, in the modest Grand just as plainly as in the demanding Tarrou, in the priest Paneloux just as plainly as in Dr. Rieux, and also, as Camus obviously intended, in Judge Othon just as plainly as in Cottard. In all these people we see flashes of the truth "that there are more things to admire in men than to despise." [26]

### The Inner Structure

The plague is thus essentially a dialogic reality, a constructive world which does not seek to storm heaven with its constructivity but merely to make the horizontality of humanness secure. It is what we have in another context called constructive horizontality.[27] All attempts to go beyond man, to attain an ideal which lies "above" him, miscarry or lead to death: "But for all those who had aspired beyond man toward something they could not even imagine, there had been no answer. Tarrou did seem to have reached that elusive peace he used to talk about, but he had found it only in death, when it could no longer do him any good." [28]

The peace which in the early essays Camus found in unquestioned oneness with oneself and nature, the peace to which, on a loftier level, the Stranger opened himself in death, remained beyond Tarrou's reach because in aspiring toward this ideal he had set his sights too high; he had tried to achieve a kind of sainthood without God. But the fact that he did not attain his ultimate goal does not affect the immanent meaning of his actions, the constructive task he, along with Dr. Rieux and others, performed during the plague.

Thus without abandoning the horizontality of a humanness without ideals, *La Peste* goes an important step beyond *L'Etranger*; it is a constructive reality which offers viable meaning. Its internal formal principles confirm this. Comparing it with the dualistic, discrete reality in *L'Etranger*, we find that the partners in the dialogue have become much more important and that the use of tenses is quite different. Whereas in *L'Etranger* Camus relied almost exclusively on the perfect, as a tense which, used in a monotonous way, could express aloofness, unrelatedness, and alienation, here the tenses echo the contrasting play of events and place them clearly in their setting in accordance with the principle of constructivity.

> On the morning of April 16, Dr. Bernard Rieux left his office and stumbled over a dead rat in the middle of the hallway. Instinctively he kicked it aside without paying any attention to it and went on downstairs. But when he reached the street it occurred to him that the rat had no business being there, and he turned back to tell the concierge.[29]

This is how, after a prologue, the story of *La Peste* begins, and it is easy enough to see that the place and time of the story are being firmly established by the use of tenses and adverbial clauses. But what we have here is not, as we might be inclined to think, *the* style of *La Peste*. On the contrary, in this work Camus shows how many styles he has at his disposal. He makes frequent and often very abrupt shifts of style (and this bears out the idea that the inner form of *La Peste* is constructive horizontality, that is, a construction which is not continuously projected but falls back from time to time into the horizontal plane).

An example of one of these abrupt shifts occurs between the prologue and the beginning of the narrative; another marks the transitions from Part I to Part II, from Part II to Part III, and from Part IV to Part V. Only between Parts III and IV do we find no abrupt shift, and this is because the whole of Part III is written in the style that in the other parts is confined to the openings. It is as though Camus were trying to make the individual parts of his work to some extent formally self-contained, like the cantos of an epic, to build them up from below by introducing each one by a kind of formal prologue. (Part IV has a prologue of this kind too, but it does not depart from the style of Part III.) This formal prologue always consists of a few paragraphs in which the writer assumes the tone of a sober, theory-conscious observer and reporter.[30] Characteristically, it is the third "canto" that maintains this tone throughout, and here there is no dialogue. This is significant thematically—as what we have called the ecstasy of the plague—and also formally, inasmuch as the continuity of the curve depends to a great extent on this third canto of the five. What is going on here is similar to something we have already seen in Sartre's *Les Mouches*: the outward continuity of the curve is broken from time to time, referred back to horizontality by the inner form.

This is confirmed again and again. There are, for example, the numerous vignettes Camus offers us in *La Peste*, some of them painted in affectionate detail, some in a few bold strokes: the funny old man and his antics with the cats; Judge Othon and his family; the asthmatic old Spaniard who takes a senile delight in the emergence of the rats (p. 1228); the man leaning against a lamppost, laughing silently while the sweat runs down his ashen face in great beads; the woman who suddenly flings

open a window, screams twice, and then slams the shutters
closed (p. 1310); the newspaper boys, still half asleep, drowsily
offering their wares to the lampposts (p. 1314). Every one of
these scenes shows how far the cosmic development has pro-
gressed, but at the same time they all stand alone in a blaze of
light which makes the shadow separating them look even
darker. Hence none of them has any sequel; each stands, absolute in itself, alongside other scenes and events which are not
continuations of it. Only occasionally will it resurface, distorted by the general development, only to drop out of sight
again.

We may cite one last and particularly characteristic example of this lack of continuity within the fundamental process
of development. This one is drawn from the special atmos-
pheric symbolism which Camus repeatedly suggests: the play
of light and shadow. Here again, as we shall see, there is no
continuous buildup of meaning (that is, light), but a dialogue
of light and shadow which shifts back and forth between
alternatives and shows only a barely discernible directional
trend. This is an ideological discussion between Tarrou and Dr.
Rieux which goes on for several pages and which is accompanied by a curious interplay of light and shade.

Dr. Rieux stands in the shade while he restates the negative
part of his creed, his atheism: "Without moving out of the
shadow, the doctor said that he had already replied, that if he
believed in an omnipotent god he would give up healing men
and leave that to Him." When Tarrou tries to pin him down to
his positive faith, to the truth of a fight against creation, he
steps back into the lamplight: " 'More or less,' replied the
doctor, moving back into the light." [31] Later, though, when
Tarrou is leaving and Dr. Rieux is seeing him to the door, the
hall light does not work, so that Tarrou has to make his idealistic confession of faith in the dark, and his clear "yes" stands in
complete isolation in the night: "The reply came in the darkness, spoken by the same tranquil voice: 'Yes.' " [32] Only when
they both set ideology aside and move on to the dialogue of
horizontality, to the natural impulse of human friendship, does
the light fall on them both, and now for the first time it is the

light of heaven, the light of the world. "Standing by the car, Rieux asked Tarrou if he wanted to come in, and Tarrou accepted. A faint glow from the sky illuminated their faces" (*ibid.*). In the car they resume their ideological conversation, but Rieux does not see Tarrou's face again until they reach the house of the old asthma patient, that is to say, until the moment they turn back to the self-evident business of helping people.

Thus the dialogic element can stand separate and alone— and not merely in this instance. It does indeed point to the fundamental role of dialogue, but the dialogic element does not join with others in the continuous construction of a vertical transcendence, nor is it the prelude to a vertical structure of meaning which will not emerge until the end. It reminds us of the towers of some modern churches, which do not draw the architectural space of the church upward from the portal in a symbol of all-embracing, continuing redemption, but have an existence of their own and no longer fit into the structure of the whole.

This may help us to recognize that we are confronted here with an epochal phenomenon, that constructive horizontality is a characteristic of modern literature which, differently practiced, is also typical of *Les Mouches*, for instance, where, it will be remembered, the verticality of the external buildup of tension was overcome from inside and forced into the horizontal plane.

Thus these so dissimilar writers seem linked by something—and perhaps by something very essential. In a letter to Camus, Sartre even went so far as to say: "We were linked by many things and separated by few." [33] Whether this is so or not we shall not venture to decide, but we shall certainly have more to say about what the two have in common.

## chapter 12

# Exile and the Kingdom

*L'Exil et le royaume*
(Exile and the Kingdom) —
*La Chute* (The Fall)

### A New Phase

The analysis of *Les Justes* and *La Peste* has shown that in these works of revolution the dialogic and constructive element becomes stronger and the vertical tension increases in comparison with the works of the first phase (the phase of the absurd). The well-balanced hero Rieux is now joined by true idealists such as Tarrou or Yanek in *Les Justes*. Whereas the developmental curve of Meursault merely rose slightly under outer pressure from the level of worldness and then, in the execution, led back into reaffirmed oneness with himself and the world, the heroes, or at least some of them, are now themselves thrusting beyond horizontality; they are on the way to an ideal.

This tension will increase still more in what we may call the third phase. In fact it already announces itself plainly and programmatically in the title, which juxtaposes two polarized concepts. And when we remember that one novella, the story called *La Chute*, which was almost certainly intended originally as the final one, detached itself from this collection to stand alongside *L'Exil et le royaume*, then it looks as though the extreme vertical tension of this latter work was quickly followed by a fall.

In examining these interconnections we should not start with the dates of publication. (*La Chute* appeared in 1956, a year before *L'Exil et le royaume*.) Quite obviously *La Chute* was intended as the seventh and last novella in the volume entitled *L'Exil et le royaume*. In the process of being written, however, it developed an independence incompatible with the overall plan. Camus therefore took it out of the original design and completed it before putting the finishing touches to the larger complex of *L'Exil et le royaume*.

Thus *La Chute* is the last link in a chain of development which Camus certainly intended to pursue. Death, however, which, as Sartre said, always comes either too soon or too late, put an abrupt end to it, and what remains is a Camus who undoubtedly had further plans in mind but also a corpus of work which for better or worse must be regarded as his *oeuvre*. Of this work it can be said that its three phases show an increasing verticalization, a growing tension, which reaches its highest intensity in *L'Exil et le royaume* and sinks down again in *La Chute*, to sound its final chord on a breaking string, so to speak. Yet even this extreme tension in *L'Exil et la royaume* and even the strangely torn final chord of *La Chute* have their harmony and their cosmic character.

### The Unity of *L'Exil et le royaume* [1]

The choice of genre in *L'Exil et le royaume* already indicates the growing tension we have spoken of, for here Camus turns to a literary genre which in a way pulls extremities together, which tries within a narrow scope to capture the antinomy of mutually exclusive things—a genre which does not seek the harmony of wholeness but discovers in details the tension of something that cannot achieve wholeness.

And yet Camus cannot deny his "better" self, the constructive Camus, for he overcomes the "meaninglessness" of the single novella [2] by means of a meaningful overall design, integrating the stories into the unity of a well-planned collection, into the totality of a cosmos of meaning. No doubt the novella lends itself by nature to the creation of such a collection—Sartre too collected several in *Le Mur*—but for Camus the comprehensive title of this collection will denote more than a thematic bracketing together; for him the collection as a whole will acquire to some degree the character of a continuous work. We only need to recall the titles of the individual novellas in sequence and to coordinate them systematically:

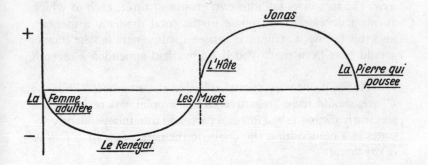

The movement starts from the cosmic unity glimpsed for fleeting moments by the "adulterous woman" in her ecstatic exaltation, drops into the negativity of the perverse search for meaning carried to its nadir by the Renegade, and rises gradually in *Les Muets* (The Silent Men) inasmuch as this story expresses the need for some word to resolve the tension between employees and employers. In *L'Hôte* (The Guest) the movement unmistakably thrusts forward for the first time into the positive range—the "guest" concept itself is significant—and in *Jonas* (The Artist at Work) it reaches its high point (strongly interspersed with irony): the writer's prophetic mission. Finally in *La Pierre qui pousse* (The Growing Stone) it sinks back almost to the horizontality of true cosmic meaning which lies between positivity and negativity. Thus in the final story the movement returns to the level of *La Femme adultère* (The Adulterous Woman), with a slight but important shift of accent.[3] The engineer D'Arrast will not commit adultery with the cosmos; instead he will carry to his friend's hut a stone which is supposed to be taken to the church and drop it into the open fire so that it is half covered with dirt and ashes. This is the answer the movement holds for us: the answer of world-related solidarity with the poor, the suffering, and the exiled.

Thus the novellas in *L'Exil et le royaume* form a whole, and there is good reason to suppose that this was one of the factors that led Camus to take out *La Chute* and let it stand alone. For the unity of *L'Exil et le royaume* is built around an axis. The six stories fall into two groups of three, each of which forms a developmental phase in the total thematic argument, and this balanced structure, whose duality parallels its theme, would have been destroyed if Camus had appended a seventh story.[4]

And is it not very remarkable that the amputated limb, *La Chute*, should have "regenerated" to a point where it too has six clearly distinguished integral parts and thus independently re-states as a composition the dualistic thematic ideas of *L'Exil et le royaume*?

### Exile and Existence

The term "exile" coupled dualistically with the positive notion of "the kingdom" suggests that we are not far from the Sartrean notion of "existence," and in fact it does mean something similar, as we have already shown in our analysis of *L'Envers et l'endroit*, though of course with the important difference that here again Camus thinks dynamically while Sartre does not. The word "exile" itself (from ex-salire—to jump out) denotes this as distinct from "existence" (from ex-sistere—to stand out). Camus, however, also uses the word "existence," and this requires some clarification, especially since the context might sometimes mislead us into taking this "existence" to mean the Sartrean notion of existence. Such a mistake could easily arise, for instance, from a careless reading of the scene in *La Femme adultère* in which Janine, the adulterous woman, explains why she finally yielded to the endless entreaties of the law student and married him: "By so often making her feel that she existed for him, he made her really exist. No, she was not alone." [5] The words *"exister réellement"* here might mislead us into assuming that Camus is speaking of the *"existence vraie"* that Sartre attributes to Brunet in *La Mort dans l'âme* or Hugo in *Les Mains sales*. Neither would it be tenable to impute to *"réellement"* some of its etymological sense and make this connection with Sartre: through the student's entreaties Janine is raised to become a thing (*res*), and it is this "status" of thingness that she seeks in marriage. Objectively speaking, an interpretation of this kind would not be false, but the next sentence, "No, she was not alone," shows that Camus does not mean any such thing. For him "really exist" obviously means the ending of her aloneness. Paradoxically enough it means exactly the opposite of what the word *exister* actually denotes; it means the overcoming of "standing outside," the knowledge of belonging.

Thus for Camus existence is not the basic premise of being, not an ontic point of departure. Rather it is what is implied in phrases like "to create an existence for oneself." It is structure-building, the reinforcement of being. This is shown very clearly in a conversation between Jonas in *The Artist at Work* and his friend Rateau, where he says that even the greatest artists are not sure that they exist: "So they look for proof; they judge; they condemn. This fortifies them. It's a beginning of existence." He is joking, of course, but a little later he sums up what he thinks of his own existence in all seriousness: "No, I can't be certain I exist. But I shall exist, I'm sure." [6] Thus "to have existence"—which is the way we really have to express it in Camus—means to have found a meaning, to have created a structure, which provides a basis for answering the one vital question: the question of life's value.

Jonas concretely demonstrates the creation of a structure that will make it possible for him to say *yes* again to life when he builds inside his apartment a kind of loft where he can paint. This structure he gives himself, this fixed place between exile and the kingdom, between heaven and earth, enables him to devote himself to art without denying his relatives and friends. It offers him the possibility of true—and for Camus this means meaningful—existence worth living.

Thus in Camus "existence" is not to be confused with "exile," for exile really means loss of meaning. It means—and in this case the meaning coincides with the etymology—to fall out of meaning. We have already encountered this kind of exile in *L'Etranger* and *La Peste*, but nowhere does it emerge in such "programmatic" clarity as in the novellas of *L'Exil et la royaume*. Whereas in *La Peste* and *Le Malentendu* it took the form of being cut off and excluded from the happiness of sea and shore, now corresponding forms of exile move into the foreground, variations on separateness, such as growing fat and old. Thus none of the main heroes in *L'Exil et le royaume* with the exception of Daru in *L'Hôte* and the Renegade have the unquestioned oneness with themselves that the Stranger possessed before the death of his mother, nor are they at what we have called the existential age, that is, between thirty and forty, as all Sartre's heroes are. They are all in their early forties or they reach forty in the course of the story. They all have to realize that they are getting fat, that they are relegating their last illusions to the reassuring structure of a set framework—turning them into souvenirs of illusions. As Sartre puts it, they have reached the age of their "last chance." Janine is *La Femme adultère* becomes conscious of her exile as she sits beside an unimaginative cloth merchant in a cross-county bus; she becomes aware of how ridiculous her name now sounds, this youthful, girlish, bright "Janine," how unsuited to a middle-aged woman who has put on so much weight that she has difficulty in bending over to get to her suitcase. Yvars in *Les Muets*, who is lame in one leg, rides his bicycle painfully over the cobblestones still wet with dew. Slight as he is, he feels the heaviness of age creeping up on him as he sits on the saddle, and he is forced to admit to himself that he long ago gave up looking out to sea on his daily ride to work. Jonas finds his creativity paralyzed and can paint nothing but sky. D'Arrast, the engineer in "*La Pierre qui pousse*," with his massive "*corps de colosse*," arriving in the kingdom of natives who dance as they walk, realizes that he is too heavy. All these illustrations go to show that Camus is trying here to exemplify the exile inherent in human existence.

Here we have something new, something that was not present in *L'Etranger* or *La Peste*. Here Camus breaks away from literature as World, and there is no doubt that this is connected with his choice of the novella genre. Although this whole novella cycle does depict a kind of panorama, in the individual stories the thematic emphasis is more important than the cosmic one, and this brings Camus closer to Sartre's concept of literature. In *L'Etranger* and *La Peste*, although the literary reality was centered in the theme, adapted to and integrated into a message-communicating structure, it was still a self-sufficient literary universe. Now, however, meaning is so far divorced from its literary incarnation that we miss an essential component of this work if we fail to discover a viable meaning in it.[7] Dr. Rieux, for instance, and Meursault too were individuals whose reasons for being what they were lay in themselves and in circumstances. But the reason for the adulterous woman's being fat and clumsy does not lie entirely in her lack of fulfillment in marriage; it is an indication of a given fact which can and must be divorced from the context: the exile inherent in human existence. Camus's use of physical heaviness to symbolize this notion of exile unquestionably represents a return to a Neoplatonic way of thinking; it reflects the opposition between matter and spirit that the early Camus was unwilling to admit.[8] He does, to be sure, shift the accent to fit his "Mediterranean religion." For the principle of a spiritualizing rise out of the bodily condition he substitutes a flexible capacity to adjust to cosmic reality (the kingdom of the nomads), indeed of unity with it.

Janine, who represents the purest embodiment of this Neoplatonic thematic idea, is driven by a longing for such perfect unity. A delicate fly circling around in the cross-country bus and settling on her husband's hand, a slim Frenchman who seems to be entirely constructed of bone and sand, the fine-limbed Arabs she sees during their stop at the oasis, the nakedness of the desert itself, and the "oneness" of the nomads who offer the only sign of life—all this becomes a call to leave her corporeality behind and find her way back to "lost time." But her husband's world of heavy, brightly colored fabrics holds her, and not until she tears herself away from his side to yield to the sky's cosmic force on the terrace of the fort does she recapture for a few minutes of ecstatic rapture her oneness with herself and feel herself in touch again with the sources of her being.

### Exile and the Kingdom

But we must not forget that Camus calls this union with night and stars adultery,[9] and that before going off on her "adventure" with the cosmos Janine told herself that she wanted "to be liberated, even if Marcel and the others never were" (p. 1571). This for Camus was the great sacrilege—an error like those of Martha in *Le Malentendu* and Victoria in *L'Etat de siège*, who set their personal happiness above solidarity with other people. Although in these two plays Camus had already abandoned his youthful pagan fantasy of an unproblematical feeling of oneness with nature, although in *La Peste* sun and water were able to regain their status as symbols of unity only after the gigantic struggle for human solidarity, now "the kingdom" has become completely divorced from "the real." It has become a dream of restless nomadic existence close to nature,[10] such as Janine can now only experience as a tourist. It is the sea which Yvars long ago gave up looking at.[11] It is nature, into which the engineer D'Arrast briefly enters, though only as a foreigner, as one who does not know the language of the country. It is the idealistic utopia in which the Renegade gets lost.

Is Camus then liquidating in *L'Exil et le royaume* his childhood dream of sun, seashore, and carefree oneness with world? Hardly. He is merely reducing it to proportions commensurate with the demands of human engagement and the reality of a life structure. In her adultery with night and stars Janine finds her way back to the sources of her being, to her roots, but this will not help her clumsiness and the symptoms of old age, neither will it save her from realizing that she must stand the test elsewhere: at her husband's side. Like Sartre's Goetz in *Le Diable et le bon Dieu*, the Renegade can try to establish successively a kingdom of absolute good and a king-

dom of absolute evil,[12] but his intention leads to self-ali
and murder. Yvars may persist in his dream of a far-off
happiness;[13] he may tell himself that the other man is to blame,
but these are nothing but subterfuges. What was needed was
the right word at the right moment.[14] Daru in *L'Hôte*—and
here we approach the positive side of the curve [15]—was right to
risk losing "the country in which he was happy," because
loyalty to a guest, even one forced upon him, demanded it, but
this does not change the threatening message he discovers on
the familiar school blackboard: "You turned in our brother.
You will pay for it." [16] Jonas would like to give full play to
human solidarity, but he comes to realize that this is injurious to
his art and finally makes it impossible for him to paint. He does
indeed find a solution in the end: the loft he builds inside his
apartment enables him to remain within the bosom of his family
and at the same time devote himself to art in comparative peace
and seclusion. But we must remember that the next morning
finds him sitting, exhausted, in front of a blank canvas,[17] just as
Daru's solution brings him aloneness and possibly death. These
are no longer ideal solutions but positions which, while providing a positive answer, bring out just as strongly the insoluble
antinomy, that is to say the absurdity, of what they are supposed to be an answer to.

The main thing is to keep the middle way between the inviting kingdom of the absolute and solidarity with one's fellow
men, to retain the longing for a kingdom of absolute happiness
without yielding to it entirely, to remain *à mi-chemin* like
Jonas [18] or like D'Arrast, who follows the path leading to the
church only so long as it is still the path to his friend's hut too.
But it is also important to realize that this "both/and" attitude
does not by any means dispel the absurdity of human existence
and that even the "growing stone," [19] like the rock of Sisyphus,
will never stop rolling down from the heights of joyous-painful
fulfillment [20] toward the foot of the hill, where Sartre and
Camus meet.

### La Chute

*La Chute*, the very title of which captures the downhill movement, will lead us back to the foot of this hill and hence—
though not by any means finally—back to Sartre.[21] This is already suggested by the book's outward structure, which not
only recalls *L'Etranger* (which had met with Sartre's approval)
in its axis-centered design but breaks the principle of continuous tension, thus removing one of the essential obstacles to a
meeting of Sartre and Camus. A diagram and short résumé of
the "plot" will explain this.

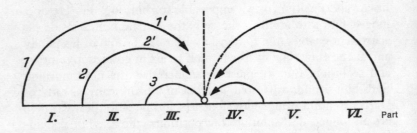

In the Mexico City Bar in Amsterdam the "hero," a former
lawyer, is telling his life story to an imaginary listener. He
cautiously approaches the central event (0) which plunged him
into the duplicity of guilt. In the first part [22] he merely circles
around this event at a distance (1), only venturing an open
allusion to it (1') toward the end. In the second part he first
draws away again (2) but then allows more and more references
to it to creep in (2'). Finally, in the third part, he goes straight
to the cause and effect of his guilt complex (3), postponing the
actual account of the event that was to become the focal point
of his entire thought and action until the end of this part, just
before the midpoint of the book.[23] A young woman had thrown
herself into the water (the fall), and he passively lets her drown,
thus plunging into guilt (the metaphorical fall). Parts IV to VI,
which are no less closely connected with this fall, now recount
his efforts to come to terms with his guilt. In a parallel to the
first half of the book these efforts now lead, at the end of Part

VI, to yet another recapitulation of the fall—this time as a purely imaginary chance to make amends for the injustice. Even this imaginary chance is denied, so that his fall into guilt is now explicitly affirmed.

The action of *La Chute* is an inward happening; the book is a kind of interior monologue, its phases concerned with one single phenomenon, with an omitted—that is, a negatively performed—action, allowing somebody to die, which is how the "hero," formerly a competent, helpful lawyer, became guilty. Thus we have here something similar to Frantz's "negative" action in *Les Séquestrés d'Altona* in which he passively watched a rabbi being strangled. But the analogy is limited. Frantz could not have intervened because his captors were holding him, whereas the lawyer could certainly have acted, though perhaps with little hope of success. There is also a strong analogy with the "negative" action of the Stranger, who let himself be driven by the sun. Otherwise, though, *La Chute* in comparison with *L'Étranger* and *Les Séquestrés* must be said to offer an extraordinarily novel and fresh approach to a basically analogous theme. The lawyer does not shut himself up in a room to atone for his guilt, nor is he forcefully sequestered in a prison cell which might offer him the opportunity to find himself. On the contrary, adopting a position between the sovereign Orestes and the remorseful Electra of *Les Mouches*, he steps up "into the pulpit" to become *juge-pénitent* and simultaneously judge. In a manner of speaking, he takes the initiative, anticipates other people's verdict through his self-accusation, but he turns his confession into a mirror which indicts all mankind.[24]

In *La Chute* we follow the circlings of this judging self-indictment. The *juge-pénitent* has selected an appropriate background for it, a setting as ambiguous as his interior monologue, as disjointed as he is himself. For the stone desert of Amsterdam and the Mexico City Bar [25] do not represent, as the beaches, sea, and sky of the Mediterranean do, the quintessence of oneness with oneself and the world. Their significance is much more like that of Prague in *L'Envers et l'endroit*: they represent the image and reality of non-oneness.

We have the steaming cauldron of a sea wreathed in dark drifts of fog, and this gives people a kind of duplicity: "I like these people, swarming on the sidewalks, crammed into a little area of houses and canals, hemmed in by fog and cold land, and by a sea that steams like washing. I like them because they're split. They're here and they're somewhere else too." [26] This is a people whose real destiny lies in the sunny South Sea islands; hence it becomes a living symbol of paradise lost—or paradise betrayed: it can no longer fulfill its destiny except in dreams. There is something ghostlike about this nation which, enveloped in fog, persists in its "golden dream."

> Holland, Monsieur, is a dream, a dream of gold and smoke, smokier in the daytime, more golden at night. And night and day this dream is peopled with Lohengrins like these, riding dreamily by on their black bicycles with high handlebars, funereal swans incessantly circling, all over the country, around the seas and along the canals.[27]

This is a city crisscrossed by canals and hemmed in by fog, rather like an Inferno.[28] And finally, as an absolutely concrete symbol of the dichotomy, there is the "gorilla" who controls the destinies of the Mexico City Bar, who makes only relucant use of any of the civilized languages heard in his seamen's bar, who envelops himself in the silence of his "native" virgin forest to become a perverted, almost extinct dream of far-off Java.

Thus the setting is an image of what is in the mind of the *juge-pénitent*; it is language participating in the confession he is about to make—though not without first having made sure that his silent listener is properly qualified to hear it and to identify with it, for its final purpose is to implicate all mankind in this guilt. Jean-Baptiste Clamence, as the *juge-pénitent* now calls himself, in a deliberate allusion to John the Baptist, the *vox clamans in deserto*,[29] has an eventful life behind him. Not unlike Camus's Renegade or even Sartre's Goetz, he has accumulated an essentially twofold experience. Twice he has set out from entirely different premises on a course which he expected to prove absolutely meaningful. Now in the Mexico City Bar he takes stock and draws some of the conclusions.

The first meaning to offer him anything to hold on to prior
to that "certain evening" was the sense of paradisiac ideality.[30]
In those days the present *juge-pénitent* was still a practicing
attorney, which enabled him to regard his professional activity
as consistent with his ideal of kindness (unlike the profession of
judge, which he despised). His favorite cases were those which
concerned widows and orphans. In private life too he personified helpfulness and amiability; he liked to help old people
to cross the street, and the pleasure he derived from this gave
him a feeling of sublimity: "At all hours of the day, within myself and among other people, I would ascend to the heights and
light visible fires there, and a joyous greeting would rise toward
me." [31] Since he was always successful in love too, he had every
reason to feel that he was one of the chosen, to regard himself as
a man who certainly did not owe his advantages to mere
chance.[32]

Yet even as he is talking about this "ideal" reality, this Eden
he lived in, he keeps remembering the evening when his ideality
proved to be an illusion, the evening when he was thrown back
upon the naked reality of himself.[33] Perhaps he would not have
been able to help the young lady dressed in black who jumped
into the water from the Pont Royal and whose cry he heard
drifting downstream, but he did not even try; he remained a
silent witness, an accomplice in death.

His ideality was shattered by this guilt, exposed as a lie, as
merely factitious reality. This guilt had made him realize that
his ideal reality was ultimately only a pretext for dominating
other people, for doing in his own way exactly as all the others
were doing, who, whatever their social position, could always
find someone a little beneath them to "look down on," even if it
were their own child.[34] It was not long before his proud
wholeness was shattered outwardly too, and he permitted himself unforgivable *faux pas* which revealed what was going on
inside him. He once lost his temper in the street and cursed a
motorcyclist—he even felt like boxing his ears—because his
stalled vechicle was blocking traffic and he wouldn't get out of
the way so that he, Clamence, and the other waiting cars that
were impatiently blowing their horns could pass. The episode

had ended in obvious defeat for the self-conscious widows' and orphans' attorney: a looker-on had intervened and punched the lawyer in the face to teach him that just because he was an automobile driver he had no right to curse and threaten a poor motorcyclist. Finally somebody in the crowd had added the crowning touch by calling him a "*pauvre type*."

And this was but one of several aggravating incidents. There was no doubt about it now: he was not a lawyer; ultimately he was a judge too. His "ideal" practice of the law was merely a pretext to make it easier for him to judge, to dominate more effectively. The punch in the face and the "*pauvre type!*" had shown beyond question that even he himself was not exempt from being judged. The one categorized him as heedless of social justice, the other as a poor devil deserving pity. And as this dawned upon him, he heard behind him a burst of laughter which destroyed his dream of being a complete man (p. 1501).

Since then (the beginning of the second half of *La Chute*) his one concern has been to come to terms with this sense of guilt, to find a new modus vivendi. First (Part IV) he tried to do this by looking the other person searchingly in the face, demasking him, and exposing ill will as the general rule of human conduct: "The only defense is to hit out yourself. That's why people are in a hurry to judge, so as not to be judged themselves." [35] He discovered that the love of truth is a merciless passion (p. 1515), and he could only shake his head in wonder at those extraordinary creatures who would die for the sake of money, fall into despair if they lost their job, and sacrifice themselves so that their families could live comfortably—in brief, those who so obviously had no ideals (pp. 1517 ff.). But these diversionary tactics did not help for long. The thought of death arose in him, prompting him to tell his lies to at least one other person before he died. The idea of challenging the laughter that haunted him, the idea of forestalling it by hitting a child in the subway for no reason at all or something of that sort—this too remained a dream. The only solution would have been "to accuse himself in a quite specific way," [36] as he now does as a *juge-pénitent*. At the time, however, he was not yet able to do that.

Then came his attempt (Part V) to break through to absolute meaning through debauchery.[37] Here, however, memory played him an ugly trick. He was on the deck of a ship, enjoying his lofty position (his old love of the lofty and the ideal, perverted now), when he noticed a black dot on the ocean. No matter what he did, he could never escape his guilt. There remained only one hope: the fact that all men are guilty.[38]

But he was not yet able to draw the conclusions from this insight. From his sickbed he tells how he made another attempt to escape into sublimity (Part VI). It was in a prison camp. He had been elected "pope," but his instinct for self-preservation was to topple him abruptly from this lofty position. He had drunk some water intended for a dying man, telling himself (in another of his *faux pas*) that they had more need of a pope than of a dying man. And then at last he had drawn the conclusions, recognized that justice and innocence are irreconcilably separated, and moved into the Mexico City Bar to practice the solution that had for so long been thrusting itself upon him: to forestall the other person's judgment by confessing his guilt, but to turn his confession into an indictment.[39] Nevertheless, along with *juge-pénitent's* utilitarianism goes a doctrine, and this doctrine, the quintessence of his experiences, will bring us very close to Sartre.

### Camus and Sartre

It is not as if *La Chute* were very far from Sartre's position anyway! On the contrary, to take one example, it obviously deals with the problem of "the other." The *juge-pénitent's* recognition that the hidden motive for his behavior was the will to dominate, and his consequent admission that, having become guilty, his only chance consisted in becoming a judge himself, contain much of that confrontation with "the other" that Sartre developed as a central phenomenon of existence. Aegisthus too became a *juge-pénitent* of this sort when he evaded judgment for his act of murder by "preaching" collective guilt and repentance. As for the *"pauvre type!"* which the lawyer had to swallow, its effect is very close to what Sartre calls objectification. In both cases the victim defends himself by seizing the initiative in order to master his opponent and try to get him into his power.

To be sure, the means they use and the place where the confrontation takes place are quite different. In Camus, as the fundamental dynamics of his thinking requires, it takes place in the vertical plane; it is a question of above and below, not of being or not being. The *juge-pénitent* is concerned to maintain his dominance or recapture it. For him it is essential to attain a hold over "the other" from above, to secure himself a "*cathedra*." For the Sartrean heroes, on the contrary, everything takes place on the horizontal plane; for them the decisive form of encounter is face to face; hence the glance, the duel in which each man takes the other's measure with the eye, is the standard confrontation. And what is at stake in this duel is not superiority or inferiority but death and life or objectness and being.

In *La Chute*, however, these differences for the first time appear more like slight divergences from a profound agreement, as for instance when the *juge-pénitent* encounters *his* equivalent of the crabs in *Les Séquestrés d'Altona*: the burst of laughter behind him. Laughter and these crabs are both signs of a guilt feeling, a feeling that one is being judged. Camus's symbol for this is vertical: a laugh that can become a cry. Sartre makes the sense of guilt concrete horizontally: as the undifferentiated thingness of "dumb" animals. Essentially, however, both symbols mean the same thing. Yet in the end the differences recede when the *juge-pénitent* comes to the quintessence of what he has to say, when his reminiscences become a statement of belief, a theory which he reveals as an existential oracle, as he lies in bed like some wounded king of the Holy Grail.

The first thing he has to say is that there is no excuse, no good intention to be pleaded. Rather, it is all a question of what has happened, a question of addition: you take a look, determine what has happened, and then you know with whom you are dealing. The next thing is that one is simply confronted by a choice in which one gets no help from the rules or from a father, and this freedom is a torture from which most people seek escape in discipline.

> But that's just it. There's no father, there are no rules
> any more! They're free, and they have to do the best they
> can, and as the one thing they don't want is freedom and its
> verdicts, they ask to have their fingers rapped, they invent
> terrible rules, and they rush out to build stakes for burning
> people, to replace churches.[40]

Man is afraid of this freedom, which also represents judgment: "But on the Paris bridges I learned that I too was afraid
of freedom." [41] This freedom deprives him of all possibility of
excuse, confronts him inescapably with the fact of having
failed. In this situation masters are precious and remorse is
precious too.

> So long live the master, whoever he may be, to replace
> the law of heaven! "Our father, who art provisionally
> here. . . . Our guides, our delightfully strict masters, O
> cruel and beloved leaders. . . ." In the end, you see, the
> essential thing is to cease being free and repentantly to obey
> somebody smarter than yourself. (Ibid.)

Obedience and repentance help one to avoid the real issue:
freedom and the personal guilt it inescapably confers. They
help one to attain what Sartre calls *mauvaise foi*.

It would take a lot of ingenuity to find any difference from
Sartre surviving in this attitude. The rock of Sisyphus has
rolled down the hill, and Sartre and Camus meet, with all their
differences behind them. Yet it is rather surprising that Camus
should use Sartrean terminology for this meeting in the abyss—
or at least a terminology behind which Sartre's specific position
is all too recognizable. Since throughout his work Camus shows
a fondness for irony, we are tempted to suppose that he would
like this agreement ultimately to serve the purpose of an argument with Sartre. This supposition is confirmed by what follows.

After the *juge-pénitent* has revealed this insight that man is
condemned to freedom, he will decide to get rid of this freedom, so important and so desirable to Sartre as ontic truth, as
quickly as he can because it separates him from his fellow men.

Since all mankind is afraid of freedom and flees from it, he will seek to become like the rest of humankind in this respect. He will opt not for inhuman, philosophically defined freedom but for the freedom of hounded mankind. He will become one of the despised and the persecuted, partly through his own doing, through his self-accusation, for in this way he can better "show his full worth" as a man. Only in this way can he be natural, whereas a desire to be free in the philosophical sense would force him into inhumanity.

> Isn't it good to live like the rest of society, and to do so isn't it necessary for society to be like me? [42] Intimidation, dishonor, the police—these are the sacraments of this resemblance. Despised, hounded, coerced, I can then show all I'm capable of, rejoice in what I am and be natural at last. And that, my dear friend, is why, after having solemnly saluted freedom,[43] I decided on the quiet that it should be passed on without delay to somebody else—anybody else.[44]

This passage leaves nothing to be desired in the way of clarity. Camus is again taking his distance from Sartre. Like Sisyphus, Jean-Baptiste Clamence has had to retrace his steps down to the valley, where he has "met Sartre" and been forced to agree with him as to the absurdity of his actions and existence. But he does not stop here any more than Sisyphus does. He is ultimately concerned, not with recognizing an ontic fact, but with wresting a meaning from absurdity itself.

The awareness of his absurdness will help him to do so: "But I'm better off because I know it, and this gives me the right to speak." [45] Accepting his situation also represents meaning to him: "I have accepted duplicity instead of getting upset about it." [46] And finally he experiences a triumphal flash of meaning when he can deflate one of the bourgeois citizens sitting with him in the Mexico City Bar in all his trumped-up verticality and make him beat his breast and become a man, aware of his guilt. That is the big moment of this "new Sisyphus": "Then I grow taller, my dear friend, I grow taller. I breathe freely. I am on the mountain, and the plain stretches before my eyes." [47] Paradoxical and absurd as it is, this is accepted and hence immanently meaningful absurdity—as meaningful as the closing sentence of *Le Mythe de Sisyphe*: "One must imagine Sisyphe happy." "Then, soaring in my thoughts above this whole continent, over which I hold sway without its knowing it, drinking in the absinthe-like daybreak, intoxicated finally with evil words, I am happy. I am happy. I am happy, I tell you. I forbid you not to believe that I am happy. I am happy enough to die!" (*Ibid.*)

Thus Camus remained true to himself to the end, and there is no reason to want to make *La Chute* an exception or to regret that he should have died right after such a "nihilistic" work. *La Chute* is not only one of the best things he ever wrote from the point of view of language and compositional technique; [48] as a formulation of the ideas he was trying to set forth it is in no way inferior to *L'Etranger* and *La Peste*—and perhaps even more fascinating. This is a formulation which, for all its irony and multiplicity of levels, shows Camus to be a writer who, like Sartre, takes the existentiality of existence as his given point of departure but accepts it as no more than a basis from which man must come to grips with the only vital question: whether life is worth living, whether there can be any meaning in being a man.

# Notes

*Introduction and Chapter 1*

1. These concepts, on which my book *Das Epos in den romanischen Literaturen* (Vol. 34 in the series *Sprache und Literatur*) is based, may be briefly explained as follows. Horizontality denotes essentially juxtaposition, being for itself, and identity.
   (Thus, for instance, parataxis in syntax; the "single-level" principle of the representative assembly and of democracy in sociol-
   ogy; the horizontal line and the plane in geometry; the independence of whatever is in metaphysics.) Verticality, conversely, is essentially stratification, connection, and differentiation
   (hypotaxis is syntax; monarchy and the court in society; space
   in geometry; the link between the here-and-now and the beyond
   in metaphysics).
2. I have therefore attempted no systematic discussion of the secondary literature—except for occasional footnotes. Such a discussion would undoubtedly have diverted me from my primary
   objective: to lead the reader to the literature itself.
3. Simone de Beauvoir indicated that Sartre's original intention in
   writing *La Nausée* was "to express metaphysical truths and feel-

ings in a literary form" (*La Force de l'âge*, Paris, 1960, p. 293). A. Manser in *Sartre: A Philosophical Study* (London, 1966) rightly stresses that the philosophical content is much denser in, say, *La Nausée* than in *Les Chemins de la liberté*. (See also note 7.)

4. We should not forget, however, that Sartre is enough of a writer not to deny this "lying element" in writing. He says in *L'Etre et le néant* (Paris, 1943, p. 687): "Above all, the writer must never stop lying."

5. See W. Engler's very useful survey *Der französische Roman von 1800 bis zur Gegenwart* (Bern, 1945, p. 240).

6. See pp. 39–40.

7. Manser stresses this danger of misunderstanding: "The danger that Sartre runs in exposing his philosophical views in the way and to the extent that he does in the novels is that his point will be missed, that people, knowing he is a philosopher, will take certain things to be expressions of his views when they are meant quite otherwise" (*Sartre*, pp. 175 ff.).

8. L'Etre et le néant (Paris, 1943, p. 96).

9. *Ibid.*, p. 95.

10. A suggested reading list to provide a background of Sartrean philosophy sufficient for the appreciation of his literary works would begin with Sartre's own short, somewhat popular *L'Existentialisme est un humanisme* (Paris, 1946), even though it may be said to present him in too "positive" a light. Among the secondary literature, R. Campbell's *Jean-Paul Sartre ou une littérature philosophique* (3rd ed., Paris, 1947) deserves first mention. This work starts out from philosophical categories and looks for them in literature. This procedure is unsatisfactory as literary criticism but is a useful heuristic device. O. F. Bollnow's *Französischer Existentialismus* (Stuttgart, 1965) is also recommended as an introduction. *Le Problème moral et la pensée de Jean-Paul Sartre* (Paris, 1947) by F. Jeanson deals with the questions of Sartrean ethics in a way which Sartre himself approved, but the book is not really a suitable introduction to the literary reality. A. Niel's *Jean-Paul Sartre. Héros et victime de la "Conscience malheureuse"* (Paris, 1966) is stimulating though slightly biased. For Sartre's politics and philosophy, G. A. Zehm's *Historische Vernunft und direkte Aktion* (Stuttgart, 1964) is recommended. (Zehm also deals with the literary themes. The often distinctly polemical tone is unfortunate.) On the philosophical power of Sartrean literature itself (as distinct from Campbell's thematic

external approach), see Manser *(Sartre)*. On the philosophical power of his style, see F. Jameson's extraordinarily stimulating study *Sartre: The Origins of a Style* (New Haven, London, 1961). (This book will yield its full value only to a fairly leisurely reading.)

## Chapter 2

1. As M. Kruse notes in an essay on *La Nausée* ("Philosophie und Dichtung in Sartres *La Nausée*" in Romanistisches Jahrbuch, IX [1958], p. 215), Sartre was in all likelihood acquainted with Aurel Kolnai's phenomenological study "Der Ekel" (*Jahrbuch für Philosophie und phänomenologische Forschung*, 10 [1929], p. 515). Sartre's avoidance, despite this theoretical approach, of the danger of disincarnation is all the more admirable.

2. Jeanson's acute definition of *nausée* does not quite do justice to the element of *lucidité*: "Nausea is the feeling of existing, it is existence reduced to feeling oneself exist" (*Sartre par lui même: Ecrivains de toujours*, Paris, 1955, p. 124).

3. We do not see this, as Kruse does, as a contradiction of Sartre's philosophical position and hence as an argument against the philosophical significance of *La Nausée*. Kruse says: "Nowhere in *La Nausée* does the notion of *exister* contain the ethical demand for self-realization found in Sartre's later works" ("Philosophie und Dichtung in Sartres *La Nausée*," p. 216). The Sartrean philosophy incarnated in *La Nausée* is indeed not yet an ethics. Sartre was forced to set aside this part of his philosophy in order to capture the philosophical phenomenon of nausea within a closed esthetic structure. To point to responsibility would have been to distract the reader from the specific phenomenal aspect with which *La Nausée* was exclusively concerned and to give him a moral reassurance "harmful" to existential thinking. (See also my critical observations on the ending of *La Nausée* on p. 26.)

4. See Sartre's *L'Etre et le néant*, p. 14: "Being will be unveiled to us through some immediate means of access—boredom, nausea, and so on—and ontology will be the description of the phenomenon of being just as it reveals itself, that is, without intermediary." This reveals how ontological the whole conception of *La Nausée* unquestionably is.

5. B. T. Fitch is therefore right when he says in *Le Sentiment d'étrangeté chez Malraux, Sartre, Camus et Simone de Beauvoir* (Paris, 1964, p. 136): *La Nausée* enjoys an incontestable novelistic autonomy and . . . thus it is not the novelized philosophical treatise that one might have supposed." This is what justifies a purely literary study of the kind undertaken by Kruse. To prevent misunderstandings it should perhaps be added that a novel which is not a "philosophical treatise" may very well have philosophical significance.

6. See *La Nausée* (Paris, 1938), p. 26.

7. *Ibid.*, p. 30.

8. *Ibid.*, p. 30.

9. See also Sartre's attitude to François Mauriac in *Situations l* (Paris, 1947), pp. 36 ff, and his essay "Qu'est-ce que la littérature?" (Paris, 1947).

10. Simone de Beauvoir confirms the validity of this view inasmuch as she indicates in *La Force de l'âge* that Sartre, seemingly in response to her suggestion, deliberately tried to give this book a novelistic structure: "In its very first version *La Nausée* was a long, abstract meditation on contingency. I urged Sartre to give Roquentin's discovery a novelistic dimension, and to add a bit of suspense, which we enjoyed in detective novels. He agreed" (p. 111). In *Les Chemins de la liberté* this striving for a structure which, though esthetic, is still suited to the philosophical content moves even more into the foreground. Thus he draws inspiration for his novelistic technique from others. (See note 1, Chapter 3.) But this explicit intention was obviously unfavorable to the unity of the work and led to a divergence between his esthetic and philosophical purposes, so that the philosophical element sometimes shows up as a reflective reality almost alien to the work.

11. *La Nausée*, p. 44.

12. *Ibid.*, p. 42.

13. Here Kruse calls attention to Rilke's *Malte Laurids Brigge* as a possible literary model ("Philosophie und Dichtung in Sartre's *La Nausée*." pp. 220 ff.). In 1936, in *L'Envers et l'endroit*, Camus had used the metaphor of a stay in Prague to present an analogous existential experience. In *L'Emploi du temps* (1956) Michel Butor was to offer yet another formulation of this myth of an alien, unmasterable city so common in modern literature.

14. *La Nausée*, p. 142.

15. Roquentin indicates that he is to be numbered among the "existentialists" when he says of the autodidact that he is a man of the same type as M. Achille, the type that betrays out of ignorance and goodwill (*La Nausée*, p. 154).
16. *La Nausée*, p. 94.
17. *Ibid.*, p. 127.
18. *Ibid.*, p. 128.
19. *Ibid.*, p. 130.
20. *Ibid.*, p. 131.
21. *Ibid.*, pp. 133–157.
22. *Ibid.*, p. 155.
23. *Ibid.*, p. 156
24. *Ibid.*, pp. 161–171.
25. The full significance of the visionary nature of this understanding, as Kruse rightly stresses, emerges only from the context of the novel ("Philosophie und Dichtung in Sartres *La Nausée*," p. 218). However, this does not negate the philosophical importance of what it is that Roquentin has come to understand or of the experience itself.
26. *La Nausée*, p. 161. By "bench marks" (*reperes*) Sartre means man's frantic, hopeless efforts to make himself part of an essential structure.
27. *La Nausée*, p. 161.
28. *Ibid.*, p. 163.
29. *Ibid.*, p. 164.
30. *Ibid.*
31. *Ibid.*, p. 166.
32. *Ibid.*, p. 169.
33. *Ibid.*, pp. 172–194.
34. This reflects Sartre's first philosophical "phase," the phase of imagination, as it expressed itself in the philosophical treatises *L'Imagination* (1936), *Esquisse d'une theorie des émotions* (1939), and *L'Imaginaire* (1940).
35. *La Nausée*, p. 190.
36. *Ibid.*
37. *Ibid.*, p. 193.
38. *Ibid.*, pp. 195–197.
39. *Ibid.*, pp. 201–211.
40. *Ibid.*, p. 211.
41. *La Nausée*, p. 218. Here Kruse refers to Goethe's *Die Leiden des jungen Werther*, a "novel in letters" which has the same

"diary" character. Here, in a letter dated July 16, Werther speaks of a tune Lotte used to play on the piano which would relieve him of all "suffering, perplexities, and general gloominess" ("Philosophie und Dichtung in Sartres *La Nausée*," p. 224). More pertinent, though, seems to be her reference to the meaning of the *"petite phrase de Vinteuil"* in Proust's *A la Recherche du temps perdu*.

42. Zehm calls attention (*Historische Wernunft*, p. 31)) to a little essay Sartre published in 1948 in which he says of American jazz (as quoted by Zehm): "The musicians concentrate on the best they have in them, all that is dryest and most free, which seeks not melody but the muted explosion of the moment" (Sartre: *"Au Nick's Bar"* in *Caliban*, 7 [1948]).

43. *La Nausée*, p. 221.

44. *Ibid.*, p. 217.

45. *Ibid.*, p. 216.

46. The almost devotional ending of *La Nausée* has disappointed many readers, and in fact it is not very convincing. (See Fitch: *Le Sentiment d'étrangeté*, p. 138.) With some justification, C. E. Magny links this ending with Sartre's philosophy of imagination and, referring to *L'Imaginaire*, written in 1940, attributes the unconvincingness to the fact that "at the very moment of writing *La Nausée*, Sartre already knew that this salvation is also illusory. An unreal universe is not really even a world—this is as true for the novelist's or the painter's universe as for those of the madman or the mythomaniac" ("Le Système de Sartre" in *Esprit*, I [1945], pp. 569 ff.). See also p. 26 of the present study.

47. The fact that we distinguish between novelistic and inner structure shows that we are attempting here to see two aspects of a single reality: the reality of the novel *La Nausée*. In "Sartre ou la Duplicité de l'Etre" in *Les Sandales d'empédocles* (Neuchâtel, 1945, pp. 137 ff.) Magny speaks of two novels, one inside the other, and distinguishes between a series of meditations by Roquentin and a *"trame proprement romanesque."* We find no such esthetic cleavage; on the contrary, we believe we have shown that in *La Nausée* the meditations and the action achieve a convincing structural unity.

48. As already mentioned, Kruse has noted the kinship with *Die Leiden des jungen Werther*. In support of her thesis that Rilke in *Malte Laurids Brigge* and Sartre in *La Nausée* reworked Goethe's *ennui* theme, she points out ("Philosophie und Dich-

tung," p. 224) that Sartre mentions the young Werther (*La Nausée*, p. 217)).

49. *La Nausée*, p. 106.

50. *Ibid.*, p. 83.

51. Another point to note here is the "horizontal" present—the tense not only of *La Nausée* but of most of Sartre's novellas and of *Les Chemins de la liberté*. See R.-M. Albérès: *Jean-Paul Sartre* (7th ed., Paris, 1964), p. 38. As J. Bloch-Michel says in "Une Littérature d'ennui" in *Preuves*, 131 (1962), pp. 17 ff., this is the tense of "strangeness" and "solitude," the tense which creates "a world of objects divested of all meaning and existing only through their presence." Thus the present tense produces an effect quite in keeping with Sartrean ontology.

52. *La Nausée*, p. 12.

53. *Ibid.*, p. 22.

54. This does not exclude a deliberate drawing away from Husserl and Heidegger such as Manser (*Sartre*, Chapter 1) posits for *La Nausée*.

55. *La Nausée*, p. 23. Here, and throughout, the italics are Sartre's own. They usually denote that in this instance the word is to have an ontological dimension. Sartre's use of capitalization on the other hand (as in "*Homme*") always has an almost idealizing, sometimes even allegorizing function.

56. *La Nausée*, p. 23.

57. *La Nausée*, p. 96. This transformation of the hand into an independent thing occurs elsewhere in modern literature, too. Albérès (*Sartre*, p. 4) mentions Malraux and Rilke; Fitch (*Le Sentiment d'étrangeté*, p. 108, note) cites Claude Simon's *Le Tricheur* (Paris, 1945, p. 113) and Samuel Beckett's *Molloy* (Paris, 1951, p. 100). In Camus there are only suggestions of this, as for instance when Meaursault is embarrassed because the director of the old people's home holds his hand so long that he doesn't know how to withdraw it. (*L'Etranger*, Paris, 1942, p. 5).

58. *La Nausée*, pp. 127 ff.

59. We cannot therefore accept without qualification Magny's statement: "Wherever Roquentin's experience acquires ontological significance, Sartre changes from a writer into a philosopher" (*Sartre ou la duplicité de l'être*, pp. 166 ff.).

60. *La Nausée*, pp. 33 ff. This avoidance of all deduction finds its counterpart in the style, as Jameson has shown. The example from *L'Age de raison* (pp. 54 ff.), his point of departure, is

particularly telling (*Sartre*, pp. 20 ff.). Here Sartre juxtaposes the two polar extremes of an event. Mathieu sees a vase, picks it up, and smashes it on the floor. Sartre reduces this to two images, Mathieu seeing the vase and the vase lying in fragments on the floor, thus making both of them absolute as image. See also Jameson (pp. 29 ff.) on the description of a park on Sunday in *La Nausée*.

61. Cf. the ideas Sartre expresses on the nature of story-telling in *La Nausée* (pp. 57–59) and Jameson's remarks on them (*Sartre*, pp. 25 ff.).

62. See René Girard: *Mensonge romantique et vérité romanesque* (Paris, 1961) and Lucien Goldmann: *Pour une sociologie du roman* (Paris, 1964).

63. P. Thody says in *Jean-Paul Sartre: A Literary and Political Study* (London, 1960, p. 37): "Each one of the stories . . . has a conciseness which comes from being written to illustrate a particular philosophical point."

64. J. Weightman in "Jean-Paul Sartre" in *The Novelist as Philosopher*, ed. J. Cruickshank (London, 1962, pp. 106 ff), says that "the stories are not uniformly successful" and speaks of "the least convincing of the stories."

65. *Le Mur*, p. 239. Page numbers of quotations from *Le Mur* refer to the Gallimard edition (Paris, 1939).

66. *Le Mur*, p. 102.

67. *Ibid.*, p. 152. It should be explained that Lucien's nonauthenticity does not lie in what he actually decides to do but in the subjective perspective which leads to his decision.

## Chapter 3

1. As G. Zeltner-Neukomm notes in *Des Wagnis des französischen Gegenwartsromans* (Reinbek, 1960, p. 45), Dos Passos' trilogy *U.S.A.* was probably among the works that inspired Sartre here. On Sartre's technique in *Le Sursis*, see also P. de Boisdeffre: *Métamorphose de la littérature* (Paris, 1963), Vol. II, pp. 272 ff.

2. *L'Age de raison* (Paris, 1945), p. 113.

3. *Ibid.*, p. 124.

4. *Ibid.*, p. 122.

5. *Ibid.*, p. 123. In this quotation the language of the "temptations" takes on a Biblical, Christian tone.

6. *L'Age de raison*, p. 125.

7. *Ibid.*, p. 129. Here it becomes quite obvious that Mathieu is not to be taken as an ideal figure.

8. *L'Age de raison*, p. 200. Variations on the theme of self-injury recur throughout Sartre. In *Le Diable et le bon Dieu* it acquires a quite different significance. See K. Douglas: "The Self-inflicted Wound" in *Sartre*, ed. by E. Kern (Englewood Cliffs, N. J., 1962), pp. 39–46.

9. *L'Age de raison*, p. 221.

10. *Ibid.*, p. 249. The maxim *l'existence précède l'essence* comes out very clearly here.

11. *L'Age de raison*, p. 308.

12. *Ibid.*, p. 309. Note the masterful ending which recapitulates the title word for word, rounding off the book and at the same time making a final point.

13. *Le Sursis* (Paris, 1945), p. 26.

14. *Ibid.*, p. 70.

15. *Ibid.*, p. 87.

16. *Ibid.*, p. 168.

17. *Ibid.*, p. 285.

18. *Ibid.*, p. 286.

19. *La Mort dans l'âme* (Paris, 1949), p. 94.

20. *Ibid.*, p. 197.

21. That Sartre originally had no intention of making Brunet an ideal figure is shown by this sentence from Simone de Beauvoir's *La Force de l'âge* (p. 387): ". . . Sartre explained to me how, in the third volume of *Les Chemins de la liberté*, Brunet would become disgusted by the German-Soviet pact and leave the Communist Party; he would go to Mathieu for help—something that Sartre considered a necessary reversal of the situation developed in the first volume."

22. *La Mort dans l'âme*, p. 202.

23. Manser says: "Brunet avoids all Mathieu's errors" (*Sartre*, p. 171). But he also adds: ". . . but develops others of his own." We shall soon see proof of it.

24. *La Mort dans l'âme*, p. 284. Note the peculiar way in which this image of a little girl holding a hoop becomes for Sartre an expression of superannuation—and this in one of the few cases where Sartre creates a "real" child. (In Lucien, by contrast,

there is from the outset something adult, something unusually reflective.)

25. *La Mort dans l'âme*, p. 281.

26. *Ibid.*, p. 296. Here Sartre strongly stresses the analogy with a community of religious belief. In both cases, only one who "has the faith" can be helped.

27. *La Mort dans l'âme*, p. 298. There is a suggestion of symbolism here which recalls the autodidact's final departure from the Bouville Library.

28. Nonetheless Simone de Beauvoir writes in *La Force de l'âge* (p. 529): In *Les Mouches*, Sartre was urging the French to free themselves from remorse and to reclaim their freedom."

29. *Les Mouches*, in *Théâtre I* (Paris, 1947), p. 27.

30. *Ibid.*, p. 14.

31. See K. Hamburger: *From Sophocles to Sartre*, trans. by Helen Sebba. (New York, 1969).

32. *Les Mouches*, p. 29.

33. *Ibid.*, p. 40. The novel, structured on continuity and development, could never have permitted such an ideal shift in Sartrean thinking.

34. *Les Mouches*, p. 68. Note the italicized *"in"*—a sign that this word carries ontological weight. Here Sartre was particularly concerned with the phenomenon of space whose dimensions structurally include man.

35. *Les Mouches*, p. 69.

36. *Ibid.*, p. 72.

37. *Ibid.*, p. 85. Both are oriented toward creating a structure; both want to obliterate the horizontal reality of freedom.

38. *Les Mouches*, p. 86.

39. On remorse and freedom in Sartre, see M. Otto: *Reue und Freiheit. Versuch über ihre Beziehung im Ausgang von Sartres Dramen* (Freiburg, Munich, 1961). Otto says: "For him [Sartre] remorse is the essence of corruption and to resist its temptation is the real test of freedom" (p. 27).

40. *Les Mouches*, p. 105.

41. *Ibid.*, p. 111.

42. *Ibid.*, p. 119.

43. Otto makes this excellent observation on the freedom Orestes has won: "It is freedom assaulted and ferociously torn apart by its own meaning; it releases man from slavery only to offer him nothingness instead."

44. Cf. B. Guyon: "Sartre et le Mythe d'Oreste" in *VIIe Congrès Aix-en-Provence* (Paris, 1964), pp. 42–54.

## Chapter 4

1. *Les Mouches*, for instance, having three acts, was to some degree subject to the principle of tension. However, this division into three acts was superseded from within by the division of the middle act into two scenes. See also the detailed analysis on p. 76.

2. The syntax too shows a horizontal cast. Short sentences without subordinate clauses follow one another paratactically. Anacolutha are common. The following passage is typical: "And we blink our eyes. A wink, it was called. A quick black flash, a curtain that falls and is raised: the incision is made. The eye is moistened, the world is destroyed" (p. 130).

3. "Epic theater" in this sense is not to be equated with Brecht's concept of epic theater in *Kleines Organon für das Theater*. On this whole question, see also M. Kesting: *Das epische Theater* (Stuttgart, 1959) and R. Grimm (ed.): *Episches Theater* (Cologne, 1966). "Epic drama," regardless of other connotations, should be seen from the viewpoint of the internal formal principles of dramatic writing rather than the audience-stage relationship on which Brecht bases it.

4. *Huis clos in Théâtre I* (Paris, 1947), p. 174. The italicization of "*can't have*" is significant. It is intended to make this *inability* to run away an absolute statement against which practical reality fades into irrelevance.

5. *Huis clos*, p. 175.

6. *Ibid.*, p. 179.

7. Butor makes Léon Delmont, the hero of *La Modification*, even older—and this is no accident. The age Butor is interested in is the age at which man is already determined, hemmed in by structures. (See my essay in *Der moderne französische Roman*.)

8. *Morts sans sépulture* in *Théâtre I*, p. 201.

9. *Ibid.*, p. 228.

10. *Ibid.*, p. 211.

11. *Ibid.*, p. 234.

*Chapter 5*

1. On the political aspect of this section, see Zehm's *Historische Vernunft*, pp. 88 ff.
2. *L'Age de raison* appeared so much later because no publisher was prepared to bring out *"un roman aussi scandaleux,"* and the manuscript lay in Sartre's drawer for years. (See Simone de Beauvoir: *La Force de l'âge*, pp. 528 ff.)
3. See M. Cranston: "Jean-Paul Sartre" in *Der Monat*, V, 1962 and M. Natanson: "Sartre's Philosophy of Freedom" in *Social Research*, II, 1952; also Zehm's book, cited earlier, on Sartre's politics and philosophy, to which I am indebted.
4. See Jeanson's *Le Problème moral*, p. 46.
5. On Sartre's politics, see Zehm's already cited studies; P. de Boisdeffre's *Métamorphose*, pp. 301–315, and P. Thody's *Jean-Paul Sartre*, pp. 172–179 and 235 ff.
6. As quoted in Zehm's *Historische Vernunft*, p. 168.
7. See Thody, *Jean-Paul Sartre*, p. 88. On the unintentionally comic effect of *La Putain* in America, see Eric Bentley: "Sartre's Struggle for Existence" in *Sartre*, ed. E. Kern (Englewood Cliffs, N. J.), pp. 73 ff.
8. In this connection it is worth noting that in *Morts sans sépulture* we are confronted with a whole group of people right away. Hitherto we have always been introduced into the world of the play by two characters only.
9. *La Putain respectueuse in Théâtre I* (Paris, 1947), p. 294.
10. *Ibid.*, p. 315.
11. The existentiality of existence is, however, unaffected by this; this existentiality is what is real, what is merely glossed over by the structure.
12. *The Times* (London), September 24, 1954, as quoted by Zehm (*Historische Vernunft*, p. 210).
13. *Les Mains sales* (Paris, 1948), p. 142.
14. *Ibid.*, p. 240.
15. *Ibid.*, p. 242. Meursault in Camus's *L'Etranger* gives the same answer to his judges.
16. *Les Mains sales*, p. 257. The name Raskolnikoff, an allusion to the hero of Dostoevski's *Crime and Punishment*, may suggest a source of Sartre's problem theme of action. Raskolnikoff had planned a murder, but committed it out of completely different

motives. For a long time afterward he fought against taking refuge in remorse and atonement (cf. especially *Les Mots*) and deliberately tried to think of his murder purely theoretically.

17. Cf. Sartre's interview with Kenneth Tynan in *Die Zeit*, July 7, 1961.

18. Boisdeffre says "This rich, long, enigmatic work, like a mirror that is too faithful, reflects Sartre's major philosophical themes" (*Métamorphose*, p. 294).

19. This might, as Manser suggests, be interpreted as a formal parallel to the kinship between *Les Séquestrés d'Altone* and *Critique de la raison dialectique*. Manser notes passages which coincide word for word.

20. In *Nouvelles littéraires*, October 1, 1959. It is not surprising of course that a "social" play which takes place within a family setting should have earned the particular approval of Gabriel Marcel.

21. Sartre believed he had invented the name, but actually he had chanced upon the name of a family opposed to the National Socialist regime!

22. *Les Séquestrés d'Altona* (Paris, 1959), p. 19.

23. In an interview Sartre indicated the multiple meaning of the title: "Léni is a *séquestrée* because she is incestuous; old Gerlach is the powerful industrialist—*un grand bourgeois*—who is a *séquestré* because of his class. Frantz is also a *séquestré* from the beginning" (*Tulane Drama Review*, V, 1961, p. 14). On other interpretations of the title, see also H. Lausberg: *Interpretationen dramatischer Dichtung*, Vol. I (Munich, 1962), p. 110.

24. *Les Séquestrés d'Altona*, 44.

25. In his essentially allegorical interpretation of the play Lausberg tries to see both Johanna and Léni as personifications of art, while admitting that he is proposing this reading more or less independently of the "marked intention of the author" (*Interpretationen*, Vol. I, p. 181). F. N. Mennemeier in *Das moderne Drama des Auslandes* (Düsseldorf, 1965) interprets *Les Séquestres* as "a tragedy of fascism" (pp. 183–192).

26. *Les Séquestrés d'Altona*, p. 202.

27. *Ibid.*, p. 206. Cf. Sartre's interview with O. F. Pucciani in which he sees Frantz's real guilt as lying not in his actions but in his reactions to actions: "The first sign that Frantz was really guilty of torture, that he was actually the first to torture, is his reaction to the Jewish prisoners. He was disgusted by their dirt

and their degradation rather than revolted by their plight. This is not the sort of reaction to have." (Note the ethical imperative—"to have"—which Sartre here applies to action.)

28. Cf. the parallel of the old women in *Les Mouches* who can hardly hide the pleasure they derive—though behind closed windows—from the murder of the king.

29. *Les Séquestrés d'Altona*, p. 218.

## Chapter 6

1. *Les Jeux sont faits* (Paris, 1966), p. 91.

2. *Ibid.*, p. 93. Sartre certainly used the word "authentically" quite deliberately. His concern is the claim to authenticity of the "myth" of love.

3. *Les Jeux sont faits*, pp. 141 ff. In picking these names, did Sartre have in mind a parallel to the account of Paradise in Genesis (Adam and Eve)? There is considerable support for the assumption.

4. *Les Jeux sont faits*, p. 161. Ontologically Pierre's statement is correct; practically it is false. Here, as so often, Sartre is playing with two possible points of view.

5. *Les Jeux sont faits*, p. 162.

6. *Ibid.*, p. 165.

7. *Ibid.*, p. 180. It is worth noting that despite Eve's great excitement and insistence, Sartre does not italicize "can't." This is a kind of negative confirmation that Sartre's italics always denote that an ontological statement is to be taken as absolute.

8. From the back cover of the Gallimard edition (Paris, 1951).

9. *Le Diable et le bon Dieu* (Paris, 1951), p. 93.

10. *Ibid.*, p. 117.

11. *Ibid.*, p. 133.

12. *Ibid.*, p. 155.

13. In the eighth and ninth scenes, pp. 235 ff.

14. One might say that now for the first time Raskolnikoff (see note 16, Chapter 5 of this volume) finds his Sonia.

15. *Le Diable et le bon Dieu*, p. 185.

16. *Ibid.*, p. 193.

17. *Ibid.*, p. 199.

18. *Ibid.*, p. 213.

19. *Ibid.*, p. 215.

20. *Ibid.,* p. 219. Contrast the impossibility of togetherness in *La Nausée* (pp. 119 ff. of the present work) and *Les Chemins de la liberté*.
21. *Le Diable et le bon Dieu,* p. 263.
22. *Ibid.,* p. 275. This definition is very close to the well-known one of Saint-Exupéry: "Loving does not mean looking at one another, but looking together in the same direction" (*Terre des Hommes,* Ed. de la Pléiade, p. 252).
23. *Le Diable et le bon Dieu,* p. 280. They thus achieve what for Roquentin was to remain a vain hope.
24. Here again we feel the closeness to Saint-Exupéry, despite the strongly existentialist tone. We are reminded of Rivière in *Vol de nuit*. Two points are particularly interesting in Goetz's decision: his desire to "be with them all" and his acceptance of an imperative: "There's this war to be fought." Although this does not amount to an admission of given values, it is certainly a first step toward recognizing principles of action.

## Chapter 7

1. Interview with Guiton in *Opéra,* February 2, 1951, as quoted in Zehm's *Historische Vernunft*.
2. *L'Invitée* (Gallimard, Paris, 1962), p. 12.
3. On the nature of this kinship, see Fitch: *Le Sentiment d'étrangeté,* pp. 154 ff. In the footnote to p. 156 he quotes word-for-word similarities.
4. Whether these two people are convincingly characterized is, of course, another question. Fitch thinks they are not (*Le Sentiment d'étrangeté* p. 161) and that Simone de Beauvoir did better with Xavière. One is inclined to agree.
5. See G. Gennari: *Simone de Beauvoir: Classiques du XXe siècle* (Paris, 1958), p. 41.
6. *L'Invitée,* p. 440.
7. *Ibid.,* p. 21.
8. Fitch recognizes the danger of this closeness to biographical reality even in *L'Invitée* (*Le Sentiment d'étrangeté,* p. 150).
9. *Les Mandarins* (Paris, 1961), p. 579.
10. *Les Mots* (Paris, 1964), pp. 7 ff. My italics.
11. *Les Mots,* pp. 34 ff. Sartre is bringing out the independence of the individual elements in this cosmos of words. This is why he

chose the horizontal notion of *"mot"* for his title rather than the synthetic concept of *"parole."*

12. *Les Mots*, p. 37.
13. *Ibid.*, p. 39.
14. *Ibid.*, p. 35.
15. *Ibid.*, p. 47.
16. *Ibid.*, p. 24.
17. *Ibid.*, p. 66.
18. *Ibid.*, p. 70. That was also the experience of Roquentin and of Lucien in *L'Enfance d'un chef*. Are we to conclude that *La Nausée* and *L'Enfance d'un chef* were autobiographical or, conversely, that *Les Mots* is a work of fiction? The truth lies, as is so often the case, on both sides or—if you prefer—in the middle.
19. *Les Mots*, p. 73.
20. *Ibid.*, p. 78.
21. *Ibid.*, p. 83.
22. *Ibid.*, p. 149.
23. *Ibid.*, p. 152. Since something constructive is involved here, Sartre introduces the term *"parole"* for "word."
24. *Les Mots*, p. 209.
25. *Les Mots*, p. 211. [My italics.]

### Chapter 8

1. Quoted by R. Quilliot in his biography of Camus in *Camus: Théâtre, récits, nouvelles* (Ed. de la Pléiade), p. XXXIII.
2. Another point of contact, rightly stressed by J. Netzer in "Sartre et Camus" (in *Le Français dans le monde*, VIII, 1962, pp. 16 ff.), is that they both believed that literature has a social function.
3. A. Noyer-Weidner even goes so far as to apply "the fundamental existential thesis that existence precedes essence" at least to *Le Mythe de Sisyphe* and *L'Etranger* ("Albert Camus im Stadium der Novelle" in *Zeitschrift für französische Sprache und Literatur*, 70, 1960, pp. 1–38 and 35). The positing of practical values, however, he regards as an alien element—quite correctly so far as principles are concerned. Fitch (*Le Sentiment d'étrangeté*) is essentially justified in stressing the kinship between Sartre and Camus, but it would have been at least equally

important to bring out their differences, as Noyer-Weidner does in his point about "practical values."

4. See Zehm: *Historische Vernunft*, pp. 156 ff. Also J. Cruickshank:*Albert Camus and the Literature of Revolt* (Oxford, 1959), pp. 120–127.

5. H. Peyre takes a different view: "Our conviction is that not only *La Nausée* but *Les Chemins de la liberté* tower above most European fiction of the years 1935–1955" ("Sartre's Roads to Freedom" in *Sartre*, ed. E. Kern, pp. 31–38).

6. On Sartre's general esthetic and philosophical development, see Gaëtan Picon's survey: "Sartre par lui-même" in *L'Usage de la lecture* (Mercure de France, 1961), pp. 131–137.

7. This is not the only instance where Camus in his synthetic manner anticipates a theme which Sartre was to treat fundamentally on a broad scale. So far as I know, a study of this has yet to be made. I feel sure that it would reveal several cases where Camus influenced Sartre's choice of themes.

8. Fitch tends to underestimate the difference. Comparing *La Nausée* and *L'Envers et l'endroit*, he says: "The only difference is that for the hero of *La Nausée* things do not have a 'miraculous value' " (*Le Sentiment d'étrangeté*, p. 120.).

9. *L'Envers et l'endroit* in *Albert Camus*, Ed. de la Pléiade, p. 31.

10. *Ibid.*, p. 34.

11. *L'Eté*, Ed. de la Pléiade, p. 865.

12. *Le Mythe de Sisyphe*, Ed. de la Pléiade, p. 99.

13. Ed. de la Pléiade, p. 1169.

14. In Camus's remarks on Sartre's *La Nausée* in *Alger républicain*, October 20, 1938. Ed. de la Pléiade, pp. 1417 ff.

15. *L'Envers et l'endroit*, p. 28. Note the importance of the "*image.*" Here is another point of contact with the early Sartre through which other differences and common features could be exposed.

16. *Commentaires* on *L'Envers et l'endroit*, Ed. de la Pléiade. p. 1177.

17. In his preface to the new (1958) edition of *L'Envers et l'endroit*, Camus himself said that his "source" lay in that work. See R. de Luppé: "La Source unique d'Albert Camus" in *La Table ronde*, February 1960, pp. 30–40.

18. A. Fronton believed that such a philosophical system could be found in Stoicism. In support of this he noted that both systems are antimetaphysical and world-accepting ("Camus entre le Pa-

ganisme et le Christianisme" in *La Table ronde*, February 1960, pp. 114–119).

19. Much of this "Neoplatonic" climate, however, is quite concretely attributable to the influence of Camus's teacher Jean Grenier.

20. The teachings of the Stoa certainly offer no parallel here.

21. Cf. *Entre Plotin et Saint Augustin*, Ed. de la Pléiade, pp. 1250 ff.

22. *Entre Plotin et Saint Augustin*, p. 1286. The term "intelligence" means the second hypostasis of the One. The Logos would be its equivalent in the Christian doctrine of the Trinity.

23. *Enneads*, III. 9, 16 (quoted in *Entre Plotin et Saint Augustin*, p. 1287).

24. *Entre Plotin et Saint Augustin*, p. 1271.

25. *L'Envers et l'endroit*, p. 49.

26. C. Wigée is quite justified in stressing this aspect of the sacred in Camus ("La Nostalgie du sacré chez A. Camus" in *Hommage à Albert Camus* [*Nouvelle revue française*, March, 1960], pp. 527–536). He equates Meursault's act of murder in *L'Étranger*, the hatred of the Renegade in the story of that name in *L'Exil et le royaume*, and Janine's adultery in *La Femme adultère* (*The Adulterous Woman*), and makes this general statement on the "deadly" experience of this kingdom: "Possession of the kingdom destroys them, as far as anything essential in their lives is concerned" (p. 531).

27. This danger emerges most clearly later in Janine in *La Femme adultère* as well as in *Jonas* (*The Artist at Work*). As *Discours de Suède* shows, Camus sees the writer exposed to a similar danger if he devotes himself wholly to beauty.

28. Nguyen-van-Huy, who sees the One as a central theme in Camus, although he does not mention Neoplatonism, disregards this decisive difference and hence fails to grasp the true problem of this search for the kingdom and for oneness (*La Métaphysique du bonheur chez Albert Camus*, Neuchâtel, 1962).

29. *L'Envers et l'endroit*, p. 37.

30. *Ibid.*, p. 38.

31. Cf. *Entre Plotin et Saint Augustin*, pp. 1282–1286.

32. *L'Envers et l'endroit*, p. 38.

33. *Ibid.*, p. 39.

34. Quilliot rightly gives this word of warning with regard to the early essays: "The mystical nature of this feverish vocabulary should not mislead us. The only mystique here is of a carnal

nature . . . ." (*La Mer et les prisons*, Paris, 1956, p. 57). G. Brée speaks of "gods of this earth" (*Camus*, New Brunswick, N. J., 1959, pp. 77–85). N. Kohlhase, introducing the notion of "immanent transcendence," says that in Camus "the tendency to unbelief is closer to a 'negative theology' of unbelief than to the temptation of nihilism" (*Dichtung und immanente Transzendenz. Eine Gegenüberstellung von Brecht und Camus*, Munich, 1965, p. 192).

35. *Noces*, Ed. de la Pléiade, p. 84.
36. *Le Mythe de Sisyphe*, Ed. de la Pléiade, p. 198.
37. *Ibid.*, p. 175.
38. In *Alger républicain*, October 20, 1938, pp. 14117 ff.
39. *Le Mythe de Sisyphe*, p. 177.
40. G. Brée: "By every means at his disposal Camus creates closed worlds which recall the closed, self-contained universe of classical tragedy" (*Camus*, p. 107).
41. *Le Mythe de Sisyphe*, p. 174.
42. *Ibid.*, p. 178.
43. *Ibid.*, p. 179.

## Chapter 9

1. See my *Das Epos in den romanischen Literaturen* (Stuttgart, 1966, pp. 17 ff.).
2. R. Champigny (*Sur un héros païen*, Paris, 1959), M. G. Barrier (*L'Art du récit dans "L'Etranger,"* Paris, 1962), and B. T. Fitch ("Narrateur et Narration dans *L'Etranger* d'Albert Camus" in *Archives des Lettres Modernes*, 3, 1960 and *Le Sentiment d'étrangeté*) have written on the time of the Stranger's narrative. They all conclude—in my opinion wrongly—that the time of narration is just prior to the final revolt, that is, the execution. Champigny's explanation of specific designations of time ("today," and so on) is that the Stranger is thinking himself back into the situation (*Sur un héros païen*, p. 147). Why, then, does he stop doing so in Part II? Barrier maintains that it is the nature of the Stranger to relive past events as a memory from which no distance separates him (*L'Art du récit*, p. 26). This is certainly no longer true of the Stranger of Part II. A clear distinction must be made between the Strangers of Part I and Part II. In Part I the time of narration moves along with the events, always following

them closely, whereas in Part II, after the murder, it is the static moment posited by Champigny and others. This again shows how excellently planned *L'Etranger* is, for the difference corresponds to the different factual situation. The time of Part I is, as it were, cyclical and cosmic, whereas in Part II time "stands still" in keeping with the Stranger's imprisonment.

3. A. King says in *Camus* (Edinburgh, London, 1964, p. 61): "From the first page, a feeling of judgement against Meursault is gradually built up. He feels vaguely at fault." It should, however, be added that these feelings develop in curves, not in a straight line. The guilt feeling temporarily drops again.

4. The sixth sentence is an explanatory addition; from the point of view of meaning it is hypotactical.

5. P. Thody says in *Albert Camus* (Frankfurt am Main, 1964, pp. 41 ff.): "When he gets the news of his mother's death, he feels nothing but slight annoyance at having to ask his office for two days off." This, however, hardly does justice to the text.

6. J.-C. Brisville says in *Camus* (Paris, 1959, p. 58): "In his very first narrative work, Camus affirms his classicism, in the premeditation of his art, his sense of proportion. . . ."

7. Brisville rightly stresses the importance of humor in *L'Etranger*: "On the esthetic level, it is not surprising that this work should have a humorous appeal. Meursault sees without understanding—or rather, without joining in the game: thus his view is ingenuous. . . . The fact that Meursault's humor is applied to a serious subject adds to its impact" (*Camus*, pp. 57 ff.).

8. In his "Préface à l'edition américaine de *L'Etranger*" (in *Hommage à Albert Camus*, p. 402) Camus says: "Meursault, to me, is not a wreck, but a poor man, a man who loves the sun and casts no shadows. Far from lacking in all sensitivity, he is enlivened by a passion that is profound, because tacit, the passion for the absolute and for the truth."

9. *Carnets* (1942–1945) (Paris, 1964), p. 45.

10. In his stimualting study *La Métaphysique du bonheur* (p. 166), Nguyen-van-Huy says: "Meursault does not think, asks himself no questions, has no memory, no imagination." D. Wellershoff takes a similar view in *Der Gleichgültige* (Cologne, Berlin, 1963), p. 43. Brée (*Albert Camus*, p. 130) and especially Thody (*Albert Camus*, pp. 46 ff.) are more perceptive. On this whole question, see Fitch's well-documented *Le Sentiment d'étrangeté* (pp. 196 ff.), where he makes the forceful point that the Stran-

ger can tell from the behavior of the people coming out of the movie theater what kind of film they have been watching (*ibid.*, p. 189; see also *L'Etranger*, p. 37). In a study of Camus which is an exemplary guide, C. Gadourek stresses that the Stranger's indifference is only apparent and that he acts quite deliberately except at the precise moment of the murder, when he lets himself be determined by "the other" (*Les Innocents et les coupables: Essai d'exégèse de l'oeuvre d'Albert Camus*, The Hague, 1963, p. 288). Gadourek also gives a very useful reference to Grenier, who called *"indifférence"* an *"ombre portée par un attachement"* (ibid., p. 87).

11. *L'Etranger* (Paris, 1942), p. 13.
12. *Ibid.*, p. 29 [My italics.]
13. *Ibid.*, p. 38. This marks the end of Chapter 2, so that again we can regard it as a structurally determined, pointedly "shameless" ending (cf. p. 129 of the present work).
14. *Ibid.* Cf. Chapter 3, first paragraph.
15. Champigny uses the word "pagan" for this sense of World (*Sur un héros païen*, pp. 38 ff., 49, and *passim*). It seems doubtful whether the *société* to which this pagan sense of World feels itself opposed is so specifically Christian. Possibly Champigny is using *"société chrétienne"* merely as a historical term.
16. *L'Etranger*, p. 53.
17. Cf. *L'Etranger*, p. 154, where Meursault, now in prison, remembers his deepest pleasures. They were: "Summer odors, the neighborhood I liked, a certain sky in the evening, Marie's laugh and her dresses."
18. In this respect Meursault is a better incarnation of Sartrean ideas than, say, Roquentin.
19. *L'Etranger*, p. 55.
20. Before grief could affect Meursault it had to become something tangible—an image. The abstraction of a telegram was powerless to affect him, as was the abstracted, structured mourning of a funeral ceremony with censer-swinging acolytes, solace-dispensing priests, and literally "collapsing" fiancés.
21. *L'Etranger*, p. 76.
22. On sun in *L'Etranger*, see R. Barthes: "L'Etranger: Roman solaire" in *Bulletin du club du meilleur livre*, 12 (1959).
23. See also footnote 2 to this chapter.
24. Quilliot rightly points out that this imprisonment also stands for the fate of mankind (*La Mer et les prisons*, p. 96). On the

notion of oneness, the reader is referred back to our reservations regarding the metaphysical meaning.

25. *L'Etranger*, pp. 175 ff. What Camus is getting at here is the evidence of an immanent certainty of salvation violently surging up within the Stranger. D'Arrast in *La Pierre qui pousse* experiences something similar: a certainty of salvation which in *L'Etranger* is made up of anger and joy, in *La Pierre qui pousse* of despair and joy: "And there, rising to his full height, suddenly enormous, inhaling in desperate gasps the odor of misery and of ashes that he recognized, he heard rising within him the current of an obscure, panting joy he could not name."

26. Meursault counters it with Camus's credo of belief in the world, so strikingly formulated in *Noces* (p. 87): "The world is beautiful, and there is no salvation outside of it."

27. Cf. *L'Envers et l'endroit* (p. 24): "The world sighs to me in a long rhythm and brings me the indifference and tranquillity of things that do not die."

28. *L'Etranger*, p. 179. Note how "positively" the word "indifference" is used here. (See also the preceding note.) It means being merged with the world: distanceless ("in-difference") worldness.

29. It should be stressed again that this happiness (as opposed, say, to Neoplatonism) does not consist in turning away from the merely bodily and the merely worldly. A sentence in *Noces* applies here: "The great truth which, patiently, it teaches me is that the spirit is nothing—nor even the heart itself" (p. 89).

30. On the significance of the mother in Camus's work, see Nguyen-van-Huy: *La Métaphysique du bonheur*, pp. 161 ff.

31. In this connection we should remember that the constructive second part, built on the principle of sustained tension, has five chapters, whereas Part I, in which Meursault is relatively balanced, has six. Discussing the chapter arrangement, P. G. Castex says in *Albert Camus et L'étranger* (Paris, 1965 p. 103): "The novel's architecture testifies, in fact, to an extraordinarily painstaking care. The two parts are of equal length, within a few lines. The first part comprises six chapters, the second only five; but Chapter 6 in the first part is a pivot." The parallelism between the two parts is indeed striking (cf. Gadourek: *Les Innocents*, p. 86), and Camus himself drew attention to it: "The meaning of the book consists precisely in the parallelism of the two parts" (*Carnets*, Vol. II, p. 30). On the other hand, indisputable as it is,

this must not be taken too rigidly. The two-level quality and the contrast are just as important as the parallelism; indeed the latter serves the two-level world of *L'Etranger*, giving it greater esthetic forcefulness.

32. *L'Etranger*, p. 161.
33. *Ibid.*, p. 163.
34. Cf. *Noces*: "Aside from the sun, certain kisses and wild fragrances, everything seems futile to us" (p. 56).
35. This connection with Christ is no discovery of mine. In the preface to the American edition of *L'Etranger* Camus himself calls Meursault "the only Christ we deserve" (in *Hommage à Albert Camus*, p. 402).
36. So the novel ends.

## Chapter 10

1. Possibly Camus was inspired here by the stage technique of the *autos sacramentales* in which carts were drawn up, furnishing the setting for each scene.
2. Caligula was overwhelmed by this absurdity when Drusilla, his sister and mistress, died.
3. See *Caligula*, Ed. de la Pléiade, pp. 25, 35, 106. Brisville makes the point that: "As an absurd man, Caligula proves, through the absurd, that absolute freedom, even if it can be justified philosophically, leads in fact to nihilism" (*Camus*, p. 81).
4. As we have already mentioned, Sartre wrote *L'Age de raison* long before it was published (see p. 67). This does not apply, however, to the crucial Volume II, in which Mathieu breaks through to the freedom of terror.
5. *Caligula*, p. 34.
6. According to Brisville the darkness and despair of this play reflect the circumstances in which it was written. (Camus wrote *Le Malentendu* in 1942, during the German occupation.) P.-H. Simon (*Présence de Camus*, Paris, 1961, pp. 89 ff.), seeking an explanation for this unexpected nihilism in Camus, mentions its closeness to Sartre's *Huis clos* and recalls that both plays were written during the occupation.
7. Quilliot rightly notes: "Here, on the artistic level Camus seems to have justified the strenuous work of coherence and clarifica-

tion embodied in *Le Mythe de Sisyphe*" (*La Mer et les prisons*, p. 136).

8. R. de Luppé developed this partly plausible interpretation in *Albert Camus* (Paris, 1952), but the play does not ultimately support such a reading.

9. See *Préface à l'édition américaine du théâtre*, Ed. de la Pleiade, pp. 1727 ff.

10. Victoria: "I am whole! I know only my love" (*L'Etat de siège*, Ed. de la Pléiade, p. 262). This shows that *L'Etat de siège* too can be considered part of Camus's treatment of the theme of oneness. In this sense Victoria is a counterpart of Martha in *Le Malentendu*, who dreams of the happiness of feeling at one with herself at the seashore. But it should not be overlooked that now, in the phase of rebellion, the desire for oneness conflicts sharply with man's mission as brother of his fellow men.

11. See Simon, *Présence de Camus*, p. 94. Also W. Mönch: "Albert Camus. Ein Versuch zum Verständnis seines dramatischen Werkes" in *Zeitschrift für französische Sprache und Literatur*, 75 (1964), pp. 289–308.

12. Simon strongly emphasizes the analogies with Sartre's *Les Mains sales*, but his equating of individual characters is sometimes unconvincing. He sees Yanek as Hugo, Annenkov as Hoederer, Stepan as Louis, and Dora as Olga. But he admits himself that their differences are equally great (*Présence de Camus*, p. 97 ff.).

13. As we have already mentioned, Sartre has also written one five-act play. This is—and not by chance—*Les Séquestrés d'Altona*, the story of a community. Characteristically, it is among his weakest plays, whereas Camus as a dramatist reaches his peak in this form. Verticality, a danger to Sartre, is the compositional element through which Camus fulfilled himself.

14. Lausberg has suggested an allegorical interpretation of *Les Justes* according to which Dora stands for pure, humane nature, Yanek for the positive act of rebellion, Stepan for Aristotelian excess, Alexis for Aristotelian deficiency, and the leader for a recapitulation of Dora's role (*Interpretationen*, I, pp. 41 and 47 ff.).

15. In a preface Camus stressed the historicity of the events. They are taken from an attack on the Grand Duke Sergius in 1905, when the young intellectual Ivan Kaliayev (Yanek in the play) threw the bomb.

16. Cf. Stepan: "You'd like me to go soft, to drag the bomb like a cross?" (p. 356). Shortly before this, Yanek had crossed himself before an icon.

17. Lausberg is right in seeing these temptations of Yanek in prison as an analogy to the three temptations of Jesus in the wilderness as recounted in Matthew 4: 3–4 (*Interpretationen*, I, p. 64).

18. Thus, when F. N. Mennemeier speaks of the "tragedy of the just" (*Das moderne Drama des Auslandes*, Düsseldorf, 1965, pp. 183–192), we are obliged to qualify this with a reminder that it is a triumphant tragedy. "Yanek! A cold night and the same rope! Everything will be easier now" is indeed a "terrible sentence" (*Ibid.*, p. 216), but it is also a sentence of faith in a goal. The same reservation applies to Mönch (*Camus*, p. 305).

19. *L'Homme révolté*, Ed. de la Pléiade, p. 424.

20. See Lausberg, *Interpretationen*, I, p. 25.

21. *L'Homme révolté*, p. 707.

22. Cf. Quilliot: *Commentaires* on *Les Justes*, Ed. de la Pléiade, p. 1814.

23. In an interview with F. Rauhut in *Deutschland-Frankreich. Ludwigsburger Beiträge zum Problem der deutsch-französischen Beziehungen*, Vol. II, Stuttgart, 1957, p. 180.

24. It should not be forgotten that *Le Malentendu* deals with a community, albeit an imperfect one—the community of a family.

25. The rigid opposition is relaxed a little in *L'Etat de siège* inasmuch as Diego and Victoria do engage in dialogue, though of a very disrupted kind.

26. Like the oneness with the world of the early essays and of the Stranger, the constructivity remains immanent. It is, as it were, a phase devoid of objective and lacking all origin, which becomes its own goal. Hence it cannot be called metaphysical in the strict sense.

## Chapter 11

1. "And when, then, am I truer than when I am the world?" (*L'Envers et l'endroit*, p. 124).

2. On other treatments of the plague in literature, see H. J.

Grimm: *Die literarischen Gestaltungen der Pest in der Antike und in der Romania. Freiburger Schriften zur romanischen Phillologie*, 6, 1965.

3. Brisville: "The book's momentum carries everything forward together: the internal evolution of the principal characters, as well as the evolution of the collective feelings" (*Camus*, p. 60).

4. The warlike, militant element persists only in the metaphors. (See A. Noyer-Weidner: "Das Formproblem der Pest von Albert Camus" in *Germanisch-romanische Monatsschrift, Neue Folge*, 8, 1958, pp. 260–289, also p. 271.)

5. *La Peste*, Ed. de la Pléiade, p. 1294.

6. *Ibid.*, p. 1367.

7. In an interview with C. Chonez in *Paru*, 47 (pp. 7–13), quoted by Gadourek in *Les Innocents* (p. 117), Camus said that *La Peste* was the most anti-Christian of his books. It is quite conceivable that he intended it to be—and Sartre would no doubt have said the same of *Le Diable et le bon Dieu*—but in both cases an inescapable law holds that in literature direct opposition always entails an involvement with the "opponent" and hence if not dialogue at least dialectic. And this, if one understands dialectic correctly, is a form of *rapprochement*.

8. *La Peste*, p. 1225.

9. *Ibid.*, p. 1235.

10. *Ibid.*, p. 1248.

11. *Ibid.*, p. 1256.

12. *Ibid.*, p. 1407.

13. *Ibid.*, p. 1427.

14. *Ibid.*, p. 1425.

15. *Ibid.*, p. 1284: "Joseph Grand had also suffered in turn. He could have begun again, as Rieux pointed out to him. But you see, he had no faith."

16. This is what Camus in *La Chute* calls Lake Ijssel in the Netherlands.

17. *La Peste*, p. 1404.

18. It should not be forgotten that it was from the womb of the earth that the plague issued forth. Here again, as in *L'Envers et l'endroit* (pp. 113 ff.), the "reverse side" of the world, that which transcends man in the world, has two aspects: a dark one (corresponding to night, death, and old age, as well as Prague in *L'Envers et l'endroit*) and a light one (Vicenza).

19. On the light and water symbolism, see J. Tans: "La Poétique

de l'eau et de la lumière d'après l'oeuvre d'Albert Camus," in *Style et littérature* (The Hague, 1962).

20. "Thus the subject of the plague stretches between reality and symbolism," says Noyer-Weidner in "Das Formproblem der *Pest*" (p. 269).

21. Gadourek: "The images assist in emphasizing this evolution" (*Les Innocents*, p. 119).

22. *La Peste*, p. 1237.

23. *Ibid.*, p. 1415.

24. *Ibid.*, p. 1229.

25. *Ibid.*, p. 1329.

26. *Ibid.*, p. 1471.

27. *Das Epos in den romanischen Literaturen*, pp. 159 ff.

28. *La Peste*, p. 1465.

29. *Ibid.*, p. 1221.

30. Camus's own prologue (in our sense the prologue to Part II is a special case, marked by a "rhetorical" cadence of sentence constructions which, particularly in the third and fifth paragraphs, harmonize in a triple syntactical rhythm. (As, for instance, in the third paragraph: "*comment*," "*femmes*"—"*cinéma*" —"*bains de mer*," "*se réunissent*"—"*se promènent*"—"*se mettent*," "*les associations*"—"*les banquets*"—"*les cercles*," and so on.))

31. *La Peste*, p. 1321.

32. *Ibid.*, p. 1323.

33. "Réponse à Albert Camus" in *Les Temps Modernes*, 8 (1952), p. 334.


## Chapter 12

1. To discuss the novellas in *L'Exil et le royaume* individually would have been beyond the scope of this book. The reader is referred to the dissertation of M. Pelz, "Das Novellenwerk von Albert Camus. Form- und Problemdarstellung" (Diss., Tübingen, 1962), in which they are discussed in detail.

2. G. Lukács: *Die Theorie des Romans*, 2nd ed., Berlin, 1963, p. 47.

3. Note how closely the overall development of *L'Exil et le royaume* corresponds to the curve of tension in *L'Étranger*. (See diagram on p. 140.)

4. Whether Camus was aware of these relationships is, of course, another question.

5. *L'Exil et le royaume*, Ed. de la Pléiade, p. 1558.

6. *Ibid.*, p. 1643.

7. See also Noyer-Weidner "Albert Camus," p. 37.

8. Cf. Note 29 to Chapter 9.

9. Vigée in *Hommage à Albert Camus* (p. 531) equates Meursault's act of murder, the Renegade's hatred, and Janine's adultery and says: "It is significant that, even in this kindly, attenuated form of nocturnal invasion, there remains, in the experiences of the sacred, an element which betrays its excessive character. They have the effect of a rape or an ultimate fulfillment."

10. Cf. *La Femme adultère*, p. 1568: "Since time immemorial, some men had been traveling relentlessly over the raw, bone-dry earth of this outsized land, men who possessed nothing but served no one, pitiful, free masters of a strange kingdom."

11. *Les Muets*, p. 1595.

12. In the reverse order, though. In the case of *Le Diable et le bon Dieu* there is also a synthesis.

13. The final sentence of *Les Muets* (p. 1606) reads: "He would have liked to be young, along with Fernande; they would have gone off to the other side of the sea."

14. When the factory owner against whom they had lost their wildcat strike was assailed by misfortune and his daughter was taken to the hospital, Yvars should have found a word of sympathy for him instead of leaving the initiative to the union representative—who of course did not take it. In this way the breach between employee and employer might have been healed.

15. See diagram on p. 173.

16. Daru had sheltered overnight an Arab whom he was supposed to turn over to the authorities and the next morning had given him the choice between freedom and prison. The Arab chose the road leading to prison—prompted perhaps by his inner obligations as a guest. Returning to the schoolhouse (he is an elementary school teacher in Algeria), Daru finds the threatening message written on the blackboard. In the closing sentence Camus says: "In this vast country he had loved so much, he was alone."

17. At the bottom of this blank canvas is one almost illegible word which—characteristically—could be read equally well as either *"solitaire"* or *"solidaire."*

18. How seriously Camus took the solution that he presented so humorously in *Jonas* is shown by his statement in *Discours de Suède* (Paris, 1958, p. 13) that the writer must stand midway between beauty and humanity.

19. The title *La Pierre qui pousse* refers to two factors in the story: the stone in the native grotto which is said to grow back if a piece is broken off and the stone which the cook has vowed to carry in the procession and which D'Arrast, thanks to some ineffable strength, carries into his friend's hut instead of the church.

20. Cf. D'Arrast's feelings in his friend's hut.

21. How strongly *La Chute* suggests this return to Sartre is shown by A. King's curious interpretation of this work in "Structure and Meaning in *La Chute*" (*Publication of the Modern Language Association*, 77, 1962, pp. 660–667). She sees the "hero" of *La Chute* as a caricature of Camus in which the author has portrayed himself as he appears to Sartre. This caricature of Camus, which leads the reader down into the circles of hell, later turns into Sartre himself and finally stands at the center of the earth as Lucifer. I find this interpretation untenable as a whole.

22. The word "part" requires a brief explanation. The "parts" of *La Chute* are separated only typographically. They could just as well be called chapters, but "parts" seemed to me more pertinent.

23. Meursault in *L'Etranger* commits his murder at exactly the same point in the composition.

24. The word *juge-pénitent* contains both components: judging and penitence.

25. The Mexico City Bar actually exists, as King has so admirably established (*Camus*, note 23, p. 663) and exactly matches Camus's description of it.

26. *La Chute*, Ed. de la Pléiade, p. 1480.

27. *Ibid.*

28. This is the basis of A. King's interpretation of *La Chute* ("Structure and Meaning," pp. 664 ff.). Though the conclusions she draws from it may be quite off the mark (see note 21), the interpretation cannot be entirely rejected. It should rather be reduced to its sound core, as has been done by Gadourek in her already quoted study (*Les Innocents*, pp. 189 ff.). Gadourek's interpretation stresses that Clamence is concerned above all to

lead the other person (in the Sartrean sense) through the infernal regions of self-knowledge.

29. Several critics have remarked that the name Jean-Baptiste Clamence is also intended to suggest *clémence*. (See Thody, *Camus*, p. 78.)

30. Expressions such as *avancer, viser plus haut, bonheur, joie, exulter, courtoisie, plus haut, vertu, hauteur, lumière édénique*, and *plénitude* unmistakably demonstrate this orientation toward an ideal.

31. *La Chute*, p. 1486. The little Poulou in Sartre's *Les Mots* enjoyed similar pleasures (cf. p. 106). This is by no means the full extent of the analogy with *Les Mots*, considering that it too is written in two parts ("Lire"—"Ecrire") and that, like *La Chute*, it represents a doubly false path.

32. This is a reference to the doctrine of predestination which may recall Sartre's attitude to the Platonic myth of love in *Les Jeux sont faits*.

33. Variations on this notion keep recurring like a leitmotiv.

34. A variation on the vertical plane of the Sartrean problem of "the other."

35. *La Chute*, p. 1514.

36. *Ibid.*, p. 1522. Thus in the second part too Camus approaches the essential point by way of allusions. This is in keeping with the parallel structure of the two "halves," found also in *L'Etranger*.

37. *La Chute*, p. 1525: "Despairing of chaste love, I finally realized that there was still debauchery, which can easily replace love, stop mocking laughter, restore silence, and, above all, confer immortality."

38. *La Chute*, p. 1530: "Every man testifies to the crime of all the others—that is my faith, and my hope."

39. It is made quite clear that this "solution" is not expected to eliminate absurdity: "He is led by the idea, of course, of silencing derision, avoiding judgment himself, although there is apparently no way out" (*La Chute*, p. 1541).

40. *La Chute*, p. 1543.

41. *Ibid.*

42. He attains his goal of making society resemble himself by holding up to it the mirror of his self-accusation. The whole construction is thus consciously paradoxical and absurd.

43. The irony of "solemnly saluted" may perhaps confirm the

hypothesis that Camus had deliberately adopted Sartrean ideas and is now departing from them.

44. *La Chute*, p. 154.
45. *Ibid.*, pp. 154 ff.
46. *Ibid.*, p. 154.
47. *Ibid.*, p. 154.
48. Simon says in *Présence de Camus* (p. 162): "Never has he more finely sculpted the rock of French prose than in this work." See also Brisville: *Camus* (p. 60) and T. Hanna: *The Thought and Art of Albert Camus* (Chicago, 1958, pp. 215 ff.); both critics concur in this judgment. Neither is it surprising that Sartre should consider *La Chute* Camus's finest work (*France-Observateur*, January 7, 1960).

## Original French Texts
## for Quoted Passages

*p. 12*

De Rollebon m'assomme.

Au mur, il y a un trou blanc, la glace. C'est un piège. Je sais que je vais m'y laisser prendre. Ça y est. La chose grise vient d'apparaître dans la glace. Je m'approche et je la regarde, je ne peux plus m'en aller.

*p. 14*

Tout de même . . . est-il absolument nécessaire de se mentir?

*pp. 16 and 17*

Les mots s'étaient évanouis et, avec eux, la signification des choses leurs modes d'emploi, les faibles repères que les hommes ont tracés à leur surface.

Mon but est atteint: je sais ce que je voulais savoir; tout ce qui m'est arrivé depuis le mois de janvier, je l'ai compris.

Le monde des explications et des raisons n'est pas celui de l'existence.

*p. 17*

L'essentiel c'est la contingence. Je veux dire que, par définition, l'existence n'est pas la nécessité. Exister, c'est *être là*, simplement; les existants apparaissent, se laissent *rencontrer*, mais on ne peut jamais les *déduire*.

*p. 17*

Tout existant naît sans raison, se prolonge par faiblesse et meurt par rencontre.

*p. 18*

On ne peut pas être un homme d'action.

Etonné devant cette vie qui m'est donnée—donnée pour rien.

*p. 20*

Le soleil couchant éclaira un moment son dos courbé, puis il disparut. Sur le seuil de la porte, il y avait une tache de sang, en étoile.

*pp. 20 and 21*

Et moi aussi j'ai voulu *être*. Je n'ai même voulu que cela; voilà le fin mot de ma vie: au fond de toutes ces tentatives qui semblaient sans liens, je retrouve le même désir: chasser l'existence hors de moi, vider les instants de leur graisse, les tordre, les assécher, me purifier, me durcir, pour rendre enfin le son net et précis d'une note de saxophone.

En voilà deux qui sont sauvés: le Juif et la Négresse. Sauvés. Ils se sont peut-être cru perdus jusqu'au bout, noyés dans l'existence. Et pourtant, personne ne pourrait penser à moi comme je pense à eux, avec cette douceur. Personne, pas même Anny. . . . ils se sont lavés du péché d'exister. Pas complètement, bien sûr—mais tout autant qu'un homme peut faire.

*p. 21*

Faire quelque chose, c'est créer de l'existence—et il y a bien assex d'existence comme ça.

*p. 22*

Le vieillard avait fini son roman. Mais il ne s'en allait pas. Il tapait du doigt sur la table, à coups secs et réguliers.

"Messieurs," dit le Corse, "on va bientôt fermer."

Le jeune homme sursauta et me lança un bref coup d'oeil. La jeune femme s'était tournée vers le Corse, puis elle reprit son livre et sembla s'y plonger.

"On ferme," dit le Corse, cinq minutes plus tard. Le vieillard hocha la tête d'un air indécis. La jeune femme repoussa son livre, mais sans se lever.

Le Corse n'en revenait pas. Il fit quelques pas hésitants, puis tourna un commutateur. Aux tables de lecture les lampes s'éteignirent. Seule l'ampoule centrale restait allumée.

"Il faut partir?" demanda doucement le vieillard.

*p. 23*

Je vais sans doute revoir Anny mais je ne peux pas dire que cette idée me rende précisément joyeux. Depuis que j'ai reçu sa lettre, je me sens désoeuvré. Heureusement il est midi; je n'ai pas faim, mais je vais manger, pour passer le temps. J'entre chez Camille, rue des Horlogers.

C'est une boîte bien close; on sert la choucroute ou le cassoulet toute la nuit. Les gens y viennent souper à lá sortie du théâtre; les sergents de ville y envoient les voyageurs qui arrivent dans la nuit et qui ont faim. Huit tables de marbre. Une banquette de cuir court le long des murs. Deux glaces mangées de taches rousses.

*p. 24*

Le galet était plat, sec sur tout un côté, humide et boueux sur l'autre. Je le tenais par les bords, avec les doigts très écartés, pour éviter de me salir.

*p. 24*

Les objets, cela ne devrait pas *toucher*, puisque cela ne vit pas. On s'en sert, on les remet en place, on vit au milieu d'eux: ils sont utiles, rien de plus. Et moi, ils me touchent, c'est insupportable. J'ai peur d'entrer en contact avec eux tout comme s'ils étaient des bêtes vivantes.

Et cela venait du galet, j'en suis sûr, cela passait du galet dans mes mains. Oui, c'est cela, c'est bien cela: une sorte de nausée dans les mains.

*p. 25*

A ce moment, le long de la jupe, une main se mit à descendre, au bout d'un bras raide.

Je vois ma main, qui s'épanouit sur la table. Elle vit—c'est moi. Elle s'ouvre, les doigts se déploient et pointent. Elle est sur le dos. Elle me montre son ventre gras. Elle a l'air d'une bête à la renverse. Les doigts, ce sont les pattes. Je m'amuse à les faire remuer, très vite, comme les pattes d'un crabe qui est tombé sur le dos. . . . Maintenant je sens son poids au bout de mon bras. Elle tire un peu, à peine, mollement, moelleusement, elle existe.

*p. 26*

Les bretelles se voient à peine sur la chemise bleue, elles sont tout éffacées, enfouies dans le bleu, mais c'est de la fausse humilité: en fait, elles ne se laissent pas oublier, elles m'agacent par leur entêtement de moutons, comme si, parties pour devenir violettes, elles s'étaient arrêtées en route sans abandonner leurs prétentions. On a envie de leur dire: "Allez-y, *devenez* violettes et qu'on n'en parle plus." Mais non, elles restent en suspens, butées dans leur effort inachevé.

*p. 27*

Il avait longtemps cru qu'il existait par hasard, à la dérive: mais c'était faute d'avoir assez réfléchi. Bien avant sa naissance, sa place était marquée au soleil, à Férolles.

*pp. 27 and 28*

Des générations d'ouvrier pourraient, de même, obéir scrupuleusement aux ordres de Lucien, ils n'épuiseraient jamais son droit à commander; les droits c'était par-delà l'existence, comme les objets mathématiques et les dogmes religieux.

"Je vais laisser pousser ma moustache," décida-t-il.

*p. 28*

Lulu aimait sentir contre elle ce grand corps captif. 'S'il pouvait rester comme ça paralysé, c'est moi qui le soignerais, qui le nettoierais comme un enfant et quelquefois je le retournerais sur le ventre et je lui donnerais la fessée. . . .'"

*p. 28*

Il pensa qu'il en avait assez de jouer à être Lucien.

*p. 32*

Tu as l'âge de raison, Mathieu, tu as l'âge de raison ou tu devrais l'avoir.

*p. 33*

A présent rien ne peut ôter son sens à ma vie, rien ne peut l'empêcher d'être un destin.

Tu as besoin de t'engager.

Tu as renoncé à tout pour être libre. Fais un pas de plus, renonce à ta liberté elle-même: et tout te sera rendu.

*pp. 33 and 34*

Un homme aux muscles puissants et un peu noués, qui pensait par courtes vérités sévères, un homme droit, fermé, sûr de soi, terrestre, réfractaire aux tentations angéliques de l'art, de la psychologie, de la politique, tout un homme, rien qu'un homme.

Et Mathieu était là, en face de lui, indécis, mal vieilli, mal cuit, assiégé par tous les vertiges de l'inhumain.

"Je suis un irresponsable," pensa-t-il.

*p. 34*

J'aime mes rideaux verts, j'aime prendre l'air, le soir, à mon balcon et je ne voudrais pas que ça change.

Je suis un type foutu.

*p. 35*

"Je suis un con," pensa-t-il, "Brunet a bien raison de dire que je suis un vieil enfant."

Et soudain il lui sembla qu'il *voyait* sa liberté. Elle était hors d'atteinte, cruelle, jeune et capricieuse comme la grâce.

Même s'il se laissait emporter, désemparé, désespéré, même s'il se laissait emporter comme un vieux sac de charbon, il aurait choisi sa perdition: il était libre, libre pour tout, libre de faire la bête ou la machine, libre pour accepter, libre pour refuser . . . il n'y aurait pour lui de Bien ni de Mal que s'il les inventait.

*p. 36*

Cette vie lui était donnée pour rien.

Il n'était rien et cependant il ne changerait plus: il était fait.

Il ôta son veston, il se mit à dénouer sa cravate. Il se répétait en bâillant: "C'est vrai, c'est tout de même vrai: j'ai l'âge de raison."

Je suppose. Moi, je ne m'y suis pas encore fait.

*pp. 36 and 37*

Ça y est. Je suis en train de devenir intéressant.

Je pars parce que je ne peux pas faire autrement.

La guerre, la paix, c'est égal.

Elle continuera à n'aller nulle part.

*p. 37*

Au milieu du Pont-Neuf, il s'arrêta, il se mit à rire: cette liberté, je l'ai cherchée bien loin; elle était si proche que je ne pouvais pas la voir, que je ne peux pas la toucher, elle n'était que moi. Je suis ma liberté.

La liberté c'est l'exil et je suis condamné à être libre.

*p. 38*

Mathieu bâilla; il regardait tristement les types noyés dans l'ombre; il murmura: "*Nous.*" Mais ça ne prenait plus: il était seul.

*p. 39*

C'était une énorme revanche; chaque coup de feu le vengeait d'un ancien scrupule.

*p. 40*

C'est fini de se battre, à présent, la guerre est perdue et il y a du travail à faire.

"Beaucoup de travail." Il s'étend sur la paille, il bâille, il s'endort.

*p. 41*

Dans le parc une petite fille qui tient un cerceau regarde gravement: à travers ses jeunes yeux toute une France innocente et surannée les voit passer. Brunet regarde la petite fille et il pense à Pétain; le train file à travers ce regard, à travers cet avenir plein de jeux sages, de bonnes pensées, de menus soucis, il file vers les champs de pommes de terre, les usines et les fabriques d'armement, vers l'avenir noir et vrai des hommes.

M'évader, tirer une croix sur vingt mille hommes, les laisser crever dans leur merde, a-t-on jamais le droit de dire: il n'y a plus rien à faire? . . . Il y a toujours quelque chose à faire. Il faut travailler où on est avec les moyens qu'on a.

*p. 42*

Il voudrait lui parler, l'exhorter, l'aider, il ne peut pas: ses mots sont au Parti, c'est le Parti qui leur a donné leur sens; à l'intérieur du Parti, Brunet peut aimer, peut persuader et consoler. Le typo est tombé hors de cet immense fuseau de lumière, Brunet n'a plus rien à lui dire.

*p. 42*

Il se tient sur un pied, l'autre est coincé au-dessus du plancher, dans un enchevêtrement de jambes et de souliers. Il n'essaie pas de le dégager, il a besoin de rester dans le provisoire: il est de passage, sa pensée est de passage dans sa tête, le train est de passage en France.

Demain viendront les oiseaux noirs.

*p. 44*

Moi, je suis libre, Dieu merci. Ah! comme je suis libre. Et quelle superbe absence que mon âme.

Par cette porte, je serais entré et sorti dix mille fois. Enfant, j'aurais joué avec ses battants, je me serais arc-bouté contre eux, ils auraient grincé sans céder, et mes bras auraient appris leur résistance.

Les odeurs et les sons, le bruit de la pluie sur les toits, les tremblements de la lumière, je les laisse glisser le long de mon corps et tomber autour de moi.

*p. 45*

Je suis né ici et je dois demander mon chemin comme un passant.

*p. 46*

Il y a des hommes qui naissent engagés: ils n'ont pas le choix, on les a jetés sur un chemin, au bout du chemin il y a un acte qui les attend, *leur* acte; ils vont, et leurs pieds nus pressent fortement la terre et s'écorchent.

S'il était un acte, vois-tu, un acte qui me donnât droit de cité parmi eux; si je pouvais m'emparer, fût-ce par un crime, de leurs mémoires, de leur terreur et de leurs espérances pour combler le vide de mon coeur, dussé-je tuer ma propre mère. . . .

Et tu sauras enfin que tu as engagé ta vie sur un seul coup de dés, une fois pour toutes.

*p. 47*

Comprends-moi: je veux être un homme de quelque part, un homme parmi les hommes. Tiens, un esclave, lorsqu'il passe, las et rechigné, portant un lourd fardeau, traînant la jambe et regardant à ses pieds, tout juste à ses pieds pour éviter de choir, il est *dans* la ville, comme une feuille dans un feuillage, comme l'arbre dans la forêt, Argos est autour de lui, toute pesante et toute chaude, toute pleine d'elle-même; je veux être cet esclave, Electre, je veux tirer la ville autour de moi et m'y enrouler comme dans une couverture. Je ne m'en irai pas.

Mon bras peut défendre la ville, et j'ai de l'or pour soulger vos miséreux.

*p. 48*

Ecoute: tous ces gens qui tremblent dans des chambres sombres, entourés de leurs chers défunts, suppose que j'assume tous leurs crimes. Suppose que je veuille mériter le nom de "voleur de remords" et que j'installe en moi tous leurs repentirs.

*pp. 48 and 49*

Nous avons la même passion. Tu aimes l'ordre, Egisthe.

J'ai fait de l'ordre. O terrible et divine passion.

Quand une fois la liberté a explosé dans une âme d'homme, les Dieux ne peuvent plus rien contre cet homme-là.

*pp. 49 and 50*

Je l'aime plus que moi-même. Mais ses souffrances viennent d'elle, c'est elle seule qui peut s'en délivrer: elle est libre.

Tu es le roi des Dieux, Jupiter, le roi des pierres et des étoiles, le roi des vagues de la mer. Mais tu n'es pas le roi des hommes.

*p. 50*

Un crime que son auteur ne peut supporter, ce n'est plus le crime de personne, n'est-ce pas?

*p. 53*

L'enfer c'est les autres.

*p. 54*

S'il y avait une âme, une seule, pour affirmer de toutes ses forces que je n'ai pas fui, que je ne *peux pas avoir fui*, que j'ai du courage, que je suis propre, je . . . je suis sûr que je serais sauvé!

Elle a besoin d'un homme, tu peux le croire, d'un bras d'homme autour de sa taille, d'une odeur d'homme, d'un désir d'homme dans des yeux d'homme. Pour le reste . . . Ha! elle te dirait que tu es Dieu le Père, si cela pouvait te faire plaisir.

*p. 55*

Seuls les actes décident de ce qu'on a voulu.

Tout est permis aux héros.

*p. 55*

On meurt toujours trop tôt—ou trop tard.

Tu n'es rien d'autre que ta vie.

*pp. 58 and 59*

A présent personne ne peut plus me donner d'ordres et rien ne peut plus me justifier.

Pendant trente ans, je me suis senti coupable. Coupable parce que je vivais.

Tu n'es pas modeste, Henri.

*p. 59*

Moi, je crois qu'il y a beau temps que nous sommes morts: au moment précis où nous avons cessé d'être utiles.

*p. 60*

SORBIER: (*Criant*) Hé, là-haut! Henri! Canoris!, je n'ai pas parlé! (*Les miliciens se jettent sur lui. Il saut dans le vide.*) Bonsoir!

Il n'y aura dans mes yeux que de l'amour.

Elle ne pense qu'à moi. C'est pour ne pas me livrer qu'elle endure les souffrances et la honte.

*p. 62*

On meurt par-dessus le marché.

*p. 67*

J'aime mieux la taule. Je ne veux pas mentir.

*pp. 68 and 69*

Une fille comme toi *ne peut pas* tirer sur un homme comme moi.

FRED: (*En lui tapant la joue*) Allons, tout est rentré dans l'ordre. (*Un temps*) Je m'appelle Fred. (*Rideau*)

*p. 73*

La jeunesse, je ne sais pas ce que c'est: je suis passé directement de l'enfance à l'âge d'homme.

Vous voyez, Hoederer, je vous regarde dans les yeux et je vise et ma main ne tremble pas et je me fous de ce que vous avez dans la tête.

*pp. 73 and 74*

Je l'ai tué parce que j'avais ouvert la porte. . . . Ce n'est pas moi qui ai tué, c'est le hasard.

Un type comme Hoederer ne meurt pas par hasard. Il meurt pour ses idées, pour sa politique; il est responsable de sa mort. Si je revendique mon crime devant tous, si je réclame mon nom de Raskolnikoff et si j'accepte de payer le prix qu'il faut, alors il aura eu la mort qui lui convient.

*p. 77*

Trois heures dix, Werner: tu peux te lever.

*p. 79*

Je *suis* Goering. S'ils le pendent, c'est moi le pendu.

*p. 80*

Belle partie! Vous avez joué Johanna contre Léni puis Léni contre Johanna. Mat en trois coups.

*pp. 80 and 81*

Le rabbin saignait et je découvrais, au coeur de mon impuissance, je ne sais quel assentiment.

Vous aurez été ma cause et mon destin jusqu'au bout.

Frantz, il n'y a jâmais eu que moi.

*p. 81*

Je t'ai fait, je te déferai. Ma mort enveloppera la tienne et, finalement, je serai seul à mourir.

*p. 84*

Si, par suite d'une erreur imputable à la seule direction, un homme et une femme qui étaient destinés l'un à l'autre ne se sont pas rencontrés de leur vivant, ils pourront demander et obtenir l'autorisation de retourner sur terre sous certaines conditions, pour y réaliser l'amour et y vivre la vie commune dont ils ont été indûment frustrés.

*p. 84*

Vous étiez authentiquement destinés l'un à l'autre. Mais il y a eu erreur au service des naissances.

*p. 86*

Eve et Pierre rient, puis se regardent:
"Nous aurons au moins réussi ça," constate Eve.
Elle réfléchit une seconde, et ajoute:
"Pierre, nous la garderons, si tout marche bien."
"Tout marchera bien," assure Pierre.

*pp. 87 and 88*

"Pierre . . . qu'est-ce que nous allons faire de cette vie nouvelle?"

"Ce que nous voudrons. Nous ne devons plus rien à personne."

Nous sommes seuls au monde.

*p. 88*

"Eh bien, va . . ." murmure-t-elle. "Va, Pierre. C'est la plus belle preuve d'amour que je puisse te donner."

Tu ne peux pas. . . . Ce n'est pas possible. Tu vas te faire tuer, c'est absurde. Rappelle-toi que je t'aime, Pierre. . . . C'est pour nous aimer que nous sommes revenus.

*p. 92*

Je veux être ton bordel.

*p. 92*

Essaie donc d'aimer ton prochain.

Et pourquoi ne l'aimerais-je pas, si c'était mon caprice?

Au secours, les anges! Aidez-moi à me vaincre!

Seigneur, délivrez-moi de l'abominable envie de rire!

Encore un qui va me faire le coup du baiser au lépreux.

*p. 93*

Ne soie pas mon ennemie.

Je souffre dans tous les corps, on me frappe sur toutes les joues, je meurs de toutes les morts.

*p. 94*

Parbleu, je suis trop bête; aide-toi, le Ciel t'aidera!

Ne crains plus rien, mon amour. Je touche ton front, tes yeux et ta bouche avec le sang de notre Jésus.

Ton sang, Goetz, ton sang. Tu l'as donné pour moi.

Ne leur fais pas de mal.

Ils sont à moi. Enfin.

*pp. 94 and 95*

Ma soeur. . . . Tu nous gênes.

Tu es lumière et *tu n'es pas* moi, c'est insupportable. Je ne comprends pas pourquoi nous faisons deux et je voudrais devenir toi en restant moi-même.

Elle, c'est moi. Parle ou va-t-en.

*pp. 95 and 96*

GOETZ:   Nous prenons la décision ensemble?
HILDA:   Oui. Ensemble.
GOETZ:   Et nous en porterons les conséquences ensemble?
HILDA:   Ensemble quoi qu'il arrive.

Autrefois je violais les âmes par la torture, à présent je les viole par le Bien.

S'aimer, c'est haïr le même ennemi.

*p. 96*

Parbleu, Hilda, cet homme est aussi seul que moi.

Je leur ferai horreur puisque je n'ai pas d'autre manière de les aimer, je leur donnerai des ordres, puisque je n'ai pas d'autre manière d'obéir, je resterai seul avec ce ciel vide au-dessus de ma tête, puisque je n'ai pas d'autre manière d'être avec tous. Il y a cette guerre à faire et je la ferai.

*p. 99*

Ma liberté exige pour s'accomplir de déboucher sur un avenir ouvert: ce sont les autres hommes qui m'ouvrent l'avenir.

*p. 99*

Quand elle n'était pas là, cette odeur de poussière, cette pénombre, cette solitude désolée, tout ça n'existait pour personne, ça n'existait pas du tout . . . il fallait la faire exister, cette salle déserte et pleine de nuit.

*pp. 100 and 101*

Ce qui l'enchantait surtout, c'était d'avoir annexé à sa vie cette petite existence triste . . . rien ne donnait jamais à Françoise des joies si fortes que cette espèce de possession.

Les gestes de Xavière, sa figure, sa vie même avaient besoin de Françoise pour exister.

*p. 102*

Puisque mon coeur continue à battre, il faudra bien qu'il batte pour quelque chose, pour quelqu'un.

*p. 105*

Outré, le docteur Sartre resta quarante ans *sans adresser la parole* à sa femme; à table, il s'exprimait par signes, elle finit par l'appeler "mon pensionnaire." Il partageait son lit, pourtant, et, de temps à autre, *sans un mot*, l'engrossait.

Pris entre le mutisme de l'un et les criailleries de l'autre, il devint bègue et passa sa vie à se battre contre les mots.

. . . s'empara de cette grande fille délaissée, l'épousa, lui fit un enfant au galop, moi, et tenta de se réfugier dans la mort.

*p. 106*

Des phrases en sortaient qui me faisaient peur: c'étaient de vrais mille-pattes, elles grouillaient de syllabes et de lettres, étiraient leurs diphtongues, faisaient vibrer les doubles consonnes; chantantes, nasales, coupées de pauses et de soupirs, riches en mots inconnus, elles s'enchantaient d'elles-mêmes et de leurs méandres sans se soucier de moi.

Je n'ai jamais gratté la terre ni quêté des nids, je n'ai pas herborisé ni lancé des pierres aux oiseaux. Mais les livres ont été mes oiseaux et mes nids, mes bêtes domestiques, mon étable et ma campagne; la bibliothèque, c'était le monde pris dans un miroir.

*p. 106*

Les phrases me résistaient à la manière des choses.

Platonicien par état, j'allais du savoir à son objet; trouvais à l'idée plus de la réalité qu'à la chose, parce qu'elle se donnait à moi d'abord et parce qu'elle se donnait comme une chose.

A la longue je pris plaisir à ce déclic qui m'arrachait de moi-même.

*p. 107*

L'Univers s'étageait à mes pieds et toute chose humblement sollicitait un nom, le lui donner c'était à la fois la créer et la prendre.

Mon grand-père croit au Progrès, moi aussi: le Progrès, ce long chemin ardu qui mène jusqu'à moi.

L'ordre du monde cachait d'intolérables désordres.

Je sentais mes actes se changer en gestes.

Ma raison d'être, à moi, se dérobait, je découvrais tout à coup que je comptais pour du beurre et j'avais honte de ma présence insolite dans ce monde en ordre.

*pp. 107 and 108*

Les cailloux du Luxembourg, M. Simonnot, les marronniers, Karlémami, c'étaient des êtres. Pas moi: je n'en avais ni l'inertie ni la profondeur ni l'impénétrabilité. J'étais *rien:* une transparence inèffaçable.

Dieu m'aurait tiré de peine: j'aurais été chef-d'oeuvre signé; assuré de tenir ma partie dans le concert universel, j'aurais attendu patiemment qu'Il me révélât ses desseins et ma nécessité. Je pressentais la religion, je l'espérais, c'était le remède.

C'était plus que je n'osais rêver. Mais, par la suite, dans le Dieu fashionable qu'on m'enseigna, je ne reconnus pas celui qu'attendait mon âme: il me fallait un Créateur, on me donnait un Grand Patron; les deux n'étaient qu'un mais je l'ignorais.

*p. 108*

Faute de prendre facine en mon coeur, il a végété en moi quelque temps, puis il est mort.

Mes frères, décidai-je, me demandaient tout simplement de consacrer ma plume à leur rachat.

Je dresserais des cathédrales de paroles sous l'oeil bleu du mot ciel. Je bâtirais pour des millénaires.

Je poussais, herbe folle, sur le terreau de la catholicité, mes racines en pompaient les sucs et j'en faisais ma sève. De là vint cet aveuglement lucide dont j'ai souffert trente années.

*p. 109*

N'importe: je fais, je ferai des livres; *il en faut*; cela *sert* tout de même. La culture ne sauve rien ni personne, elle ne justifie pas. *Mais* c'est un *produit* de l'homme: il s'y projette, s'y reconnaît; seul, ce miroir critique lui offre son image.

*p. 110*

Du reste, ce vieux bâtiment ruineux, mon imposture, c'est aussi mon caractère: on se défait d'une névrose, on ne se guérit pas de soi.

*p. 115*

Autour de moi, un million d'êtres qui avaient vécu jusque-là et de leur existence rien n'avait transpiré pour moi. Ils vivaient. J'étais à des milliers de kilomètres du pays familier. Je ne comprenais pas leur langage. Tous marchaient vite. Et me dépassant, tous se détachaient de moi. Je perdis pied.

*p. 116*

Et c'est pourtant par là que le voyage s'illumine. Un grand désaccord se fait entre lui et les choses. Dans ce coeur moins solide, la musique du monde entre plus aisément. Dans ce grand dénuement enfin, le moindre arbre isolé devient la plus tendre et la plus fragile des images.

*p. 116*

Au plus noir de notre nihilisme, j'ai cherché seulement des raisons de dépasser ce nihilisme.

Juger que la vie vaut ou ne vaut pas la peine d'être vécue, c'est répondre à la question fondamentale de la philosophie.

Je juge donc que le sens de la vie est la plus pressante des questions.

Je n'ai jamais vu personne mourir pour l'argument ontologique.

*p. 117*

Un roman n'est jamais qu'une philosophie mise en images.

*p. 118*

Oui, recueillir seulement la transparence et la simplicité des paradis perdus: dans une image.

*p. 119*

Après tout, je ne suis pas sûr d'avoir raison.

*p. 120*

Méditation de solitaire, amoureux du monde dans la mesure où il n'est qu'un cristal où se joue la divinité, pensée toute pénétrée des rythmes silencieux des astres mais inquiète du Dieu qui les ordonne, Plotin pense en artiste et sent en philosophe, selon une raison toute pénétrée de lumière et devant un monde où l'intelligence respire.

Non, encore une fois, mépriser le monde, mépriser les dieux et toutes les beautés qui sont en lui ce n'est pas devenir un homme de bien.

Ce n'est pas l'apparence que Plotin recherche mais plutôt cet envers des choses qui est son paradis perdu.

*p. 121*

Un homme contemple et l'autre creuse son tombeau: comment les séparer? Les hommes et leur absurdité? Mais voici le sourire du ciel. La lumière se gonfle et c'est bientôt l'été! Mais voici les yeux et la voix de ceux qu'il faut aimer. Je tiens au monde par tous mes gestes, aux hommes par toute ma pitié et ma reconnaissance. Entre cet endroit et cet envers du monde, je ne veux pas choisir, je n'aime pas qu'on choisisse.

*pp. 121 and 122*

Ce silence intérieur qui m'accompagne, il naît de la course lente qui mène la journée à cette autre journée.

A Prague, j'étouffais entre des murs. Ici, j'étais devant le monde, et projeté autour de moi, je peuplais l'univers de formes semblables à moi.

Ce que je touchais du doigt, c'était une forme dépouillée et sans attraits de ce goût du néant que je portais en moi.

Ce pays me ramenait au coeur de moi-même et me mettait en face de mon angoisse secrète.

*pp. 122 and 123*

J'y puisais la force d'être courageux et conscient à la fois.

Cette entente amoureuse de la terre et de l'homme délivre de l'humain—ah! je m'y convertirais bien si elle n'était déjà ma religion.

Cet univers desormais sans maître ne lui paraît ni stérile ni futile. Chacun des grains de cette pierre, chaque éclat minéral de cette montagne pleine de nuit, à lui seul, forme un monde.

*p. 123*

Car l'oeuvre d'art aussi est une construction.

La création c'est le grand mime.

*p. 126*

Pendant un demi-siècle, les bourgeois de Pont-l'Evêque envi- èrent à Mme Aubain sa servante Félicité.

*p. 130*

Il s'approchait de la bière quand je l'ai arrêté.

*pp. 131 and 132*

Comme je ne comprenais pas, j'ai regardé l'infirmière et j'ai vu qu'elle portait sous les yeux un bandeau qui faisait le tour de la tête.

Il y a eu encore l'église et les villageois sur les trottoirs, les géra- niums rouges sur les tombes du cimetière, l'évanouissement de Pérez (on eût dit un pantin disloqué), *la terre couleur de sang* qui roulait sur la bière de maman, *la chaire blanche des racines qui s'y mêlaient,* encore du monde, des voix, le village, l'attente devant un café, l'inces- sant ronflement du moteur, et ma joie quand l'autobus est entré dans le nid de lumières d'Alger et que *j'ai pensé que j'allais me coucher et dormir pendant douze heures.*

*p. 133*

J'ai pensé que c'était toujours un dimanche de tiré, que maman était maintenant enterrée, que j'allais reprendre mon travail et que, somme toute, il n'y avait rien de changé.

*p. 134*

J'ai eu très envie d'elle parce qu'elle avait une belle robe à raies rouges et blanches et des sandales de cuir.

*p. 134*

Elle a eu l'air triste. Mais en préparant le déjeuner, et à propos de rien, elle a encore ri de telle façon que je l'ai embrassée.

*pp. 137 and 138*

Pour la première fois peut-être, j'ai *pensé vraiment* que j'allais me marier.

. . . comme quatre coups brefs . . . sur la porte du malheur.

*pp. 138 and 139*

On me remettait alors entre les mains des gendarmes.

Personne ne peut imaginer ce que sont *les soirs* dans les prisons.

*p. 139*

. . . comme si les chemins familiers tracés dans les ciels d'été pouvaient mener aussi bien aux prisons qu'aux *sommeils innocents*.

Je déversais sur lui tout le fond de mon coeur avec des bondissements mêlés de joie et de colère.

La merveilleuse paix de cet été endormi entrait en moi comme une marée.

*pp. 139 and 140*

Pour la première fois depuis bien longtemps, j'ai pensé à maman.

Je m'ouvrais pour la première fois à la tendre indifférence du monde.

*p. 141*

Comment n'avais-je pas vu que rien n'était plus important qu'une exécution capitale et que, en somme, c'était la seule chose vraiment intéressante pour un homme!

En réalité, la machine était posée à même le sol, le plus simplement du monde.

On se fait toujours des indées exagérées de ce qu'on ne connaît pas. Je devais constater au contraire que tout était simple: la machine est au même niveau que l'homme qui marche vers elle. Il la rejoint comme on marche à la rencontre d'une personne.

La montée vers l'échafaud, l'ascension en plein ciel, l'imagination pouvait s'y raccrocher. Tandis que, là encore, la mécanique écrasait tout: on était tué discrètement, avec un peu de honte et beaucoup de précision.

*p. 142*

Pour que tout soit consommé, pour que je me sente moins seul, il me restait à souhaiter qu'il y ait beaucoup de spectateurs le jour de mon exécution et qu'ils m'accueillent avec des cris de haine.

*p. 146*

Perdre la vie est peu de chose et j'aurai ce courage quand il le faudra. Mais voir se dissiper le sens de cette vie, disparaître notre raison d'exister, voilà ce qui est insupportable. On ne peut vivre sans raison.

*p. 152*

Ne pleurez pas. Non, non, ne pleurez pas! Vous voyez bien que c'est le jour de la justification. Quelque chose s'élève à cette heure qui est notre témoignage à nous autres révoltés. Yanek n'est plus un meurtrier. Un bruit terrible! Il a suffi d'un bruit terrible et le voilà retourné à la joie de l'enfance.

Donne-moi la bombe. . . . Oui, la prochaine fois. Je veux la lancer. Je veux être la première à la lancer.

*p. 153*

Toute valeur n'entraîne pas la révolte, mais tout mouvement de révolte invoque tacitement une valeur.

Cette part de lui-même qu'il voulait faire respecter, il la met alors au-dessus du reste, et la proclame préférable à tout, même à la vie.

*p. 153*

Elle est donc amour et fécondité, ou elle n'est rien. La révolution sans honneur, la révolution du calcul qui, préférant un homme abstrait à l'homme de chair, nie l'homme de chair, nie l'être autant de fois qu'il est nécessaire, met justement le ressentiment à la place de l'amour.

*p. 158*

La pluie redoublait au-dehors et cette dernière phrase, prononcée au milieu d'un silence absolu, rendu plus profond encore par le crépitement de l'averse sur les vitraux, retentit avec un tel accent que quelques auditeurs, après une seconde d'hésitation, se laissèrent glisser de leur chaise sur le prie-Dieu.

*p. 158*

Notre amour sans doute était toujours là, mais, simplement, il était inutilisable, lourd à porter, inerte en nous, stérile comme le crime ou la condamnation. Il n'était plus qu'une patience sans avenir et une attente butée.

*pp. 160 and 161*

Je trouve cela intéressant, oui, positivement intéressant.

Là était la certitude, dans le travail de tous les jours. Le reste tenait à des fils et à des mouvements insignifiants, on ne pouvait s'y arrêter. L'essentiel était de bien faire son métier.

Rieux répondit qu'il n'avait pas décrit un syndrome, il avait décrit ce qu'il avait vu.

*p. 161*

Les religieux n'ont pas d'amis. Ils ont tout placé en Dieu.

*p. 162*

En somme . . . ce qui m'intéresse, c'est de savoir comment on devient un saint.

Justement. Peut-on être un saint sans Dieu, c'est le seul problème concret que je connaisse aujourd'hui.

Ce qui m'intéresse, c'est d'être un homme.

Oui, nous cherchons la même chose, mais je suis moins ambitieux.

*p. 164*

Pauvre juge. . . . Il faudrait faire quelque chose pour lui. Mais comment aider un juge?

*p. 166*

Oui, s'il est vrai que les hommes tiennent à se proposer des exemples et des modèles qu'ils appellent héros, et s'il faut absolument qu'il y en ait un dans cette histoire, le narrateur propose justement ce héros insignifiant et effacé qui n'avait pour lui qu'un peu de bonté au coeur et un idéal apparemment ridicule.

. . . qu'il y a dans les hommes plus de choses à admirer que de choses à mépriser.

*p. 166 and 167*

Pour tous ceux, au contraire, qui s'étaient adressés par-dessus l'homme à quelque chose qu'ils n'imaginaient même pas, il n'y avait pas eu de réponse. Tarrou avait semblé rejoindre cette paix difficile dont il avait parlé, mais il ne l'avait trouvée que dans la mort, à l'heure où elle ne pouvait lui servir de rien.

*p. 167*

Le matin du 16 avril, le docteur Bernard Rieux sortit de son cabinet et buta sur un rat mort, au milieu du palier. Sur le moment, il écarta la bête sans y prendre garde et descendit l'escalier. Mais, arrivé dans la rue, la pensée lui vint que ce rat n'était pas à sa place et il retourna sur ses pas pour avertir le concierge.

*p. 169*

Sans sortir de l'ombre, le docteur dit qu'il avait déjà répondu, que s'il croyait en un Dieu tout-puissant, il cesserait de guérir les hommes, lui laissant alors ce soin.

"A peu près," répondit le docteur en revenant dans la lumière.

La réponse vint dans le noir, portée par la même voix tranquille: "oui."

*p. 170*

Devant l'auto, Rieux demanda à Tarrou s'il voulait entrer et l'autre dit que oui. Un reflet du ciel éclairait leurs visages.

Beaucoup de choses nous rapprochaient, peu nous séparaient.

*pp. 174 and 175*

A lui faire sentir si souvent qu'elle existait pour lui, il la faisait exister réellement. Non, elle n'était pas seule.

Alors, ils cherchent des preuves, ils jugent, ils condamnent. Ça les fortifie, c'est un commencement d'existence.

Non, je ne suis pas certain d'exister. Mais j'existerai, j'en suis sûr.

*p. 182*

La Hollande est un songe, monsieur, un songe d'or et de fumée, plus fumeux le jour, plus doré la nuit, et nuit et jour ce songe est peuplé de Lohengrin comme ceux-ci, filant rêveusement sur leurs noires bicyclettes à hauts guidons, cygnes funèbres qui tournent sans trêve, dans tout le pays, autour des mers, le long des canaux.

*p. 183*

A toute heure du jour, en moi-même et parmi les autres, je grimpais sur la hauteur, j'y allumais des feux apparents, et une joyeuse salutation s'élevait vers moi.

*p. 184*

La seule parade est dans la méchanceté. Les gens se dépêchent alors de juger pour ne pas l'être eux-mêmes.

*p. 187*

Mais justement, il n'y a plus de père, plus de règle! On est libre, alors il faut se débrouiller et comme ils ne veulent surtout pas de la liberté, ni de ses sentences, ils prient qu'on leur donne sur les doigts, ils inventent de terribles règles, ils courent construire des bûchers pour remplacer les églises.

Vive donc le maître, quel qu'il soit, pour remplacer la loi du ciel. "Notre père qui êtes provisoirement ici. . . . Nos guides, nos chefs délicieusement sévères, ô conducteurs cruels et bien-aimés. . . ." Enfin, vous voyez, l'essentiel est de n'être plus libre et d'obéir, dans le repentir, à plus coquin que soi.

*p. 188*

N'est-il pas bon aussi bien de vivre à la ressemblance de la société et pour cela ne faut-il pas que la société me ressemble? La menace, le déshonneur, la police sont les sacrements de cette ressemblance. Méprisé, traqué, contraint, je puis alors donner ma pleine mesure, jouir de ce que je suis, être naturel enfin. Voilà pourquoi, très cher, après avoir salué solennellement la liberté, je décidai en catimini qu'il fallait la remettre sans délai à n'importe qui.

J'ai cependant une supériorité, celle de le savoir, qui me donne le droit de parler.

J'ai accepté la duplicité au lieu de m'en désoler.

*pp. 188 and 189*

Alors je grandis, très cher, je grandis, je respire librement, je suis sur la montagne, la plaine s'étend sous mes yeux.

Alors, planant par la pensée au-dessus de tout ce continent qui m'est soumis sans le savoir, buvant le jour d'absinthe qui se lève, ivre enfin de mauvaises paroles, je suis heureux, je suis heureux, vous dis-je, je vous interdis de ne pas croire que je suis heureux, je suis heureux à mourir!

*p. 193*

L'être nous sera dévoilé par quelque moyen d'accès immédiat, l'ennui, la nausée, etc., et l'ontologie sera la description du phénomène d'être tel qu'il se manifeste, c'est-à-dire sans intermédiare.

*p. 208*

La possession du royaume les anéantit dans ce que leur vie pouvait avoir d'essentiel.

*p. 210*

Meursault, pour moi, n'est pas une épave, mais un homme pauvre et un amoureux du soleil qui ne laisse pas d'ombres. Loin qu'il soit privé de toute sensibilité, une passion profonde, parce que tacite, l'anime, la passion de l'absolu et de la vérité.

*p. 211*

. . . des odeurs d'été, le quartier que j'aimais, un certain ciel du soir, le rire et les robes de Marie.

*p. 212*

Et là redressant toute sa taille, énorme soudain, aspirant à goulées désespérées l'odeur de misère et de cendres qu'il reconnaissait, il écoute monter en lui le flot d'une joie obscure et haletante qu'il ne pouvait pas nommer.

Le monde est beau et hors de lui, point de salut.

Le monde soupire vers moi dans un rythme long et m'apporte l'indifférence et la tranquillité de ce qui ne meurt pas.

La grande vérité que patiemment, il m'enseigne, c'est que l'esprit n'est rien, ni le coeur même.

*pp. 212 and 213*

Le sens du livre tient exactement dans le parallélisme des deux parties.

Hors du soleil, des baisers et des parfums sauvages, tout nous paraît futile.

*p. 214*

Je suis entière! Je ne connais que mon amour.

*p. 215*

Tu voudrais que je m'attendrisse et que je traîne la bombe comme une croix?

*p. 215*

Et quand donc suis-je plus vrai que lorsque je suis le monde?

*p. 216*

Joseph Grand à son tour avait souffert. Il aurait pu recommencer, comme le lui fit remarquer Rieux. Mais voilà, il n'avait pas la foi.

*p. 218*

Depuis toujours, sur la terre sèche, raclée jusqu'à l'os, de ce pays démesuré, quelques hommes cheminaient sans trêve, qui ne possédaient rien mais ne servaient personne, siegneurs misérables et libres d'un étrange royaume.

Il aurait voulu être jeune, et que Fernande le fût encore, et ils seraient partis, de l'autre côté de la mer.

*p. 218*

Dans ce vaste pays qu'il avait tant aimé, il était seul.

*p. 220*

Désespérant de l'amour de la chasteté, je m'avisai enfin qu'il restait la débauche qui remplace très bien l'amour, fait taire les rires, ramène le silence, et, surtout, confère l'immortalité.

Chaque homme témoigne du crime de tous les autres, voilà ma foi, et mon espérance.

Il est orienté par l'idée, évidemment, de faire taire les rires, d'éviter personnellement le jugement, bien qu'il n'y ait, en apparence, aucune issue.

# Index